CW00543373

PORNOGRAPI
AS POWERFUL AS ......

Rich Moreland's book takes a fresh look at women and trans folk in porn, giving as much credence to young alternative and sex-positive performers and filmmakers as to their feminist foremothers. His discussion is enhanced by a look at the history of explicit movies, so modern porn gets a well-researched backstory. This curious and open-minded explorer has delved into a side of the X-rated world given too little attention by mainstream viewers *and* critics. Read and learn!

Carol Queen, PhD, Founding Director, Center for Sex & Culture Author, *Real Live Nude Girl: Chronicles of Sex-Positive Culture*

I really love this book! Rich Moreland gets deep inside the hearts and minds of the innovative feminist pornographers of today, and yesterday. Finally there is some text about our XXX sisterhood that is accurate! What a relief!

Annie Sprinkle, PhD, Porn Star turned Ecosexologist/Artist

A great read exploring the duality of adult entertainment performers. For those who are what we call "civilians" it's an eye opener about porn star politics and feminism. Sex workers are the Norma Raes of the 21st century and Rich Moreland illustrates that point with candid interviews and eloquent insights. A must read for anyone curious about porn and porn stars beyond the screen, revealing a group of streetwise, savvy and independent women and possibly feminist leaders of tomorrow.

Lainie Speiser, Author, *Confessions of the Hundred Hottest Porn Stars* and *The Manhattan Madame Guide to Great Sex*

Finally a book that explores feminism as a force in adult film.

Tracing the early history of filmed pornography from the take charge women of the old stags to modern feminists shooting scenes today, Rich Moreland uses a journalist's pen to challenge old myths. Relying on interviews and a behind the scenes look at a controversial industry, the author invites the reader to rethink timeworn attitudes.

Jacky St. James, Award winning feminist writer and director

For anyone who doubts the existence of feminist pornographers, Rich Moreland's book, based on years of thorough research and astute observations, offers proof positive, SEX POSITIVE. It's an intimate and exciting read.

Veronica Vera Cottingham, Doctor of Human Sexuality (DHS) Author and founder of Miss Vera's Finishing School for Boys Who Want to Be Girls

We've seen him asking questions and taking notes at every important porn-industry event during the past two years. Rich Moreland has really done his homework and knows what he is writing about.

Dan O'Connell, Director of lesbian erotica and founder of Girlfriends Films, XCritic.com's 2012 Adult Studio of the Year

A fascinating overview of feminism as a force in the pornography business, Rich Moreland brings a historian's perspective to an industry that sorely lacks documentation. A record of female voices ranging from the trenches of Porn Valley to the queer porn enclave of San Francisco to the Feminist Porn Awards in Toronto. Performer respect, safer sex, patriarchal attitudes, and BDSM fetishes as an individual pleasure are subjects powerful women in adult film talk about in this engaging book.

Eli Cross, Award winning adult film director, former managing editor of Adult Video News

Pornography Feminism:
As Powerful as She Wants to Be

Pornography Feminism: As Powerful as She Wants to Be

Rich Moreland

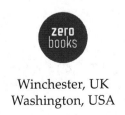

Winchester, UK
Washington, USA

First published by Zero Books, 2015
Zero Books is an imprint of John Hunt Publishing Ltd., Laurel House, Station Approach,
Alresford, Hants, SO24 9JH, UK
office1@jhpbooks.net
www.johnhuntpublishing.com
www.zero-books.net

For distributor details and how to order please visit the 'Ordering' section on our website.

Text copyright: Rich Moreland 2014

ISBN: 978 1 78279 496 7

All rights reserved. Except for brief quotations in critical articles or reviews, no part of this
book may be reproduced in any manner without prior written permission from the publishers.

The rights of Rich Moreland as author have been asserted in accordance with the Copyright,
Designs and Patents Act 1988.

A CIP catalogue record for this book is available from the British Library.

Design: Stuart Davies

Printed and bound by CPI Group (UK) Ltd, Croydon, CR0 4YY

We operate a distinctive and ethical publishing philosophy in all
areas of our business, from our global network of authors to
production and worldwide distribution.

CONTENTS

Acknowledgements   x
Introduction: Neglected Stepchildren   1
Remember Where You Started   12

Part One   23

Chapter 1 *Real* Sex Merchants   24
Chapter 2 A "Gaze" of Their Own   47
Chapter 3 My Body, My Rules   70
Chapter 4 Her Own Amateur Porn Movie   89

Part Two   111

Chapter 5 An Attitude, Not a Movement   112
Chapter 6 Space for Everyone   136
Chapter 7 *Real* People *are* the Medium   156
Chapter 8 My Porn-Art Daughter   170
Chapter 9 Too Much Gray   186
Chapter 10 A Safe Place for All of Us   208
Conclusion: Once Was   230

Endnotes   235

In Memoriam:
Carlos Batts 1973-2013
Gloria Leonard 1940-2014

Acknowledgements

This book began as a curiosity that transitioned into a popular history. I am indebted to my colleagues in academia for their support and kind words particularly when frustration set in, as it does with any historian who takes on the task of writing a manuscript. On my campus, Dr. Michael Powell mentored me from the outset, reading chapters and offering valuable guidance.

Other colleagues, Corwin Parker and Dr. Edward Taft in particular, lent a sympathetic ear and a bit of help here and there. Dan Fout, newly retired from Library Services, obtained many of the research documents I needed. The advice of scholars is invaluable and I could not have successfully navigated this project without it. Special thanks are given to Dr. Anne G. Sabo of Northridge, Minnesota, Dr. Joe Thompson of Montgomery College, Germantown, Maryland, feminist writer Susie Bright and UCLA graduate student and researcher Cristina Rodriquez-Hart. Dr. Robert Lawrence and Dr. Carol Queen of San Francisco's Center for Sex and Culture made my research trip to that city a success. First Amendment Attorney Reed Lee provided insightful advice and documentation on the government's investigation of pornography.

The genesis of the subject matter came from long discussions with my very close friend, Garey Rice, who encouraged me to take a dream and turn it into a literary reality.

No writer can produce a manuscript without getting overly immersed in his own words. A handful of my former students patiently read and edited my chapters, offering their opinions and fixing my errors. These young women transcribed interviews, a Herculean job, and served as my sounding board. They are Brandy Abel, Yana Babii, Amy Davis, Rachel Lowry, and Morgan Mullen. Other readers who offered advice and corrected mistakes are Bettie Bell Erb of Cedar Park, Texas, Brigitte Farrell,

Terry Hershey, Susan Harwell-Moeller, Melikahiwa Paulson Schmieder and Ann L. Thomas, who has stood with me and supported my endeavor from the beginning. I am forever grateful to all of you.

I traveled extensively to familiarize myself with the adult film industry. Because I am not a photographer two friends took on this job, offering support along the way. I am beholden to Bill Knight and my academic associate, Josh DeVree. Their assistance was invaluable.

It goes without saying that the ladies of Club 90 went the extra miles to help me tell their story and offered guidance as I delved into the history of adult film. Their narrative is the driving force behind this book. A heartfelt "thank you" is extended to Veronica Hart, Candida Royalle, Annie Sprinkle, and Veronica Vera, with a special posthumous recognition going to Gloria Leonard whose tragic passing was a loss for everyone. Two other adult film legends, Nina Hartley and Georgina Spelvin, and their respective spouses, Ira Levine and John Welsh, deserve much gratitude.

To the adult industry I owe more than I can ever express. First and foremost, a special salutation is offered to Bill Margold, the preeminent living historian of adult film, and Steve Nelson, Editor in Chief of *Adult Industry News* who gave me space to write a column on industry affairs and the opportunity to learn the inner workings of the business. Off Broadway and Hollywood producer/writer David Bertolino provided ongoing encouragement and, like Bill and Steve, an irreplaceable friendship. Without their support this book would never have seen the light of day.

Adult performer Casey Calvert contributed her views on the adult industry and checked my work for accuracy, offering corrections where necessary. Casey's support, knowledge and willingness to be a sounding board and informal consultant gave my words valued authentication.

I cannot express sufficient gratitude for the courtesy of Peter Acworth who accommodated my desire to take a close look at *Kink.com*, its facility and its product. Without his input the understanding of the BDSM lifestyle and film genre, a mission he values highly, would be severely lacking.

As I ventured more deeply into the adult business, I relied on the thoughts and reflections of those individuals who were willing to talk with me. The list below contains performers, directors, producers, company owners and others affiliated with the business of adult entertainment. Through their insights, I learned about a part of American culture that helps define our social history.

In alphabetical order, they are: Adrienne, Carlos Batts, Peyton Bell, Michael Bisco, Joanne Cachapero, Chris Cane, Alex Chance, Dick Chibbles, Bob Christian, Kikki D'aire, Dana DeArmond, Doron, Diane Duke, Paul Fishbein, April Flores, Chloe Foster, Tara Lynn Foxx, Jill Hagara, Sara Hide, Tina Horn, Armando Huerta, Jaiya, Jesse Jane, Carlyle Jansen, Mark Kernes, Daisy Layne, Alison Lee, Jiz Lee, Michelle Leon, Sasha Lexing, Lea Lexis, Lochai, Erika Lust, Sonny Malone, Christian Mann, James Mogul, Madelyn Monroe, Moose, Nica Noelle, Dan O'Connell, Trish Pastel, Penny Pax, Chanel Preston, Bryn Pryor, Caroline Ray, Tasha Reign, Justin Rich, Jessa Rhodes, Imani Rose, Lila Rose, Selena Rose, Lew Rubens, Jared Rutter, Christopher Ruth, Dylan Ryan, Steven St. Croix, Jacky St. James, Sabrina, John Sander, Andy San Dimas, Serena, Shea Simon, Rikki Six, Leena Sky, Lainie Speiser, John Stagliano, Bobbi Starr, John Steven, Tim Stokely, Tristan Taormino, Farrell Timlake, Courtney Trouble, Ed Vincent, Stuart Wall, Billy Watson, Jamye Waxman, Chris Wessman, John Wilkes, Madison Young, and Katy Zvolerin.

My sincere appreciation is extended to all of you.

Rich Moreland July, 2014

Introduction

Neglected Stepchildren

A few years ago a colleague and I began an extended conversation over an idea I had for a research project. In the early 1990s a young couple from our area ventured to Southern California with the expressed purpose of working in adult film. Their story offered an interesting starting point for writing a history of filmed pornography, but were biographies a viable angle for a manuscript?

Although further talks over coffee and an occasional lunch led me to abandon our local "stars," researching adult film kept at me. Mulling over possible topics, I discovered that some performers self-identify as feminists. That struck me as nonsensical. Feminism in pornography? What did that have to do with winning the vote, securing reproductive rights and smashing the glass ceiling? After all, New Left feminists of the 1960s and 1970s railed against pornography as harmful to women with some feminists still adhering to that view today.

In fact my university years taught me that the anti-pornography view is conventional wisdom among feminists. Feminism is about empowerment and women cannot be in control of their minds and bodies if they are sexually and emotionally victimized by a patriarchal industry. Anyone can see porn degrades and objectifies women... or so I assumed. What I failed to take into account are feminists who believe that participating in adult film is an expression of their personal sexual agency, their art and their politics. They are an ignored part of "individualist feminism" as described by feminist writer Wendy McElroy. A woman is privileged to do with her body as she pleases, McElroy insists. If this is true with regard to the professional display of explicit sex, I wanted to hear it directly from those who step in front of the camera.[1]

Some months later I approached the Sands Convention Center in Las Vegas. The occasion was the father (or mother) of adult film conventions, the *Adult Entertainment Expo*. When I walked onto the floor, the spectacle that greeted me was suggestive of the Robert Heinlein title, *Stranger in a Strange Land*. This was not my environment. Shutting out the distractions of urban hip hop, models signing autographs and giant posters advertising the pornographic body, I headed directly for the *Evil Angel* booth where a self-proclaimed feminist performer told me she would be. We talked briefly and arranged to meet over breakfast the next morning.

My fieldwork began at that moment.

The traditional feminist approach to pornography is outright condemnation. Hardcore adult film is destructive to women, humiliating and demeaning them through sexual exploitation. The solution is disabling porn through education, legal action and censorship. In this self-appointed mission, traditional feminism offers little about the women who make the film, especially those who claim a feminist label. They are the neglected stepchildren of the movement, pushed into the corner to eat their gruel and suffer for their errant ways. But circumstances do not quiet the persistence of an important question. What does it mean to be an adult film feminist and are these women creating change in an often maligned industry that uses them for profit?

Adult film's moneyed empire is patriarchal. Male control of the cinematic pornographic image dates to the first stag film and has since conceded mere bits and pieces of its predominance. Yet there have been, and continue to be, moments of challenge. Explicit sex still rings the porn cash register, but some of the dollars now have a different look. Female performers and directors are exercising a greater influence over how women are portrayed on film. They seek to manipulate the sexual message while demanding a voice in the male occupied boardroom where the profits accumulate. Respect facilitates these goals, though building it is an ongoing struggle. As retired performer and now director Veronica Hart told me, respect in porn is earned and money fuels the love. Adult film feminists must work both sides of the camera *and* make a profit: a tall order.[2]

Early in feminism's second wave, strident voices of "porn is violence against women" drumbeaters, Andrea Dworkin and Catharine MacKinnon in particular, virulently condemn the adult film industry. Other feminists counter with a pro-sex identity that touts a woman's right to pleasure. These feminists refuse to allow their choices to be defined and restricted by a conservative moral and political view. In time, academic feminism gave space to women who identify as sex positive. They support a woman's right to consume pornography though they may not necessarily do so themselves.

But right-wing political winds in the 1980s reoriented the argument, moving it away from satisfaction in the bedroom to a larger public forum. As a result, much of the pro-sex energy was diverted from female sexual empowerment to the issue of censorship, redefining the sex-positive feminist, pro-porn engine as it battles its anti-porn sisters. Generated through feminist papers and conferences, the "sex wars" over whose interpretation of the pornographic image is best for women clutter the movement's landscape. During this contentious period, a handful of adult film actresses formed a support group in New York City to ease their transition away from the camera's eye. They named themselves Club 90 and quietly brought feminism into adult entertainment.[3]

Eventually feminism's second wave fades by the mid-1990s, a victim of infighting and the anti-porn feminist sellout to the government's investigation of pornography. Adult film remains a contentious issue but disagreements are reduced to running on vapors. Through it all sex-positive feminism survives to claim a nascent space in adult filmmaking. By the new century female performers and directors are amplifying a woman's voice in pornography.

Eventually a newer version of popular feminism, the third wave, emerges and younger women redefine the sexual. Women who drift into adult film at this juncture take second wave feminist gains for granted, including their right to make pornography a career. Their personal statement of erotic satisfaction maintains a sex-positive aura but has little to do with the earlier "movement" perspective. Because there is not a definable fit for these performers, I believe they have shaped a new version of feminism unique to adult film: "pornography feminism."

These women achieve a degree of success in a business marked by career flameouts and high turnover rates. Though few in number, pornography feminists call their own shots as filmmakers, influence their working conditions and collect a portion of the profits along the way. They are claiming their own sexual "gaze," celebrating an authentic filmed eroticism that emphasizes their personal satisfaction and pleasure while reconfiguring the adult product for an increasingly female customer base.

This manuscript traces the journey of adult film feminism from a historian's view, beginning with the earliest stags and moving through to today's post-feminist age. Where possible, I rely on the words of performers and directors. The result is a brief overview that can serve as a reference for future study. For example, pornography feminism is a product of two adult film worlds: the traditional Porn Valley of Southern California and the sexually fluid queer community of San Francisco. Performers from both cultures work easily and naturally within each environment, largely unaware of how important this crossing over is in greater story of adult film.

Pornography feminism is in constant flux, reevaluating and

reshaping itself within a traditional "ole boy" network. It is a journey that began three decades ago and, like the adult film industry itself, is edging closer to mainstream American culture. Today a feminist attitude helps performers to weather porn's unpredictability and harsh physical demands with coping skills that define survival. Though most performers do not identify as feminists, women who build careers in this unforgiving business mirror feminist traits.

As we move into the twenty-first century the shadow of a conservative retrenchment of sexual attitudes, what feminist Ellen Willis calls "neo-Victorianism," remains, though in a quieted state. The new internet and social media driven age will, if anything, offer greater conduits for the commercialization of adult film. Pornography is not going away, but it can be produced in a manner that celebrates the women who choose to perform in it and those women who are its consumers. As professors Carmine Sarracino and Kevin M. Scott assert, pornography made by women for women is decidedly the best example of the adult film genre out there.[4]

A Few Comments on Words

The definitions of *pornography* and *erotica* are dependent on the time and culture of their use. For this book *pornography* can be soft or hardcore, with the latter being defined as filmed penetrative sex of all varieties. However, usage is fluid. What was considered pornography decades ago amuses our modern society. *I am Curious Yellow* is tame by today's standards but was considered beyond the pale in 1968 though it contains no explicit sex and is remembered as a political film. *Erotica* can be defined as a softer form of explicit sex framed within storylines. Typically it contains mutual male/female and female/female sexual interchange and a depiction of female sexual activity flavored with romantic overtones.

Yet distinguishing erotica from pornography depends primarily on point of view. Erotica claims to be less offensive while pornography offers a coarser flavor. In the end it is a matter of semantics. As the old joke goes in claiming the high road of moral determination, erotica is what turns me on; pornography is what turns you on. Or on a more amusing note, Annie Sprinkle suggests that "erotica uses the feather, porn uses the whole chicken," while her Club 90 pal Gloria Leonard insists the only difference between the two is the lighting.[5]

When discussing the *queer* community's contribution to pornography feminism, I intend for the word queer to be overarching. It includes individuals who identify as LGBTQQKI (lesbian, gay, bisexual, transgendered, queer, questioning, kink, intersex) and their personality preferred sexualities. Queer reflects the diversity of gender identity and sexual orientation. For *genderqueer* I will follow the advice given me by genderqueer performer Jiz Lee who divides the term into two components. The first is gender, which Jiz believes defines a "social identity," and the second is queer, which Jiz defines as "sexual orientation." Because a person's social identity and sexual orientation cannot be assumed, queer seems most appropriate as an umbrella term for the adult film of this community.[6]

Lesbian presents a difficulty. Possible approaches were suggested by Jiz Lee and Carlyle Jansen, creator of Toronto's *Feminist Porn Awards*. Jiz believes it is best to ask the individual. Although this is my methodological choice, it was impossible to follow completely because I did not have the opportunity to speak personally with everyone included in this text. On the other hand, Carlyle believes lesbian has a generational bias. Women over thirty-five are more comfortable with the term while it is generally avoided by younger women.

There is yet a further complication. In its conventional heterosexual product the Southern California film industry identifies girl-on-girl scenes as lesbian, the porn tradition dating back to the early stag films. All-female performer companies, *Girlfriends Films* a prominent example, commonly use lesbian in their movie titles. In that respect, its usage difference may lie within environments, with the San Francisco queer porn community minimizing the label.

The *BDSM* (bondage/discipline, dominance/submission, sadism/masochism) fetish is more easily defined. Its expression has historical variety and those involved in the BDSM community have different views on how their preferences are identified. The modern usage of BDSM is universally recognized to encompass specific sexual and political practices that surround it, including D/s relationships (Dominant/submissive) and tops and bottoms as they are used in BDSM "play." S&M is more traditional, showing up in older texts and historical literature. It's narrowly interpreted, referring to pain as an erotic mechanism. As a result I use BDSM as an all-inclusive term, reserving other identifiers like SM, S/M, s/m and S&M to written sources and my interviews with people who have their own preferences in discussing the practice.

The Script

The first half of the book begins with a thumbnail history of visual non-print pornography beginning with the earliest stag films and moving to the first hardcore features in 1970. Chapter One pays homage to the empowered woman from the first notable stag in 1915 through the sexploitation movies of the 1960s. By the fading days of that turbulent decade, hardcore penetrative sex sneaks into adult movie theaters known as grindhouses and America stands on the doorstep of a boom in commercialized filmed sex.

The coming of the modern adult film era in 1972 is the beneficiary of America's cultural liberalization. Part of this progressivism is feminism's second wave. Though seeking greater freedom for women, mainstream feminism is no friend of adult film. Yet some women in the pornography business do have feminist leanings. Club 90, founded in New York City in the early 1980s, informally introduced feminism into adult film. Its formative years are the centerpiece of the second chapter while the third presents adult film's legendary feminist and Club 90 friend, Nina Hartley. She is part of Pink Ladies, another support group formed in the late 1980s. Despite its short life, Pink Ladies is indicative of the need for a degree of political organization within the ranks of adult film performers.

Chapter Four concludes with a brief look at feminism's second wave, pornography and censorship, summarizing feminism's debate over porn and the government's attack on the industry. Though mainstream feminists and adult film feminists hold different views, they have a striking similarity: the battle with a patriarchal culture. Mainstream feminists enjoin the fight within broader society while adult film feminists compete for a space in a male-dominated industry. The dissimilar feminisms cross swords when the anti-porn feminists ally with political conservatives to condemn pornography as violence against women. Carried into the 1990s, this battle over censorship abets the demise of the movement's second wave.

By the turn of the new century feminism shifts to an individual posture, becoming a personal construct closely aligned to the third wave's "do me" feminism and the coming post-feminist era. A woman can be sexually active on her own terms and with whomever she desires. Empowerment means she can demand orgasms and no longer needs to defend her actions. Chapter Five begins the second half of the book and introduces this transformation, developing the argument for pornography feminism.

Chapter Six is dedicated to marginalized sexualities and their specific pornographies. San Francisco's queer community with its gay, transgendered and BDSM adult film, heavily influences

8

modern pornography feminism and is integral to it. The Queer Porn Mafia, a loosely formed support group of performers and directors, is a descendant, at least in spirit, of Club 90 and Pink Ladies.

Modern adult film lives in a world far removed from the days of *Deep Throat* with its shocking oral sex financed by organized crime. Chapter Seven covers two post-porno chic developments. First, sex toys and associated novelties as they are marketed to women take center stage. Female owned and operated shops like Toronto's *Good For Her* offer products and workshops tailored to female sexuality. This includes an array of filmed pornography designed for and made by women, which leads to the second important topic. Adult film has its public displays of affection. The *Feminist Porn Awards*, a Toronto festival, differs in presentation from mainstream porn's stage in Las Vegas where the Oscars of adult film are annually awarded. Putting differences of celebration aside, feminism exists in both milieus often with the same women whose work is honored on both stages

Adult film takes on an art and educational role when viewed with a pornography feminist lens. Feminist legend Madison Young's San Francisco gallery, *Femina Potens*, encourages creative expression among the city's queer community. A BDSM devotee and sexual masochist, Madison often receives marks when she performs. But in the political business of pornography, she leaves her mark as a director, performance artist, art curator and entrepreneur. Her story is Chapter Eight.

The adult film industry's confrontation with a major HIV problem in 1998 opens Chapter Nine. Condom use in filming, a practice routinely shunned, stares down industry executives. Out of this crisis comes a blood testing protocol administered by industry agreement. Largely unspoken among industry people, escorting is an ancillary business for many performers and raises the question of condoms beyond the camera's lens. Pornography feminists are upfront in their opinions on safer sex and the need to protect the performer community at large.

Among the major studios that support feminist ideals is San Francisco's *Kink.com*. At first glance *Kink* appears to be an unlikely candidate for feminist accolades. The company is BDSM oriented and seemingly humiliates and degrades women. Chapter Ten takes a look at this business and how it puts performers first. The company offers working conditions that are highly praised, honors choice and adheres to what personally delights the performer. *Kink's* popularity among adult film feminists is remarkable and some have filmed at the facility repeatedly.

Going Forward

This book does not claim to be the definitive study of pornography feminism. There are too many shortfalls within these pages to claim any degree of completeness. In particular my description of San Francisco's queer porn community is merely an introduction. Its story is rich with diversity and its people are a cornucopia of sexual fluidity that reflects the thoughts of pornography feminist Dylan Ryan who defines queer porn as a celebration of anybody and "any" and "every" body. That insight alone demands further examination and pages yet to be written.[7]

My fieldwork was limited to those individuals who granted me interviews and with whom I corresponded. To a degree "snowballing" did occur as performers and directors sometimes introduced me to others. For that I am appreciative. Should the reader run across a name for which there is little more than a mention, be assured I wanted to include that person's perspective but was reluctant to write about anyone whose views I could not personally document. Also there is a feminist pornography community abroad, primarily in Europe and Australia. Other than a quick look at the work of Spain's Erika Lust, my research is limited to this side of the Atlantic. I recommend Anne G. Sabo's

After Pornified: How Women are Transforming Pornography and Why it Really Matters (2012) as an authority on the overseas adult film world.

Finally, I am grateful to those performers, directors and others associated with the adult film business for their interest in my research. To give the narrative here a less formal and more personal voice, I choose to refer to the people I interviewed and their contemporaries on a first name basis. Meeting them and learning from them was entirely my pleasure.

Remember Where You Started

On a day awash in sunshine, a limo motors across the Bay Bridge from San Francisco into Oakland. In the backseat is an exotic beauty on the underside of thirty sporting a black miniskirt too short to cover her stockings and garters. Her white blouse is unbuttoned to expose a goodly portion of her black bra; a dark necktie hides just a bit of cleavage. Princess Donna is a bondage model and BDSM dominant with a reputation for aloofness. Today she presents the mien of a whorehouse madam, carrying a serious "I have a job to do and hope all goes well" look on her face.

The limo pulls into the passenger pickup area of the Oakland airport. An All-American Miss with a cover girl complexion hands her luggage to the driver and ducks into the backseat. Sporting jeans, t-shirt and tennis shoes, she is a few years beyond twenty. Her name is Bobbi Starr.

"Tell me what you're going to be doing today and how you feel about it," Donna asks.

"I'm doing an audience participation shoot. I'm a little nervous. I haven't done a bondage shoot in a while." Despite her confessed apprehension, Bobbi settles into a smile accentuated by her dimples.

"You know you're going to be tied up in a room full of people," Donna says, "And you're ok with that?"

"Yeah."

Bobbi sits with knees together, head turned toward the question. Donna is posed with side to the camera, flashing her left thigh, stocking and garter strap. The scene is one of uneven power, teacher addressing student.

Donna reminds Bobbi the event involves dominance and humiliation with selected audience members intimately inter-acting with her. Bobbi is expected to yield to various sex acts under Donna's direction and Donna wants to know if Bobbi is fine with that scenario. The tall, slender girl listens respectfully, smiling demurely as is her custom, and nods approval. Throughout the conversation Bobbi's hands fidget. She uses them when she talks, gestures reflecting a desire to channel energy somewhere. Her eyes never leave Donna, who sits calmly with hands folded on knees.

Donna wants Bobbi to understand a number of men will have their way with her and poses the question as to how many she (Bobbi) expects.

"There are supposed to be ten tested people, so I hope all ten," she replies, expressing a bit of delight, at least for the camera.

Donna explains the room is expansive and will have many guests to entertain. Bobbi, whose straight dark hair frames the buoyant rosy face of a college coed, appears enthusiastic yet nervously animated. A sense of uncertainty is detectable in her voice and body language. Bobbi mentions she does not want men urinating on her and says this with surprising conviction, making a fist with her left hand and softly striking the open palm of her right as if not to offend too much.

Tires rumbling on the metallic roadway, the limo speeds across the bridge toward San Francisco; the raised superstructure flashing past as the car picks up its pace.

Donna goes over rules for the shoot with the emphasis that Bobbi can change her limits at any time. It is every bit a business conversation.

"If we get into a scene and you decide it's too much, or you don't want to do it anymore, just let me know and we can always stop," Donna instructs. "Do you know your safewords?"

Bobbi responds "red," then adds an "uh-uh" accompanied by a headshake to demonstrate what to do when gagged. She has done her homework.

With parameters reviewed, Donna transforms her personality

into Bobbi's dominant or top and asks Bobbi if she is ready to get started. A forced smile prefaces, "I guess so." Donna instructs her to undress. Bobbi slips out of her top and jeans as if ordered by an impatient lover or a nurse in a hospital pre-op room. This is not an alluring strip tease, it's done via command. Donna informs Bobbi from here on she is not to close her mouth or legs completely or speak unless spoken to.

When Bobbi is completely nude Donna cuffs her wrists and ankles in leather restraints. The submissive's smile is gone replaced by a moment of noticeable unease before her face excuses all expression. Bobbi loses her animation, letting Donna do what she wants. The dominant tells her "property" she is to please the guests then adds the final accoutrement, a burlap blindfold.

As the car winds into San Francisco's Mission District Bobbi remains silent, hands locked behind her, sitting with legs slightly spread as instructed. Donna softly caresses her "captive" before lewdly working her over for the camera. Bobbi moans, seemingly aroused. Donna steadies her fondling and continues her gentle conversation, as is her habit in these types of shoots. Bobbi is entirely acquiescent; the blindfold stares straight ahead, minimizing the persona behind it. As the scene winds down Donna turns and relaxes with her back to the car door, placing her heeled shoes in Bobbi's lap. The power play is complete.

The limo pulls into an indoor parking area. Two men dressed in black reach into the car and remove the evening's entertainment. Hands still restrained, a non-resistant Bobbi is led away. Donna follows, heels clicking sharply on the concrete floor. Her lonely fading walk is reminiscent of a correctional institution: cold, proper and sterile.

The scene shifts to a well-lit space marked off in a cavernous basement. Thirty people are present, jackets and ties for the men and cocktail dresses for the women. Some wear masks covering their eyes as if attending a costume ball. The atmosphere has the

semiformality of an upscale suburban cocktail party in a contra-
dictory dungeon setting. Drinks abound. Conversation is affable.
People mill about. A man is heard to say to a female guest,
"Welcome to California."

Announced by the snap of her shoes, Donna enters and
stands beside a portable wooden frame positioned in front of red
drapes that pass for stage curtains. The dominatrix is tall and
raven-haired, dictatorially imposing yet oddly approachable. In
her well-honed director persona, she declares the show is "about
to begin" and asks everyone to take their seats in the semicircle
of folding chairs that face the frame. The men in black bring in
the still-shackled Bobbi, making certain she does not stumble.
Donna introduces the show's entertainment and parades her
around for the audience to inspect. She pulls Bobbi's hair, jerking
her head back, and orders Bobbi to expose her most intimate
body parts for everyone to see. Bobbi turns her back to the
audience and bends forward. Uneasy laughter is scattered
throughout the room. The dominant and her submissive travel
the stage's perimeter; Bobbi is presented as if for sale or for
punishment. After the public displays of her body cavities, she is
attached standing spread-eagled to the frame, blindfold still in
place.

Donna takes up a flogger and the whipping begins. Bobbi
writhes. The show is underway.

On this evening Bobbi Starr will be penetrated orally,
vaginally and anally, often by members of the audience in the
theater of BDSM. Donna will apply a vibrating Hitachi Magic
Wand on Bobbi's clitoris to induce the combination of pleasure
and pain the audience has come to see. Bobbi's performance is
vehement, physically taxing and filled with wrenching orgasms.
She is, after all, a pro.

The shoot is divided into a trilogy of scenes, each a part of a
larger ritual of dominance and submission.

Bobbi's status in this play is muted contradiction. The

blindfold conceals her personhood yet she is exposed by her nudity, becoming the helpless "victim." Without her eyes to animate the individual behind the blindfold, the audience is reminded it is easy to inflict torment on a woman who has no identity. In her darkness Bobbi will be assaulted by verbal taunts and name-calling. But at no time does she cede control. The submissive is at once the object and subject of the drama. Her boundaries are respected.

The audience must measure its degree of identification with Bobbi as victim, with Donna as punisher, and with themselves as spectators who have yielded to their own instincts as the play unfolds. Who is Bobbi in this narrative: a naughty girl, a licentious slut, an interrogated prisoner, a punished slave or helpless virginal fresh meat indoctrinated into a mythical castle of sadomasochistic terror? Does she feel empowered or sexually aroused with the display of her nakedness and her ability to receive punishment before a crowd she does not know or see?

At the end of the scene the Hitachi refines Bobbi's status. The prisoner/slave image fades; the wanton slut emerges. Her scourging complete, she is allowed a measure of indulgence to conflate pain and pleasure. For the audience it may be her perceived gratification that encourages them to unleash an occasional unkind word. Moral righteousness in punishing the promiscuous woman tests the inner desire to look while sexual fascination is safely played out knowing the performers are in on the game.

When the outcome for the first scene is complete, a frozen moment takes place. A kneeling and still blindfolded Bobbi places hands on thighs, holding the pose as the camera records the fading seconds. The audience sits silently. The resolution becomes the dark graphic in the film noir of the mind, establishing beginning and end. Is the submissive Bobbi ready for chastisement while already thoroughly corrected? The image moves in either direction and will be repeated twice more in the shoot.

The remaining scenes are miniversions of presentation and end. In the second Bobbi is kneeling once more, exhibited in the middle of the circle on a cushioned platform raised a couple of feet above the floor. Her hands are cuffed behind her back; a leather strap above the elbows pulls her arms together forcing her breasts forward. Leather strips bind calves to thighs with legs open. Bobbi remains blindfolded, back arched to accentuate the thrusting outward of her eroticism and submissiveness. The snapshot blends willing promiscuity and an invitation to abuse. The audience, quietly seated, awaits Donna's commands for the ritual to continue.

During the course of this part of the drama, Bobbi performs a variety of sex acts in different positions as the restraints are removed to accommodate her need to alter body positions. A few audience members approach the dais to participate in fondling or penetrating her. Bobbi is now working energetically. There is a splattering of applause accompanying cheers and whoops characteristic of rock concerts and sporting events. An occasional insult, the word "whore" is heard, breaks through the din. An unidentified female voice interjects with an empathetic, "now we're entertained!" Intense laughter pops up among the spectators who, at this point, are comfortable in their superiority. Another voice shouts, "Fuck like your life depended on it!" followed by a surly growl of "good whore." A series of multiple penetrations continues with as many as four or five audience participants around the laboring Bobbi. In the final minutes of the scene she becomes increasingly exhausted, breathing more heavily. Bobbi asks Princess Donna if she "may see?"

Donna removes Bobbi's blindfold. The audience participants peel away leaving her sitting on the cushioned platform, legs apart. She is the goddess, the center of attraction. Her worshippers retreat again into a self-conscious silence. The camera fades for the frozen moment leaving the question of whose pleasure is sated. Whose guilt and shame is assuaged?

In the third and final scene a bed is placed within the circle for another round of penetrations. Bobbi ends the narrative on the bed, her wrists and ankles attached to its four corners in the traditional spread-eagle position of total vulnerability. In the capable hands of Princess Donna, the Hitachi makes its final appearance. Bobbi writhes with dramatic orgasms, thrashing shamelessly while still restrained. Spectator insults, laughter and sporadic applause punctuate the scene. The final ovation, congratulations on a stellar performance, breaks out. Suddenly Bobbi is still, the Hitachi is finished. Someone from the audience offers her a drink of water. Bobbi is spent, her body covered with ejaculate and spit. Once entered repeatedly she is now quiet, bound to the bed and left to her own space, close at hand yet distant and untouchable.

The spectators gaze at Bobbi as one imagines the populace might have done centuries ago at an execution site in ancient Rome. The crucified slut, morally depraved and thoroughly punished is somehow frightening, disgusting and purifying. The inability to turn away captures the room. The silence that follows is loud, awkward and disquieting. Some onlookers, elbows on knees, lean forward; Donna abandons the bed and moves to the audience. Bobbi is alone. The camera captures the motionless climax that dichotomizes the sexual interchange of the entire play.

"The party's over," Donna announces, breaking the tension. Another enthusiastic round of acclaim erupts and spectator smiles warm the underground theater. Relief settles in. A female voice says, "Well done."

"Now that's entertainment!" a male voice shouts from the crowd.

Bobbi sparkles a bit as if to quip, "glad you liked it," then issues a simple, softly spoken, "thank you."

Applause returns, this time more politely as the camera pans the now emotionally glowing audience and goes to a fade out.

"Did everyone have fun?" Donna asks. The camera is back on. She stands next to the now empty bed.

The audience is pleased with the show.

"She did a great job, didn't she?"

Delight again bubbles up among several onlookers. "Yes she did!" "Absolutely!" "Very good job!"

A trim thirtyish looking woman admits segments of Bobbi's performance energized her submissive feelings. Sensing an opportunity to extend the audience mood, Donna issues a tongue in cheek invitation. "Sounds like someone is volunteering," she muses, her voice rising playfully and teasingly. Nervous laughter is suddenly reignited. Comments like "come on down" and "you're the next contestant" fire up among chortling guests.

After a short break to clean and compose herself, Bobbi is debriefed in the audience's presence. She remains nude and discusses the shoot with Donna who also participated sexually and now wears only a corset and stockings. She mirrors Bobbi; both have exposed breasts and genitalia. All pretense of inequality has evaporated. The women are like girls in the office talking about boyfriends and sex. Smiling broadly, Bobbi comments on how the blindfold was exciting. It kept her unaware of what would happen next and it was "fun to not know what was coming." She evaluates the men who had sex with her. "The guys were all really cool... they were all respectful so that was really nice, I liked that."

Pause for a moment and consider an alternative ending in this theater of fantasy. In the denouement, Bobbi transitions into the demanding sex goddess, sated and guaranteeing another harvest for the people. Reaching deep into the unconscious, the ritual resurrects the archetypal images that occupy the myths and legends when civilization was creating a history of itself. The applause is a tribute not so much for a good show but for renewal. Bobbi has offered herself to be harvested, the most resolute of gifts. She is to be honored and worshipped. The variant present in San Francisco on this night is the Sacred Feminine and her dual role as the nurturer of civilization and the purifying sufferer without whom mankind could not carry on. Perhaps that is why the woman in the audience suggested its arousal for her.

Or, is the narrative simply a hardcore film shoot with a veneer of sadomasochism?

Filmed in 2006, this episode is a product of *Kink.com*, a San Francisco based adult film company whose internet subscribers comment on the scenes they pay to see, rating the quality of the production and the model's performance. *Kink* is a giant in the online pornography business, controlling the production and distribution of its material. Promotional photos of the shoot are in the public domain on BDSM webpages.[1]

On an April morning in 2011, Bobbi Starr and I are chatting over brunch in Toronto's Strathcona Hotel. We had first talked a year earlier and I feel at ease asking her just about anything. I suggest she appeared jittery during the limo ride that delivered her to the Old National Guard Armory, the home of *Kink.com*.

"Yeah, I would definitely say that I was nervous," she chuckles.

Bobbi explains the narrative was a test shoot for the *Public Disgrace* website being developed by Princess Donna. *Kink.com* was building its brand and she, Bobbi, was "their guinea pig" for several of the company's original websites. *Waterbondage* with rigger Lew Rubens, *The Training of O* directed by the innovative James Mogul, *Public Disgrace* and *Sex and Submission* launched her career.

"Donna didn't really tell me much," Bobbi says, speaking of

what was running through her mind during the ride. "Because I trust Donna, I knew [it was] going to be fun."

"You didn't have a clear understanding of what was going to happen?"

Bobbi shakes her head and affirms she did not know exactly but quickly notes uncertainty in a *Kink* shoot is advantageous. "I feel there is an importance to authentic reactions at *Kink*," she declares.

Bobbi expands on what a *Kink* narrative means for a performer. "You have to be aware, really aware, of what you're getting into." Models must have a conversation with themselves and *Kink's* directors about what they are interested in doing. "You need to be honest with yourself," she insists. Being upfront is imperative because a *Kink* shoot has a genuine reality not found anywhere else, she says, at least in her experience, and Bobbi Starr is well traveled in porn.

Raised in an upper middle class family in California's Silicon Valley, Bobbi was home schooled early on before entering public education. As an adolescent she parlayed her athletic skills into junior Olympic swimmer status during high school. Her talents with the oboe opened the door for conservatory training and a budding career in classical music. After graduating from San Jose State University, Bobbi entered the adult film industry at age twenty-two, working fetish scenes for *Kink* before crossing over into the more conventional pornography of Southern California's San Fernando Valley.

I bring up her relationship with Donna, mentioning that she (Bobbi) is representative of Porn Valley and Donna is a part of the San Francisco queer porn community, bookends for two pornography universes. Why is Donna so loved by the models that shoot for her?

Bobbi smiles, "She has a power over people. She is manipulative in the most loving way." Donna is honest, Bobbi explains, "very skilled" in her work "because it's all been done to her." In other words, "the best submissives make the best dominants," Bobbi reminds me. Though Bobbi has moved on to assume more dominatrix roles in the company's female domination websites, she still occasionally films as a submissive, as does Donna, insisting that "it's important to remember where you started."

As we are wrapping up, Bobbi compliments Donna's ability to train performers who work with her. "When she does something to me," Bobbi says, "I'm absorbing what she's doing, I'm learning." That's significant, Bobbi insists, because as a performer, "you can't tune *Kink* out." A model cannot merely "go through the motions."[2]

The same is true in the broader sense for all adult film performers who make a career in a tough and demanding business. They share a sense of empowerment in how they conduct themselves and demand their space in the making of a product that could not exist without them. To do so requires a philosophy that elevates a woman beyond a simple receptacle for sex and gives all women permission to enjoy the sexual and consume adult film without guilt or shame.

Bobbi Starr gives us this direction. She is a feminist, as is her professional colleague, New York University graduate Donna Delore.

PART ONE

"It was a time when the prevailing attitude of most performers was that old, 'Hey kids, let's put on a play.' I earned decent money doing make-up and wardrobe while many others filled in as gaffers, gofers, and script. We actually had to learn lines and blocking for the camera, very much a team effort with nary a diva in sight."

Gloria Leonard on the early days of filmed pornography as told to the author on January 31, 2011.

Chapter 1

Real Sex Merchants

"If no one could define a skunk more closely than that, campers would be in trouble."
Walter Kendrick on Justice Potter Stewart's declaration that he knew pornography when he saw it, though he could not precisely describe what he saw. From *The Secret Museum: Pornography in Modern Culture* (1996)

A One Reel Showpiece

"In the wide open spaces where 'men are men' and 'girls will be girls', the hills are filled with romance and adventure," reads the title card that opens a 1915 silent film, *A Free Ride*. A clumsy tale of a man who picks up two girls in his Model T, the brief vignette introduces hardcore sex to a fading Victorian Age. The one reel showpiece is an early documented classic; a grainy black and white celebration of sexual curiosity wrapped around the quick and somewhat effortless seduction of willing females. It is *real* sex, the non-simulated type, and establishes "smokers" or "blue movies" as the original hardcore genre of American film. In the early decades of the twentieth century, society demanded that a proper woman, uncorrupted by immoral and lewd thoughts, stifle her sexual expression. However, beneath the humdrum and propriety of the farm, neighborly small towns and city office buildings, lay a substratum of sexual delights. Simply put, there are women not bound by decorum and *A Free Ride*'s viewers are privy to a secret: girls like to have fun, too, and can call their own shots while they are at it.[1]

Urban areas offered clandestine venues for stags. The films were whorehouse appetizers designed to titillate the imagination

24

and open the wallet. On the far side of the bawdy house were fraternal organizations, local clubs and fire halls. Here stags offered sophomoric peep shows that replaced the bordello adventure with a few guffaws and dirty jokes. Stags sneaked into these gentlemen only environs on a catch as catch can basis. Illegality was assuaged when local gendarmes looked the other way in exchange for a free pass to watch the sinful. A quick buck was the hustler's aim and a fast exit after the show expected. Like an archeological find at the end of digging season, the offending layer of the hardcore was covered over, at least until the next visit.

The short reels present a loose narrative revolving around a handful of themes sketched into a plot. Among them are the doctor's office where the female patient willingly disrobes; the bored housewife who entertains a stranger, often a delivery man or handyman or on the darker side, a housebreaker or neighborhood voyeur. The casting couch is the most direct scenario. The male professional, commonly a teacher or film producer, seduces the innocent female who yields for a promise or a little needed cash. When the modern hardcore film age enters the American consciousness, these themes are revisited with regularity. The classic *Deep Throat* (1972) is a doctor's office spoof. Over time extra characters are added. The husband comes home unexpectedly to join in his wife's deliveryman fun; the doctor's nurse, in her "usual" office wear of garters and heels, participates in the patient's "treatment." Stags emphasize chance encounters, reflective of fantasies where sex is exhibited for its own sake to entertain the "male gaze." The emotional connections of the characters are vacant, allowing the viewer unencumbered access to the carnal. In its simplest form, the central notion of a stag is that the sex is viewed with an adolescent lens and the assumption prevails that a good time is had by all.[2]

In their heyday stags were comedic, displaying society's average sort, individuals whose personhoods are of no consequence when it comes to the sex. The men are older, appearing sometimes paunchy, and the women a tad worn. If the female performers are seen as sex objects it isn't because they are degraded or humiliated. Their identities are missing by virtue of the stag's limited storyline, leaving only their sexuality to explain their presence. Yet stags are multilayered in their format. One level presents an inside look at a hooker and her "john." The motel film of the late stag period reinforces this convenient image. The audience assumes a blue movie female to be a sex worker playing herself, sexually receptive to a man she has just met. Another view is the couple next door that turns the audience into a collective voyeur. Other stags illustrate the simplest definition of the filmed pornographic narrative, disconnected persons who show up for sex. Who they are as individuals is unimportant. As writer Dave Thompson indicates, stag performers are any of us and all of us and it matters little if the women are prostitutes, entertainers, or office workers and the men merely store clerks or delivery workers. It's the fantasy that counts.[3]

The 1920s was a decade of stag popularity. A wink and a nod greeted special movie nights for local men's groups and college fraternities. The period offered up the perfect stag girl persona, the rebellious flapper. Modern and independent, bratty and middle class, she drank, smoked and partied with the speakeasy crowd. This Jazz Age sweetie might, given the right circumstances, unabashedly spread her legs for the camera. The working class stag viewer saw these tarts exposed and flat on their backs, subjects of the vulgar joke that is the film itself. But reality presented shades of difference because female stag performers, especially the unemployed Hollywood actresses looking for a break, were far removed from the upper classes.[4]

With a few exceptions, everyone has a delicious romp in the stag. Researchers Al Di Lauro and Gerald Rabkin believe the film illustrates the vulgar humor found in adolescent off-color jokes.

Typical is the early 1920s short *The Goat*. The male hero, a bit of a simpleton, is easily played for a fool by the female characters. In the pivotal scene he is standing against a fence with his penis poking through an opening in it, a primitive version of what is commonly known as a "glory hole" in modern adult film. An amused woman presses her nude body against the opposite side. The narrative's three females conspire to dominate the joke. The unsuspecting man copulates with a goat he cannot see when it replaces the female on the other side. Exhausted, he peers over the fence and announces, via the title card, to the giggling trio, "That's the best girl I ever had in my life."[5]

The film is typical of stags in which the woman plays the hand. She determines if the sex is to occur. Film historian Constance Penley believes the stag genre is feminine friendly, noting that women often start the sex and define its boundaries, a modern sex-positive feminist idea. Male sexual ignorance is exposed when the "hero" gets his comeuppance. Women are the mischievous ones and men, as revealed in *The Goat*, are duped by the gag.[6]

Despite the message that women often enjoy themselves in these blue movies, anti-porn feminism decades later will insist that stag women are objectified and harmed, victims of the male gaze. Incidentally, objectification also applies to men who, like the female performers, have no larger character development. In fact the clueless men are frequently incompetent buffoons, hardly bearers of a gaze that humiliates. Without a deeper understanding of who these early hardcore performers are and why they interact with each other, the objectification question lingers.[7]

Let in the Thieves

Modern society 1920s style was ready to break from its Victorian prudery. The promise of open sexual attitudes hovered over a post-war youth acclimating itself to fast living and the automobile. Enamored with a new urban culture, girls bobbed their hair and lifted their hemlines beyond the naughty. By age nineteen or twenty women left home for work, college or both, putting off traditional married life for the present. Flaunting their newfound independence, they rebelled against prohibition and kissed any man they wanted, much to the horror of their Victorian mothers.

For the fledging Hollywood film industry, the Jazz Age brought scandal and harassment. Movies were too dissolute, reflecting Tinseltown's weakness for parties, drugs, alcohol and sex. Accusations of murder were foisted on comedian Fatty Arbuckle in 1921, which personified Hollywood's moral turpitude. Starlet Virginia Rappe died in a San Francisco hotel room while partying with Arbuckle and his friends. The circumstances of her untimely death along with rumors of her alcohol use, past abortions and venereal disease painted Hollywood in its foulest colors. The demise of other Hollywood types under similar circumstances, director William Desmond Taylor and actress Olive Thomas in particular, sparked an outrage that pressured the film industry to self-police or face government intervention. The result was a film review board, the Motion Picture Producers and Distributors of America. Largely run by Irish Catholic Joe Breen, the committee produced a set of guidelines under the direction of former Postmaster General, Indiana Republican Will H. Hays. Launched in the mid-1930s the Hollywood Production Code, or the Hays Code as it is generally known, was a bitter dose of self-regulation. It was lax on violence but draconian in its treatment of anything sexual. The self-appointed guardian of moral values, the Catholic Church, chimed in with its own monitoring organization to lend Hays zesty support. Formed in 1934 the Catholic Legion of Decency (CLD) assumed the high-minded judgment of censorship and survived until the mid-1950s. At that point the moralists transitioned to a new censorship organization with lessons learned. The Citizens for Decent Literature (CDL) kept its Catholic roots but avoided overt displays of religious zealotry.[8]

The post World War I years offered up receptive audiences for the exploitation film, a product designed to skirt Hays by living on the boundaries of the acceptable. Marketed with carnival hucksterism, these movies traveled from town to city with a road show shtick that assured the customer a peek at the lustful, but delivered little that aroused. An elusive coterie of independent entrepreneurs, widely known as the Forty Thieves, promoted their films as adult fare. Exploitation became synonymous with low production costs and bad taste advertised with "carnivalesque ballyhoo." The producers controlled distribution by dividing the nation into regions and booking films in rented theaters or other venues not connected with the major studios. Publicity gimmicks tagged along to lure the audience. The big draw was shock and titillation. Lobby posters hinted at the depravity and wickedness that befall the naïve young women who are ensnared in lust and shame. Unforgivable vices expressly condemned by the Code and not on Hollywood's radar, prostitution, drugs, abortion, venereal disease, interracial sex, white slavery and unwed motherhood, set up the exploitation agenda.[9]

Grindhouses, small urban theaters avoided by polite society, served as the exploiter's roost, but there were too few to make a reasonable profit. Backwater towns and summertime carnivals provided more fertile territory. The rumored cheap thrills of exploitation fare tapped the shoulder of the surrounding population for a look-see. A road show stop brought the rube's golden chance, assuming his moxie held. But the local farmhand and town clerk got a mere smidgen of what he thought he was buying. Whether it was a carnival stop or a local cinema, David Friedman, the master of the exploitation racket in the post World War II era, summarized the longstanding secret to success:

promise the lewd and bawdy and show practically nothing. The locals left thinking the next time they'd see it all only to shell out their hard earned bucks for another round of disappointment.[10]

Exploitation films reinforced a Victorian ethos that shaped America's rural temperament, especially in the years between the wars. Offering a narrative packaged around the sexual, exploitation films supported formidable conservative values such as marriage and family while dealing with vices that threatened the young. Enticing titles sold morality lessons. The exploitation gem *Reefer Madness* (1936) is a tale of high school students whose marijuana use entangles them in a web of self-destruction. (In the later Cold War years, the film resurfaced as a humorous cult classic for a drug-oriented counterculture.) Other films such as *The Sin of Nora Moran* (1933), *The Wages of Sin* (1938), and *Secrets of a Model* (1940) deliver the unforgiving message that sadly naïve young women are headed for shame and broken lives whenever they abandon traditional virtues. *Slaves in Bondage* (1937) cautions the public about the evils of prostitution and how unsuspecting girls fall prey to the debauchery lurking in the big city nightscape. The "don'ts" of the Hays Code always reassured the moviegoer that home is father's haven and it is best to stay there until marriage safely opens the door to intimate bliss. In the exploitation product a woman's sexual agency is absent. Her vulnerability and exposure to transgression marks her destruction.[11]

Depression era America retained its small town homogeneity and its missionary position sexuality. Warnings of venereal disease and the evils of masturbation were the twin bogeymen that by some measure controlled physical expression among the young. Notwithstanding CLD opposition, sex hygiene films of the 1930s such as *Damaged Lives* (1933), a picture about the ravages of sexually transmitted infections, provided the only knowledge of the intimate some people ever got. The CLD condemned these films as insidious foreign imports unfit for a robust American youth. Such accusations gained traction in a time of impending war in Europe. Fascism engulfed Italy and Germany while the specter of world communism loomed out of Russia. An isolationist leaning public was wary of unwanted immigration and anyone whose roots hinted of foreign influence was seen as a threat to Americanism.[12]

The most enduring exploitation film was a post-war latecomer called *Mom and Dad* (1945), the story of an unwed pregnant high school girl and her missteps into an abyss of shame. Produced and marketed by road show extraordinaire Howard "Kroger" Babb, whose nickname comes from working in a Kroger grocery store, the fairly dull production has a hook: the birth of a baby. Billed as adult fare, separate shows were scheduled for men and women to capitalize on the mysterious and forbidden. To wrap an aura of credibility around the production and forestall the censors, Babb employed a guest lecturer, ostensibly a medical person whose name was predominant on the one sheets, and two "nurses," often hired locally for the gig. The lecturer, always identified as "Elliot Forbes," introduced the film using the "square-up," a brief statement about the social problem the film presents. Requiring everyone to sit through the lecture, Babb induced the audience to pony up extra money for a sex education book, extending his profit on every showing. Best of all, the live birth fulfilled the picture's educational purpose, keeping law enforcement at bay.[13]

Mom and Dad was showbiz hokum in its finest hour. David Friedman, who obtained the rights to the film in 1956, claimed that *Mom and Dad* earned $40 million in its heyday not counting all those books that went for a dollar each. The film had a seemingly endless shelf life, making its final run in the 1970s. In 2005 it was selected for the National Film Registry, the stamp of a classic.[14]

Veiled in Performance Art

Stag popularity was sustained through the Depression and beyond. Offering a bit of relief in exhausting times, an exhibitor with a 16mm projector and a handful of reels was in business anywhere a bed sheet could be tacked on a wall. After two decades of travel, stags continued to fill their own educational niche, revealing the mysteries of the female anatomy and the wonders of sexual techniques. It was a tribal rite of passage, particularly for college students, and a bonding experience for the local men's club. Perhaps a few ideas to try out with the wife was only a hope, but an enticing possibility nonetheless.[15]

While the Forty Thieves plied their trade with little censure, a new barker joined the tour with a risqué creation based on an old idea, the burlesque film. Long a part of vaudeville, live dancers brought the flesh too close to the customer for some morality minded communities. Gypsie Rose Lee starred at Minsky's Burlesque in Times Square until 1937 when Mayor Fiorello La Guardia won his battle against New York City's sex shows. But with the advent of the Second World War, burlesque buoyed morale. Glossies of adored dancers and movie stars circulated in the barracks and painted bodies decorated "nose art" on bombers. Burlesque was suddenly chic.[16]

The immediate post-war years experienced a brief resurgence of live dancers. Eventually theater owners discovered film to be more convenient than hiring girls whose work habits were not reliable. In turn strippers made quick money doing filmed shorts. Only a single camera was required and the resulting clips turned into easily repeatable "loops." They gave dancers wider exposure not dissimilar from today's web cam internet sites that feature fun-loving amateurs and porn models. Burlesque women were suggestively naughty and in control of their image, challenging the exploitation movie's morality tale. Like the puckishly assertive women of the early stags, burlesque queens served as bellwethers for the adult film feminism of the coming decades.[17]

Burlesque performers are feminist-like in their stage presence. Professors Carmine Sarracino and Kevin Scott note that dancers reveal "themselves as sexual beings but not as sex objects." The gimmick was the tease and the dancers manipulated the audience with seductive overtones veiled in performance art. The burlesque film 1950s style helped popularize the legendary Bettie Page, whose bangs and goddess-like figure fired the male libido. Bettie stepped over a few fetish lines in her day, introducing BDSM to a somewhat naive America as both dominant and lovely submissive with bondage, whips and paddles all part of the show. The ebony-haired beauty's free spirit wrapped her in an erotic innocence that captured the post-war male imagination. You could tie her up but was she really captured? "Bettie worship" became a cultural tradition with "Bettie power" never in doubt.[18]

Eric Schaefer spins another view of post-war stripper films: they were socially "transgressive" in an age when female sexuality was a prisoner of the morality tale. For its part, Hollywood reinforced the "passive, available, and controllable" image of women. Legitimate film stars at the time, among them Doris Day, Debbie Reynolds and the sexier Marilyn Monroe, exemplified this interpretation. Exploitation movies were likewise conservative, Schaefer suggests, presenting "gender roles" that reflected a mainstream heteronormative society. On the other hand, burlesque films clearly undercut this norm. The sexually powerful dancer was an intermediary between Hollywood's constrained, marriageable woman and stag indecency, an image that dangles "between the legitimate and the illegitimate," Schaefer asserts, offering a peek into feminism's coming second wave.[19]

Exploitation films were Hollywood's black sheep, loosely part of the family but forced to the edges of respectability. The exploitation narrative is lurid and its women stray, but the morality tale endures. Other women in adult entertainment markedly overstepped society's patriarchal norms. Stag women were up front in their sexual expression; likewise burlesque queens ruled their marginalized world, teasing and dominating the male gaze with calculated eroticism. By the 1960s the coming *sex*ploitation era will ratchet up women's erotic expression, challenging Hollywood's traditional gender role presentations.

The party was heating up with the little noticed sexual revolution a gathering cultural storm just outside the door. Within its rumblings a new feminism swirled among the clouds. As the winds picked up and rain pelted a society unaccustomed to radical change, the final offspring of a film genre that began in 1915 lurked in the dark. Hardcore pornography was ready to crash the party.

A "Cutie" with No Clothes

The bump and grind queens never showed it all, reinforcing the old exploitation saw of keep 'em coming back the next time. In the 1950s and 1960s burlesque shared the stage with two recon-figurations of the adult genre, a revamped nudist camp flick (early examples date to the 1930s) and the art house film, a subgenre that triggered censorship issues in the pre-war days. When a young Brigitte Bardot shocked the public with as much of her assets as could pass legal muster in *And God Created Woman* (1956), the times were turbulent. The Cold War gripped America and concern over the pornographic, particularly as a communist tool to debilitate democracy, arose.

To no one's surprise, filmed nakedness faced a court challenge over obscenity. A New York State Court of Appeals decision in 1957 cleared the way for nudity in motion pictures. The film in question was a Florida nudist camp production called *Garden of Eden* (1954). Its pretext is a "back-to-nature" theme under the newly concocted "social nudism," an academic gimmick designed to persuade the viewer he or she is more of a social scientist than a voyeur. With the stroke of a judge's pen the nudist subgenre, which had its run into the early 1960s, was exonerated. No real sex, but plenty of boobs and butts bouncing around on playful females. On the other hand, *imported* nudist films bypassed the professorial auspices of social nudism. To satisfy the censors, filmmakers assiduously avoided full frontal exposure.[20]

By 1959 the public was ready for something more, a little action and sexier bodies sprinkled with a bit of sleaze. Enter a "cutie" with no clothes, a comedic exploitation film that initiated the "*sex*ploitation" movie of the 1960s. Cuties monopolized female nakedness without overt carnality while cashing in on its suggestiveness. They were the endpoint of the exploitation's thirty-year carnival tour that ramped up what seeing it all means. No more skirting Hays with illicit topics as a cover for implied sex. Now it was upfront for the price of a ticket.[21]

The barker who made the "nudie-cutie" profitable was Russ Meyer, a film entrepreneur who cast his old war buddy Bill Teas in a Walter Mitty-like sexual jaunt. *The Immortal Mr. Teas* (1959) is about a non-descript middle-aged man with an aching tooth. A daydreamer who loves to ogle women, Mr. Teas leaves the dentist's office after a round of anesthesia that inadvertently changes his visual perceptions. To his surprise every woman he encounters is suddenly in the buff. Meyer characterized the film as "innocent, but leering." Shot in four days, *Mr. Teas* has lots of frolicking but no pubic hair. Nudie-cutie women are sexually irresistible and like burlesque queens in control of their image.[22]

Later Meyer classics like *Lorna* (1964), *Mudhoney* (1965), *Faster, Pussycat! Kill! Kill!* (1965), *Vixen* (1968), and *Beyond the Valley of the Dolls* (1970) are in a more somber vein. They feature strong women ensconced in the Meyer formula of "violence, melodrama, hoke, parody, [and] satire." David Friedman's *Adventures of Lucky Pierre* (1961) joined the act as did other genre spinoffs such as Ted Paramor's *Not Tonight, Henry* (1960) and Joe Sarno's *Moonlighting Wives* (1966). In the 1970s Sarno stepped up as a proponent of feminism in adult film. Of course with the cuties none of the sex is explicit. The game had to keep going, never show it all.[23]

By the 1960s the sexploitation road show was running low on fuel. The nudies found a home at the drive-in, continuing America's love affair with the automobile that began with *A Free Ride*. Though outdoor theaters dated to the Depression, their zenith occurred in the 1950s and 1960s, becoming a natural home for movies that danced around the mainstream. The nudies replaced burlesque films but didn't offer enough titillation to survive. The aging Forty Thieves and their road show, passé in an age dominated by possible nuclear annihilation, were looking at a last stand while the art house and its taste for everything foreign edged America closer to hardcore.[24]

Incidentally, the 1950s produced the modern stag classic *Smart Aleck* (1951), a film starring a sixteen-year old Texas stripper named Candy Barr (born Juanita Slusher). Shot near Nashville, Tennessee or possibly Bakersfield, California, the two-reeler is the personification of the motel film subgenre. The movie is noteworthy because Barr actively resists her male costar when he insists she perform oral sex. Engaging in playful pushing and shoving to waylay him, Barr calls in a friend to do the deed and later joins in with the couple. The assertive teenager clearly controls the manner in which the sex is presented and sets her limits. Praised by pro-sex feminists as an early example of a take-charge woman, Slusher later claimed her participation in the film as Candy Barr was not by choice.[25]

In the shadowy world of filmed sex work, truth is evasive. Journalist Gregg Barrios writes that Juanita Slusher did the film for the money. She went to an address provided by a friend and met a man who gave her a handful of ten dollar bills, a princely sum for a teenager with only a few cents to her name. After the shoot Slusher said she ate her first satisfying meal in weeks, though on film she hardly appears underfed. The teen later maintained that she was emotionally unable to fully comprehend what it meant to put herself in front of the pornographer's camera, not surprising considering her age. Incidentally, Barrios joins the location debate by suggesting that the film may have been shot in the Dallas area, highly likely if its star was financially impoverished and unable to travel far from home.[26]

Today *Smart Aleck* would be shunned as child pornography. But in the Cold War years homosexuality concerned society far more than abused children. In the eyes of conservative homophobes, closeted gays presented convenient targets for communist infiltrators. Ferreting out homosexuality was part of the national survival equation, especially among those who believed the Red Menace was civilization's nuclear endgame. Issues surrounding child pornography were tucked away for a future generation to address, thus a teenager's refusal to orally satisfy an adult is remembered as a feminist statement.

Pushing Back

Parading her coquettish qualities and superb physical assets, the aforementioned French starlet Brigitte Bardot redefined sexuality with a European flavor that oozed sensuality. Her timing was superb. Censors and local constabularies tried to stifle Bardot's on-screen adventures at every turn. The crowds paid to see her anyway, immortalizing *And God Created Woman* as a top grossing foreign film. Bardot's breezy eroticism established European imports as the new measure of sexual openness. Art house fare, a bit of elitism in an otherwise vanilla world, sought an edgier (i.e. more artistic) representation that pushed back against American prudery. Trendy urban sophisticates and college students enamored with the avant-garde flocked to the art house to savor a menu that could be Scandinavian, French or Italian. Obligatory subtitles or English dubbing allowed the most cosmopolitan moviegoer to engage in an international experience by being faux international. Led by Bardot, this foreign product was ready to bypass the old exploitation hustle of "you'll see it all the next time."[27]

Unconcerned about the CLD stamp of approval or Hays Code violations, art houses presented whatever they could short of real sex; and the more censorship aggravation, the better for ticket sales. Meanwhile the sexploitation distributors, practiced at marketing their product to independent theaters, also ignored the Hollywood Production Code, caring little for government attitudes of what is permissible. Inevitably the courts took notice.

The Supreme Court's 1957 *Roth v. the United States* decision established prurient interest, patent offensiveness and community standards as the legal framework for the sexually obscene. The High Court invested obscenity with vague legal parameters intentionally directed at *print* material. The problem of film remained and the art house subgenre forced the Court's hand. The legal system tackled the indecent again on a state level, this time over a French production *Les Amants* (1958) that included nudity and adultery. In the 1964 landmark *Jacobellis* decision, the Justices exonerated an Ohio theater manager of obscenity charges over the film's showing. *Jacobellis* will forever be remembered for Justice Potter Stewart's simple, direct and flummoxing interpretation of the lewd and licentious. He knew it when he saw it, but what was it he saw?[28]

In time two other Court decisions entered the obscenity fray and by implication, pornography. In *Stanley v. Georgia* (1969) the Justices affirmed that people could read or watch whatever they desired in the privacy of their own residence and in *Miller v. California* (1973) the Justices attempted to clarify *Roth*, leaving community standards up to local jurisdictions. The *Miller* guide-lines remain in place today.[29]

Les Amants opened the door for a decade of art house films that reached their pre-hardcore triumph with *I Am Curious Yellow*. *Yellow's* heroine – Lena Nyman, an expression of New Left politics, peace, free love and the sexual revolution – is an early feminist who wants sex on her terms. Barney Rosset's Grove Press assumed the risk of distributing the film. Rosset was willing to fight obscenity charges in the name of free speech with anti-censorship attorney Edward de Grazia defending the production as "artistically valuable and politically powerful." *Yellow* eventually walked away unscathed and the new era of explicit film was primed to accelerate.[30]

Yellow's cultural breakthrough was significant for adult film far beyond the obscenity issue. In fact feminist writer Susie Bright suggests that the film's sex is inconsequential; its notoriety focuses on "class and gender." She contends that for women and intellectuals *Yellow's* appearance was fortuitous. The movie created a broad vista for potential audiences to experience a pornographic film within the safety of their own kind. By 1972 that avenue widened a little more with the mainstream *Last Tango in Paris*, a European narrative that popularizes a stick of butter and introduces anal sex, though simulated in this case, as a much discussed on-screen topic.[31]

Having converted to hardcore by the 1970s, the art house presaged the "porno chic" era. Its films contained political messages in a time roiled with upheaval, challenging authority and encouraging marginalized groups like counterculture youth, blacks, feminists and gays to speak up. Their rebellion revisited the old lesson that sex, because it is political, outrageous and intimidates moral boundaries, can shake society. If the sexual revolution exposed cultural hypocrisy, explicit film undressed America's tried and true morality play. But the play had one more scene before the road show completed its final run.

Giving Away the Last Act

The aging road show entrepreneurs understood that Americans may confine real sex to the underground but will gladly pay for a good dose of violence. The grotesque would now sing the final chorus of the carnival swan song. David Friedman, Cornell University graduate and World War II veteran, introduced the extreme into sexploitation. The violence and sex that defines today's mainstream Hollywood slasher films seduced 1960s audiences at drive-ins and local downtown cinemas. Friedman and other directors like Radley Metzger, who under the pseudonym Henry Paris later scored a hardcore gold medal with porno chic classic *The Opening of Misty Beethoven* (1976), profited from the violence subgenre collectively known as "ghoulies," roughies" and "kinkies." They were gross and macabre but with a put-on that defined high camp.

David Friedman's *Blood Feast* (1963) and *Two Thousand Maniacs* (1964), both starring *Playboy* centerfold Connie Mason, offered up faux brutality that clung to timeworn cultural values. Females are exhibited as victims, tormented with pain, often whipped and tortured. Of course in the end justice prevails because for Friedman and Russ Meyer the morality lesson is sacrosanct. As mentioned earlier, Meyer's women quickly established his trademark. He loved heroines who cater to the American enthrallment with large bosoms. *Faster, Pussycat! Kill! Kill!* featured *Playboy*'s December 1966 Playmate of the Month, Susan Bernard, gagged and kidnapped in a story highlighting rough and tumble females. The later *Vixen* starring Erica Gavin is the first big feature sex movie in which a woman orchestrates the action. Stepping over the grindhouse into legitimate theater, *Vixen* also charmingly offended the CDL, but no one noticed. The organization's religious fervor was a mere nuisance and the Hays Code lay on its deathbed.[32]

Susie Bright describes Russ Meyer as "the king of slapstick

sadism" whose film work expressed a banality that represented the "male chauvinism" 1960s women loved to hate. Nonetheless, Meyer is remembered among some feminists as presenting a powerful female lead. Contemporary feminist filmmaker Erika Lust believes that a Meyer woman may have her shortcomings but projects a mind of her own and acts on it. Russ Meyer, like the Forty Thieves before him, soon retired from the industry. The 1970s ushered in hardcore and the old jester of the nudies could not abide the change.[33]

Whereas "roughies" were limited to rapes and general mayhem such as in *The Defilers* (1965), a film that features sexual slavery, "kinkies" were more torture oriented. A notable first is *White Slaves of Chinatown* (1964) directed by Joseph Mawra. The picture highlights scenes in which women are put in bondage and physically abused. In these productions forceful women often dominate other women, easing the consciences of male moviegoers who paid to see their BDSM fantasies come to life but preferred that an evil woman put the leather to the victims. David Friedman indulged his talents with the *Ilsa* series in the 1970s. The film's villainess is modeled on a sadistic Nazi war criminal named Ilse Koch. Friedman followed the lead of a picture called *Love Camp 7* (1968) about a prison camp during World War II in which female prisoners are routinely punished by the sadistic commander. Sarracino and Scott note that this "Naziploitation" subgenre features abuse and "sexual debasement," setting the stage for the women's prison films to come later. It's worth noting that the idea of physically punishing women was not new; a few stags displayed tamer versions and included what the "kinkies" directors eschewed: real sex.[34]

If "kinkies" entertained the sadomasochistic crowd, they contained little of the carnage that marked the "ghoulies." On the whole separating the subgenres is problematic, as *Blood Feast* could fall into either category. Like the other film types, "ghoulies" retained the teachable moments of the pre-war morality play. Women were brutalized for their overt sexuality and men get their just desserts. Castration became the rationalized answer for the ill treatment of women, the price men pay for their brutality. Are these films misogynistic, an illustration of patriarchy at its cinematic worst? From the standpoint of what filled the screen, film critics Eddie Muller and Daniel Faris believe it's an accusation that's hard to deny. Ironically, anti-porn feminists of the day were more concerned with the newly arrived hardcore feature than with the physical savagery of the fading sexploitation era. Of course the sophomoric Freidman/Meyer violence was an absurdity, a choreographed spoof and even the rube understood that. Not so with the coming of hardcore, the plots may have been simplistic à la the old stags or non-existent in some cases, but simulated sex was gone. Therein lay the rub.[35]

According to David Friedman, hardcore "killed the goose that laid the golden exploitation egg" and in a monstrous fashion "gave away the last act," real sex, something the old road show king abhorred.[36]

The Link

Shot in a three-day period at a cost of $7,000, a Bill Osco film crossed the simulation line. *Variety* dubbed *Mona: The Virgin Nymph* (1970) as "'the long-awaited link between the stag loop and conventional theatrical fare.'" *Mona* emphasizes in-charge females with the bonus of a storyline and character development to accompany the explicit sex. The heroine, played by the stylishly eyelashed Fifi Watson, explores sexuality on her own terms and uses well-practiced oral skills as her mode of inquiry, selecting the males she wishes to savor. After encountering Mona's talents one grateful recipient suggests they get together again, hinting that going further is in the cards. Mona backs him down. "I call the shots. I blow you and that's it! Understand?" Through her portrait of Mona, Watson offers an early definition of what it means to be an assertive, in-control feminist in adult film.[37]

Mona has the elements that frame modern film pornography: lots of oral sex, girl-on-girl moments, female masturbation, sex toys, and a final orgy with a bondage component. Although Mona's mother artfully seduces her boyfriend with vaginal sex, Osco's heroine is delaying that bonanza until marriage. She is intent on satisfying her desires in such a way as to retain a measure of virginity, not unusual for a young woman comfortable with the sexual revolution as an idea but cautiously approaching the new morality in practice. In short, *Mona's* female characters define the film. They control the action and seek their own pleasure, adding to the film's status as the breakthrough classic in hardcore.[38]

When *Mona* was released the sexually explicit feature film was working its way through Los Angeles, San Francisco and New York. Fortunately the grindhouse was available to host the party. David Friedman operated his own version known as the Pussycat Theaters in 1960s Los Angeles. The same patrons would show up regularly, often for weeks at a time, with afternoons catering to the corporate crowd's extended business lunches. Grindhouse etiquette insisted that customers honor each other's privacy, Friedman explained, because attending a film with a fedora strategically placed in the viewer's lap was a necessity. The measure of a good picture was taken in headwear. Three hats was tops and left the customer exhausted, while a "dog" was condemned to the "no-hatter" wilderness.[39]

Pornography's "golden age" would provide part time smut makers with regular work and a shot at notoriety. Poised to become filmed pornography's Land of Oz, San Francisco nurtured its own dirty movie connoisseurs who solicited a road show of their own without leaving town. The Mitchell Brothers' O'Farrell Theater, Alex de Renzy's Screening Room, and Lowell Pickett's Sutter Theater were hotspots for the cinematic hardcore.

These flesh-peddling entrepreneurs produced and directed their own films and operated their own grindhouses, keeping explicit sex a local product in an industry vertical trust. The Mitchells were working class boys from across the Bay and friends with Pickett, who incidentally met his future business partner, Arlene Elster, at a city medical clinic. She was helping an old high school friend, rock legend Janis Joplin, get an abortion.[40]

San Francisco porners learned their craft by recruiting agreeable young women, often free-spirited college students who could use a little extra money, for a new kind of film short called a "beaver." For hardcore to complete the transition from frontal nudity to explicitness, a final steppingstone was needed. Living on the farthest edge of acceptability, the beaver brought nudity to the final pre-insertion moment. The obvious draw was female genitalia with the "split" version involving the model spreading her legs. Recording on 16mm film, the city's pornographers wanted the girl to acknowledge the camera and the unseen spectator viewing her performance, a technique that heralds the coming of "gonzo" pornography three decades later. Though not usable for the drive-in, 16mm was perfect for beavers and garnered a profit with a minimal investment if presented just under the community radar. San Francisco smut peddlers developed the "pocket theater," a storefront venue that accommodated too few warm bodies to qualify as a legitimate theater. Inexpensive to start up, these movie houses avoided fire regulations and legal hassles. Soon a jump from beavers to the hardcore feature was inevitable and the O'Farrell, the Screening Room, and the Sutter stood ready to profit.[41]

Though beaver shorts were spiced with some whipping and submissive girls forcefully undressed by more aggressive ones, moviegoers eventually yawned at genitalia with no action. A simple case of seeing now what's been seen before complemented with a tinge of pink wasn't enough. The blossoming smut makers had to move to real sex, a decision that carried legal questions because 16mm using amateurs was merely a "folk art" in "a cottage industry." Few of the models were anything close to professionals and paying them to have sex brought possible pimping and pandering charges. So like the old stags, on-screen credits were sometimes nowhere to be found. Despite legal ramifications there were willing women on both coasts. Three of these adventuresses, a skinny South Florida loop performer and stripper, a lovely athletic blonde commercialized on a detergent box, and a veteran Broadway actress looking to pay the rent, would escort adult film into American cultural history.[42]

The City by the Bay pornographers realized their films could avoid legal confrontations if they carried plausible social value. In 1970 Alex de Renzy achieved success with *Censorship in Denmark: A New Approach*, a movie that takes on the documentary status pleasing to social scientists. Denmark legalized porn in 1968; de Renzy visited the country, collected some footage and recut the scenes into a movie. In doing so he dodged the predictable obscenity charges. Entrepreneurial porn merchants were setting trends by initiating new ideas and revisiting old ones. De Renzy's *A History of the Blue Movie* (1970) is the first hardcore compilation (it uses old stag material), while the Big Apple's first advertised feature, director Mike Henderson's *Electro Sex '75*, debuted on Labor Day Weekend 1970. Lastly a New York horror fantasy *Dark Dreams* (1971), directed by Roger Guermantes, joined *Mona* and another Osco movie, *Harlot* (1971) to begin the walk down the real sex yellow brick road. *Dark Dreams* stars the future porn legend, Harry Reems, destined for fame as Linda Lovelace's doctor in the coming classic *Deep Throat*. High in technical quality and sound, *Throat* will escort adult film into the coming hardcore bonanza.[43]

Like roadies prepping the stage for a sold out concert, loop merchants coast to coast had completed their set up work. The carnival "put on" of the exploitation era, the likes of nudist camp flicks, white coater documentaries, "roughies," "kinkies" and the art house film yielded to the storefront beaver. In their high times these pictures catered to select audiences seeking the illicit but reluctant to venture downtown into the urban gold coasts of porn. The big screen of legitimate theaters from cities to suburbia emerged as the final frontier. The undressed was dressed up for suburbia's cocktail set. The "golden age" of modern filmed pornography was on the mountain overlooking the Promised Land. Its Moses, a mild mannered New Yorker named Gerard Damiano, would direct a picture in Miami, Florida that returned the mob's $25,000 investment to the tune of $600 million by most estimates.

Deep Throat (1972) with its own bizarre and ludicrous exploitation of sex becomes the pornographer's Holy Grail, high-end hokum with promise fulfilled. For a few dollars the rube could now watch a woman relax her gag reflex and blow the door off the hinges of acceptability. Seeing it all had finally arrived. The game was over; the road show retired. Real sex was writing the first chapter of its own history beyond the shadowy under-world of the stag film. Notwithstanding, the stag and its siblings left a monumental legacy: the independent filmmaker who thrived outside the entrenched Hollywood system and the empowered woman whose sexuality sold the tickets. The modern multibillion-dollar pornography industry would forever be grateful.

Chapter 2

A "Gaze" of Their Own

"If feeling like I need answer to no one but myself makes me a feminist, I guess I am and always have been."
Georgina Spelvin as told to the author on December 4, 2009

The Adventurous Trio

Lovelace, Chambers and Spelvin, a catchy law firm name but a hardier one for three film personas, one comedic, one innocent, and the last bedeviled, whose on-screen sexual escapades initiated a film era. Audiences flocked to the big screen to fathom what the fuss was all about. Being seen was suddenly chic, "porno chic" actually, thanks to the wit of *New York Times* columnist Ralph Blumenthal in January 1973 and New York film critic Bruce Williamson later in *Playboy* that same year. Everyday people, celebrities, persons of lesser account and of much account sat in darkened theaters holding hands with their anticipations and anxieties. The once hidden was unveiled and moviegoers butted heads with their voyeuristic sense of guilty pleasures. The clandestine gag of the blue movies, explicit sex, was now in 35mm format.[1]

The adventurous trio changed America's conversation on sex, coming along just as anti-porn feminists were shaping the argument for pornography's harm to women. Their denunciations would pester the women's movement for years to come, amplifying the popular view of feminism as anti-man and anti-sex. Of the three, only Linda Lovelace was subjected to rumored abuse. Linda's husband Chuck Traynor, a "suitcase pimp" from South Florida, peddled his wife for profit and personal aggrandizement. Keeping watch over her on the set of *Deep Throat*, he reportedly bounced her around in their hotel room after the shooting day. A tale of domestic violence, Linda's story is compelling but misplaced as an indictment of adult film. Nevertheless, the connect-the-dots logic of pornography's opponents marketed her as the poster child for smut's alleged savagery toward women. Linda's testimony before the government's Meese Commission in 1986 and her biographies *Out of Bondage* and *Ordeal* suggested the fate of all women in an industry offhandedly condemned as predatory.

On the other hand, an inside look at pornographic film paints another picture. Women freely enter the business, take control of their sexual image and often make decent money in the process. Georgina Spelvin and Marilyn Chambers are early examples of these empowered choices. In speaking of her career Marilyn remarked that she wasn't coerced into making porn, nor was she wowed by the money. It was something that she wanted to do and she did it well. "Marilyn was really into sex," Veronica Hart remembers of her friend, "she was having a great time."[2]

Marilyn Chambers found porn by happenstance. Barbara Streisand, star of the romantic comedy *The Owl and the Pussycat* (1970), declined the film's publicity tour and the studio substituted Marilyn Briggs, a Connecticut teenager with a minor part in the production. She was sent to Los Angeles for the movie's premier and later drifted to San Francisco where she worked odd jobs that included stripping to pay the rent. Answering an advertisement from local pornographers Jim and Artie Mitchell, Marilyn was persuaded to star in a film about an innocent girl destined for her sexual awakening. The story's premise was a circulated fantasy among American servicemen during the Second World War. The Mitchells desired a fresh face to portray the kidnapped Gloria who is taken to a nightclub where she succumbs to a sexually decadent and liberating scene. Marilyn's athletic body, girl next door appeal and timely commercial appearance on the *Ivory Snow* detergent box made her ideal for the part. Briggs turned into Chambers, a legend was born and a porn classic, *Behind the Green Door* (1972) came to life.[3]

Legitimate theater was Georgina Spelvin's milieu, having appeared on Broadway in *The Pajama Game* and *Cabaret*. Like Marilyn Chambers, Georgina approached her decision to enter porn with clarity. She recalls at a mature thirty-six she was "old enough to know better" if she believed filming sex scenes was "dangerous" to "body and soul." To make the rent on her New York apartment Georgina signed on to cater for the cast and crew of *The Devil in Miss Jones* (1973), an adult movie shot in a rural area outside The Big Apple. Unexpectedly she became the film's star. Future movies were in the offing and an older woman's sexual appetite assumed its place in feature film. The former stage actress insists that porn sex was "exciting, exhausting, energizing, and fun" and self-satisfying, enabling her to claim, as she puts it, the "Feministic Feeling of Empowerment."[4]

Marilyn Chambers and Georgina Spelvin were feminist-like before any feminist label was applied to pornography's modern era. Marilyn had a liberating sexual attitude that accentuated a control of her career. Her later marriage to her manager Chuck Traynor, the same of Lovelace fame, would appear to question this assessment. Traynor had a low regard for women, especially disobedient ones, and was not the kind of man any feminist would admire. But Marilyn was not the docile Linda. Georgina Spelvin offers a snapshot of their relationship dynamics, describing Traynor as a loving husband, "darling" and "considerate," who Marilyn led "around by the nose."[5]

Veronica Hart characterizes the older Georgina Spelvin as "definitely a feminist who always owned her sexuality" and remarks that Marilyn Chambers was a groundbreaker in "pushing" America's perceptions of race and sex. The *Ivory Snow* girl boldly shot a scene with African American performer Johnny Keyes in *Green Door*, an astounding political and social statement in an age when interracial couplings bordered on the taboo. Both women touted take-charge personas that followed Lena Nyman, Fifi Watson, and the nameless women of stag fame whose identities are lost in films with no credits.[6]

Porno chic is the turning point in adult film history, ushering in a modern era of profits that reach into the billions. Yet one element lingers since the earliest stag days; men dominate the business. The old road show hucksterism is now a corporate patriarchy feminist writer Susie Bright characterizes as "a gin rummy game consortium" and adult film feminist Nina Hartley describes as "an all boys club" that dislikes "dealing with women in power." Today a handful of industry women are lobbying for recognition in a milieu they rightly believe cannot exist without them. Pro-porn feminism defines a core of performers and directors who are making film their way using a female "gaze" that transforms women from object into subject while channeling profits into female operated coffers. This cultural shift within the porn industry began quietly in 1983 with a baby shower in a Manhattan apartment.[7]

From Seven to Five

Until the late 1980s the production and distribution of filmed pornography was not legal and the number of regularly working female performers was about the size of a college sorority. Urban red light districts, the haunts of organized crime, were lined with strip clubs, grindhouses and adult bookstores whose lucrative peep show booths turned customer quarters into millions for porn merchants. The VCR was passing from adolescence into adulthood and some industry talent such as Linda Lovelace (though her career was brief), Marilyn Chambers and the well-endowed John Holmes, emerged as familiar names among hardcore acolytes. Stags became collectible memorabilia, 35mm features were transferred to videotape and new productions, cranked out assembly line style from Southern California's ascending Porn Valley, defined a reconfigured smut genre. Conveniently packaging dirty movies for home viewing, small town "mom and pop" video outlets moved adult entertainment to suburbia. In a feeble attempt to assuage Middle America's guilt over its sexual curiosity, pornography was confined to the store's proverbial "backroom," a modern replay of the Victorian "secret museum" where women and children dared not to venture.[8]

Adult film was the submerged Hollywood, a community which quietly flourished behind the hillside block letters that once advertised a developer's dream called "Hollywoodland." Myths about women victimized by failed childhoods and forced to commit filmed sex acts out of economic desperation, fear of physical harm and dehumanizing drug abuse, assumed their own reality. In truth porn actresses were there for a variety of reasons, financial need not always predominant. A sense of rebellion, love of the sexual and a natural inclination toward exhibitionism were among the motivations. Performers needed each other for support, albeit informally, especially when stigmatized in the public eye and employed in a patriarchal industry in which extended careers are rare. Such was the case with Club 90, the pioneers of feminism in adult film.[9]

A recently married Veronica Hart was expecting her first child. Some of her sister porn actresses and other non-industry friends gathered for a baby shower at the "Sprinkle Salon," adult film star Annie Sprinkle's Manhattan apartment at 90 Lexington Avenue. Filmed pornography was still New York oriented at the time and the actresses knew each other from the set or industry functions such as film premiers. The shower afforded them the opportunity to relax away from business. Within this celebratory gathering were the creators of Club 90, five incomparable women destined to emerge as artistically and politically significant in adult film history.

There were seven women originally with five at the end. Candida Royalle, a native New Yorker, became a feminist in college though her identification with the movement was later challenged by shifts within it. Feminism was breaking into factions over lesbianism and the anti-porn views of Andrea Dworkin and Catharine MacKinnon. The movement was too anti-male for Candida's liking and feminists were failing to come to grips with their own accountability for issues facing women.[10]

Like her sister New Yorker, Veronica Vera was raised in a Catholic home and banked on education as a passport to the future. Though she reckoned her English degree would jump start a writing career, Veronica spent time on Wall Street before contributing an article for *Penthouse Variations*. Her *Penthouse* experience led to the renowned erotic writer Marco Vassi to whom she expressed an interest in BDSM modeling. Vassi arranged a meeting with fetish photographer Charles Gatewood. He introduced Veronica to Annie Sprinkle, who had recently returned from Italy with her live-in boyfriend avant-garde artist Willem DeRidder.[11]

Raised as the demure and conforming Ellen Steinberg, Annie Sprinkle describes her middle class parents as intellectual, "open-minded [and] liberal." Annie's family moved from the States to Panama where her early teen years encountered drugs and altered states of consciousness. Her Central American experience became the catalyst for overcoming an inherent shyness. When her parents relocated to Southern California Annie's free spirit sought adventure. She and her boyfriend at the time drifted to Arizona via motorcycle where at seventeen Annie took up residence in an artist commune.[12]

Annie Sprinkle may very well have passed unnoticed into the hippie counterculture had not her employer, a local adult theater called the Plaza Cinema, shown *Deep Throat*. Arizona authorities closed the establishment, prosecuted the film's producers and distributors and subpoenaed the theater's buxom popcorn girl. In the courtroom Annie flirted with the forty-six year old Gerard Damiano and the two quickly became lovers. She was interested in the deep throat technique and the married director was equally fascinated with the amply built eighteen-year-old. At the trial's conclusion Annie followed Damiano to New York and a pornography career was a film shoot away.[13]

Annie first notable porn adventure was *Teenage Deviant* (1974), a movie she amusingly characterizes as "misogynist" and by today's standard's "politically incorrect." More was to come. New York City's libertine environment kept Annie busy. Understanding that she was foremost a sex worker, Annie began to examine issues surrounding prostitution, sex worker rights and censorship. Her political conscience led her to the newly formed COYOTE (Call Off Your Old Tired Ethics), a sex worker activist organization started by feminist Margo St. James to decriminalize the profession. COYOTE was a natural for Annie. Engagement in social causes was not unexpected; her parents were anti-war and civil rights activists.[14]

Emotionally drained by the loss of lovers to AIDS (Vassi fell victim in 1989) and troubled by a life of sex for money, Annie wanted to move beyond her "party girl" lifestyle into "more art oriented endeavors." A college degree interested her. On the day of the baby shower Gloria Leonard remembers Annie confided "that sometimes she didn't want to be Annie Sprinkle. She wished that she could just be Ellen Steinberg." Annie's reflections caused Gloria to reevaluate her own situation. Knowing that change is ongoing, Gloria "wondered how many other women in the business" shared the same concerns. An idea was floated and invitations were extended to about thirty women to form a support group.[15]

Annie Sprinkle's college dream did come to fruition. She obtained a degree in photography from New York City's School of Visual Arts and a PhD from the Institute for the Advanced Study of Human Sexuality in San Francisco, becoming the first adult film actress to do so. In the last two decades Annie has lectured at universities such as Brown, Columbia, UC Berkeley, UCLA and NYU. Her photography exhibitions have appeared worldwide with her camera work gracing the pages of *Newsweek*, *Spin* and *Penthouse*, among other publications. Her performance art is universally recognized.[16]

A native New Yorker, Gloria Leonard was a veteran porn actress by the early 1980s. Her employment beyond film reflected her intellect; she took a turn on Wall Street and later did a fourteen-year stint as publisher of *High Society* magazine. Gloria's literary years also took her into the public arena. College seminars became a forum for her views on pornography, feminism and First Amendments rights. She appeared on TV and radio talk shows because, as she puts it, she had the ability to string sentences together in a coherent manner.

A teenager in the homogenized 1950s, Gloria Leonard loved jazz and slipped into New York clubs where she discovered a comedian named Lenny Bruce talking sex. Her furtiveness paid off because the comic opened her eyes. "Here's a guy who is verbalizing all the shit everyone thinks about and talks about in private!'" Gloria recalls. Joking about sex was part of his show, she says, but Bruce never "demeaned women." The comedian's act influenced Gloria's liberal attitudes and in time she entered the adult industry. Raising a child alone made the money attractive but it was not the sole reason for her career move. Like Lenny Bruce, sex became a political statement for Gloria Leonard. After her retirement from film she served as president of the Free Speech Coalition, the adult industry's political wing. Her finest leadership moment came with the 1998 HIV crisis that briefly paralyzed the industry.

Born in Las Vegas and a graduate of University of Nevada at a youthful nineteen, Veronica Hart tried legitimate acting. Following a three-year gig in England as a model, dancer and actress, she returned home to the theater stage. Eventually

Veronica headed to New York at the behest of a casting director who had put her in *Going in Style* (1979), an Art Carney/George Burns film partly shot in Vegas. Renting a room from erotic photographer Roy Stuart, Veronica worked here and there in city theaters where onstage sex shows were regular entertainment. "I loved sex," she remembers. Quitting her desk job at *Psychology Today*, the Las Vegas actress was soon writhing in six shows daily with her boyfriend, traveling a circuit of three theaters. Every show required a "pop or a pretend pop," she says, and having more than two orgasms a day before a live audience was hard work. With real time sex losing its appeal, Veronica turned to stripping. After watching an explicit feature film at the World Theater and noticing the acting that was required, Veronica thought porn movies "might be a match" for her.

Entering adult film in 1980 under the name Randee Styles, Veronica Hart characterizes herself as an honest and enthusiastic actress, a description supported in spades by adult film historian Jim Holliday. Veronica made between 100-150 films, though only sixty fell into the hardcore arena. Her actual total of porn appearances is higher due to the bastardized "chopping and slicing and dicing" of her original shoots to create the old pornography standby, the compilation. Veronica notes she left performing in 1984 because she fell in love. The business did not burn her out; shooting sex with other men simply lost its appeal.[17]

Also in the original group were adult models Kelly Nichols and Sue Nero. When the gatherings assumed regularity they faced scheduling difficulties because of travel. Each was still performing while the others were transitioning out of the business. A natural separation occurred.

Settling on a sisterhood of five, the Club 90 friendships were forged; the women shared resources and created an atmosphere reminiscent of feminism's early "consciousness-raising." To this day they maintain contact with New York, San Francisco and Las Vegas mere mouse clicks away.[18]

A Shower then a Performance

When the baby shower concluded and the non-industry guests departed, the remaining women socialized like teenagers at a sleepover. Though the shower was "just a woman thing," Veronica Hart recalls, the group came together again a few months later under different circumstances. Each performer was in a transitional period and appreciated the emotional cleansing friendships can nurture. Regular meetings were suggested and quickly took hold. Talking with peers was a "tremendous source of strength for all of us," Annie remembers.[19]

Though locales changed everyone seemed comfortable at Annie's apartment. Meetings continued over an eight-year period, marking the first time porn actresses gathered informally. Confidentiality reigned, no press and no outsiders. "We didn't have to impress anybody," Veronica Hart says. According to Annie their conversations were sometimes gossipy, as might be expected, but the real value of their get-togethers came from the outpouring of affection and empathy over personal and professional stresses. The women loved to "dish" about the business, Veronica Hart comments, especially its sleazier aspects, retaining a "kind of camaraderie" that gave them license to be critical. Nevertheless, "we always stood up for the business like we do now" she says.

In late January 1984 Franklin Furnace, a Manhattan avant-garde art space, supported an exposition sponsored by the Carnival Knowledge Collective. The topic was feminist pornography and a segment of the program called "The Second Coming" covered a variety of expressions including erotic books and art. Candida Royalle was contacted about the show's premise, "'Could There Be a Feminist Porn?'" The request was a fortuitous moment. The Club 90 women could share their dual realities with the public and the art world. A staging of one of their meetings was scripted. The woman behind the porn star, seven times over, would celebrate her humanity in ways that would dissolve preconceived notions of sex workers. Their presentation, *Deep Inside Porn Stars*, broke ground as the "prototypical feminist performance" and used consciousness-raising, the staple of New Left feminist politics. The show heralded an interpretation of pornography that was not objectifying or degrading to women. Feminist writer Arlen Raven observed that the Club 90 women may be adult film "writers and performers," but the Franklin Furnace stage presents them as "artists."[20]

Each woman tells her story. Veronica Hart portrays a devoted mother trained in dance and acting. Gloria Leonard asserts her political views on free speech, debates members of WAP (Women Against Pornography) and fights male manipulation within the industry. Veronica Vera is a writer with a strict Catholic background. A performance artist, Annie Sprinkle describes herself as the "Yoko Ono of porn" who conflates sex and education to promote a more "open-minded and pleasure-filled" society. A feminist and jazz singer who loves cats, Candida Royalle runs her own production company, a maker of erotic film. The women who eventually exited the group, Kelly Nichols and Sue Nero, have their turn. Nichols uses a slide show to display her talent as a makeup artist. Nero is a stripper and party girl.[21]

The performance reverses audience expectations. The women come onstage wearing the "glitzy clothes" of adult performers, Candida Royalle remembers. They chat and serve coffee to each other just as they did at Annie's apartment. "Gradually, almost imperceptibly, as we talked among ourselves onstage," Candida explains, "we stripped down to our hangout 'comfy' clothes," flannel nightgowns, sweats, and oversized shirts and tights. The transition is complete. Arlene Raven comments that the program's script typifies the stories women tell, underlining the "American Dream" of family, love, monogamy, economic stability, seeking a balance between public and private personalities. The magic lay in negotiating the commonalities and conflicts all women face. *Deep Inside* demystifies this journey, revealing that a woman can explore viable solutions by creating an alternative "'exhibited self'" that fashions a safe place in which to negotiate these issues. Raven cites Annie Sprinkle as an example. She surfaces out of the reserved Ellen Steinberg who "'couldn't be outrageous'" and projects the side of her personality that could.[22]

Deep Inside Porn Stars explodes the myth that porn performers have damaging childhoods, early experiences that are different from those not "seduced" by the industry's dark elements. The backgrounds of the Club 90 women reflect the American norm: middle class families, religious upbringing and formal educations. Their early sexual experiences are not unusual, losing their virginities in their late teens typical of most American girls. To be in porn is a choice driven by desire and personal exploration, not forces that disable lives. Veronica Vera will carry this message to the United States Senate a few months later when she testifies before a committee investigating the adult industry, reminding the Senators that a porn model's childhood is no more abusive or flawed than those not in the business.[23]

Feminist Shannon Bell writes that the performance has a surreptitious quality that examines the porn actress, a sexual character with no larger reality, and the complex woman behind the porn facade. The audience is exposed to different and sometimes contradictory interpretations of what it means to be in porn, Bell notes. A woman can be emotionally felled by the business, as Candida Royalle concedes when she talks of patriarchal domination and how women are simultaneously recognized as actresses and perceived as trollops. In her monologue, Candida reveals her emotional dissonance about porn she concealed from herself while coming to the realization that a feminist voice, one speaking for all women, was needed in the business. The Club 90 women give voice to a commonality they share. A porn career is a decision fraught with conflicts and ambiguities that must be negotiated and reconciled.[24]

Deep Inside addresses the realities *all* women encounter, what it means to be female in a society that defines and circumscribes a woman's social/political self. Women who chose to be outliers from conventional society are not unlike the rest of us. Though they may lack society's stamp of approval, the Club 90 actresses use their performance art to reinforce a woman's basic humanity, illustrating that her needs and fantasies do not change with her clothes or her career.

Investors expressed an interest in the show as a Broadway production. Gloria Leonard remembers that famed producer Joseph Cates was intrigued by the concept. The women procured an agent and performed the piece in a theater district rehearsal studio. Gloria told the others, "'even if it doesn't go any further, we've done it on Broadway!'" The proposal withered because the women refused to give up creative control and the money would not have sufficiently compensated them. Believing the actresses lacked "business savvy," the investors proposed only $50,000 with the caveat that Club 90 would yield all control over the performance.

Akin to *Deep Inside Porn Stars'* short life of two performances, Franklin Furnace's future was likewise challenged, victimized by the conservative retrenchment of the 1980s. Opened in 1976, the facility depended on funding from the New York State Council on the Arts and the National Endowment for the Arts (NEA). In February 1984 the art space received an NEA reprimand for the Carnival Knowledge program. At the time, the performance art of the "NEA Four," Holly Hughes, Tim Miller, Karen Finley and John Fleck, was under fire. In June 1990 their grants were rejected over obscenity concerns putting the government, according to free speech attorney Edward de Grazia, in "the business of censorship."[25]

Performance art is often controversial and charged with

highly emotional overtones. Sexual minorities and those whose art is edgier are attracted to the medium for self-expression. Eventually Annie Sprinkle found herself on the government's radar as a result of her show, "Post-Porn Modernist," in which she shows her cervix to audience members as part of her artistic expression. Today Annie and her "porn-art daughter" Madison Young are internationally respected performance artists whose sex-positive feminism is widely admired.

Franklin Furnace resisted stifling the artists to whom it gave creative license. Though financially victimized from the political right, the art space continued its mission into the early 1990s until funding dissipated. In May 1990 the New York City Fire Department closed the facility and tagged Franklin Furnace as an "'illegal social club,'" citing issues with fire regulations, violations ignored for years. After losing its physical space Franklin Furnace shifted to cyberspace where it remains today.[26]

For Club 90 the Franklin Furnace experience was a game changer. Their show was the first collective expression of sex-positive feminism among adult film performers. As a result, Annie Sprinkle advanced her own performance art. Veronica Vera turned her performance art into a political message steeped in controversy at a 1992 University of Michigan conference. Veronica Hart journeyed to the West Coast as a producer/director for adult film companies, later directing Marilyn Chambers in a film about censorship. Candida Royalle resolved to move forward with her vision of feminist erotica, serving the market for couple's porn.

A Daylong Affair

Porno chic licensed women to peek at the hardcore, though permission did not yield a likeable product. In her 1973 essay "Hard to Swallow: *Deep Throat*," feminist writer Ellen Willis observes that pornography ignores what women find exciting.

Filled with sexual mechanics, porn is "unimaginative," she writes, and fails to address the muses hovering around the meaning of sex. Were she to write her own erotic story, Willis describes how she would use "sexual tension and suspense" to explore the subtle interactions between lovers and their erotic vulnerabilities, an emotional/psychological interplay that uncovers the reasons for sex. Challenging the assumption that women are disinterested in pornography, Willis believes what they lack is a "pornographic tradition," a different take on the old formula of sex as an anatomy lesson. By conflating the psychological, sensual and physical, Willis suggests the recipe that shapes the narrative of feminist erotica. Pornography needs to be less cartoonish and more human.[27]

A little over a decade later Candida Royalle and business partner Lauren Neimi launched *FEMME Productions*, giving adult cinema the voice Ellen Willis desired to hear. In doing so they braved waters not exactly unexplored, but certainly not frequently traveled. Women want to see explicit film, Candida says, and sex-positive feminism permits them "to explore their sexuality through it." From its inception *FEMME* offered an added benefit: men and women can share their fantasies with each other. Targeting an audience she believes the adult industry left unaddressed, Candida Royalle established feminist erotica as a realistic viewing choice. Within five years, *FEMME* was proudly touting female pleasure and continues to do so today. In adult film, success generates accolades and Candida Royalle is celebrated as its First Lady. Most important, she opened the boardroom door for others to follow.[28]

Today the adult industry continues the FEMME standard. Among the Porn Valley studios, *Hard Candy Films*, *Girlfriends Films* and *New Sensations* are notable for their female friendly products. Each company banks its profits on woman friendly scripts, an emphasis on acting and viewers who relish the intimate without the mindlessness of gonzo porn.

A *FEMME* production highlights a "feminist artistic interpretation" of sex that minimizes the hardcore label. In defining her work Candida avoids the word "romance" because a woman can take pleasure in her sexuality without being in love. Likewise "pornography" is not a fit for her films, she believes, because it connotes prostitution, something unrepresentative of the *FEMME* philosophy. Her forte is real people expressing authentic sexual desires. Consequently "erotica" becomes Candida's preference, though she understands that in the public mind and literary world *FEMME* cannot escape the porn label.[29]

Emphasizing her commitment to quality, Candida Royalle follows a standard uncommon in an industry that cranks out legions of movies at low cost. She relies on scripted plots, acting and original music, staples of the bygone porno chic days. An average time frame for a *FEMME* movie is five days. Anything shorter is rushed and unfair to everyone involved. Shooting a *FEMME* production relies heavily on a storyline. Candida remembers that Alexandra Silk, her star in *Stud Hunters* (1983), had an extensive amount of dialogue. "There were days she was on the set and shooting and never did a sex scene," Candida recalls. Time is also a factor in dealing with male actors and it is often well spent when necessary. Referencing a characteristic of male oriented porn, FEMME's creator says, "I don't want a performer who has a rock hard erection just as soon as the scene starts. It's not even realistic and I like realism." Giving an actor the space to achieve arousal naturally is a FEMME standard. If he has trouble, then "you treat it like real life," Candida says, which means not pressuring a man to be ready.

A *FEMME* script addresses who the people are in the story, why they are going to have sex and what kind of sex they are going to explore. Its centerpiece is a sensuality that avoids mechanically framed anatomical close ups. Feminist scholar and film critic Anne G. Sabo summarizes the kind of moments Candida Royalle seeks. Rather than pose for the camera, her characters are enchanted with each other, visually communicating their feelings. The heat of desire marks their reciprocity. Sabo praises Candida for elevating her characters beyond the simple porn formulas. Her scripts invite the viewer to experience the "gender equality" that nurtures mutually agreeable consensual sex. Adult film historian Linda Williams focuses on the heart of the matter. Instead of settling for porn cinematically sanitized to be more acceptable to female viewers, *FEMME* entertains the question of why the sex is happening at all. Candida Royalle invites the audience to look at the sexual "conversation" as "give-and-take," erotic interplay at its best. To illustrate her point Williams cites the nightclub dancers in *Urban Heat* (1984). They are in conversation through their movement, a choreographed sensuality they perform for each other. Such an artistic expression requires work. Extended takes are normal at *FEMME* to achieve the "mood" and "atmosphere" necessary for actors get to know each other and establish what the sex *is* all about.[30]

Women need the voyeuristic space to see the unveiling of sex in its explicit motifs. It's the quiet inner "okay" that permits a woman to indulge her fantasies and savor a playful approach to sex without fear of retribution. In comparing *Urban Heat* with Marilyn Chambers' classic *Insatiable* (1980), Professor Williams observes that women are provided with a safe place to be sexual away from society's disapproving eye. For Sandra Chase (Marilyn's character) her mansion is where she relates her past adventures. The script and dialogue has purpose, the male body is more than a prop and a woman's desire is accentuated. Candida Royalle cultivates what men often fail to comprehend, "getting ready for sex *is* sex," a blended world of fantasy and reality in which "foreplay, afterplay, [and] arousal" become a montage of eroticism. Determining when the sex actually occurs is not definitive, reflecting the female perspective of extended anticipation and gratification. Good sex is a daylong affair somewhat apart from the male perspective of an appealing body and quick gratification.[31]

Though conveniently labeled as couples porn, feminist erotica is a difficult sell for men. The criticism has merit because the male notion of what constitutes sex is sometimes quite limited. Women may want sensuality but men strive to "git her done," a very American "can do" work ethic. Concentrating on the task at hand and finishing on time is the goal of a "real" man's job. Many men configure sex in the same manner, adhering to a circumscribed intimacy that often negates emotion: a brief warm up (usually oral) that mostly services his needs, then penetration and orgasm. A self-protective impatient machismo devolves sex into masturbation using a woman's body. Hence the format of male-dominated porn, woman as object and penis as perpetrator with the money or pop shot the prescriptive end, self-evident proof he "got her done." Should he want his phallus entertained in other ways, a man can vicariously experience porn's multiple penetrations, facials and bondage, things his real world lover may not want to do. Nonetheless the journey is the same, his triumph is complete and his self-assurance reinforced.

After *FEMME*'s initial successes Candida Royalle and Lauren Neimi dissolved their partnership. Candida turned to her Club 90 sisters to assist in the production of a series of brief cinematic vignettes, granting them the freedom to personalize their fantasies however they desired. The fruits of their collaborative effort yielded a classic in feminist erotica: a three volume set titled *Star Director Series*, a filming coup Susie Bright celebrates as clearing "a helluva trail to the erotic frontier." According to Annie Sprinkle, Candida is unique in her ability to "focus on the seduction, the sensuality" in a film narrative. Her real forte, however, lay in controlling the long-time domain of men, product distribution. Through her hard work and innovation, Candida Royalle altered the business model that predominates in adult film, making a powerful feminist statement.[32]

She Got What She Wanted

Pornography with feminine appeal was not a new idea when Candida Royalle broke onto the adult scene. There were male pornographers, Joe Sarno and Mark Shoen in particular, who filmed from a feminist perspective. Sarno, who began his directing career on the sexploitation circuit in the mid-1960s, was supportive of women who forged their own way. Annie Sprinkle, Gloria Leonard, along with Jennifer Welles and Seka, made movies for the "Deep Inside" genre, films that offered intimate looks at women as initiators of sex.

Welles, whose career pre-dates porno chic, had early feminist leanings. She was exceptional in controlling her sexual presence. Gloria Leonard remembers Welles as "a stunning former Vegas showgirl who wrote her own rules," rightfully owning a spot in porn history as "the VERY first woman to exert her empowerment in the adult biz." Nowhere is this more evident than *Inside Jennifer Welles* (1977) which includes an interracial scene when such pairings were rare. Marriage brought retirement but Welles left a lasting impression on those who knew her.

Seka, whose extended career reached into the 2000s, is also remembered as a powerful on-screen personality. Her film *Inside Seka* (1980) was a Sarno project. Seka would later testify with her friend, Veronica Vera, before the Senate Committee in its investigation of porn, defending a porn performer's right of self-expression.

Sarno also guided Gloria Leonard's "inside" film, *All About Gloria Leonard* (1978). Gloria describes the filmmaker as "a wonderful, gentle man" who stood apart from other directors by nurturing his female stars. Shooting the film was delightful, "sex for sex's sake, lots of joking," Gloria recalls, though there was "one particularly uncomfortable location," a chilly parking garage that was the setting for her only multiple penetration scene. The studio let Gloria select her costars, respected veterans

Jamie Gillis and Marc Stevens both now "sadly deceased," Gloria says. Jim Holliday accounts for six "inside" films produced by Evart Productions. Jennifer Welles' movie was the first and Gloria's among the best. Holliday praises the Club 90 veteran for her political activism and bestows upon her the superlative compliment of being a genuine feminist who controlled her career.[33]

Though accounting for every "golden age" actress with a feminist touch is daunting, Marlene Willoughby stands out. She was forever the activist, Gloria Leonard remembers, with a forceful political conscience. Gloria recalls Marlene joining with her and others in a demonstration outside the New York offices of *Ms. Magazine*, edited at the time by anti-porn feminist Gloria Steinem. According to Gloria Leonard, the publication ran "a hypocritical cover," that read, "'Erotica VS. Pornography, Can You Tell the Difference?'" A partially nude woman "holding flowers in front of her boobs" was the disputed illustration. Their efforts were for naught, the publications staff "predictably ignored" them, though the women did have "proper authorization for the protest," Gloria remembers. The *Ms. Magazine* incident was an early episode in the porn wars that agitated and damaged feminism's second wave.

Annie Sprinkle's version of feminist filming, *Deep Inside Annie Sprinkle* (1981), was the fourth in the Evart library of "inside" films. Under Annie's careful attention, the movie celebrates female sexual agency and glorifies the orgasm. Critic Jim Holliday honors the film as the most pleasurable of the *Inside* series. When Annie first entered the business sexual attitudes toward women were "quite a bit different" than they currently are, she recalls. A woman had a "good girl" image and was not expected "to like sex all that much." In 1970s pornography women were seduced, "pursued" and "manipulated into the sex," she says. In her film, Annie turns that notion on its head.[34]

Annie Sprinkle believes her production, which she also

directed, contributed to "a new era of pornography made by women." In 1982 the movie was second in receipts behind *Insatiable*. Given the opportunity to tell the story from her point of view was a thrill, Annie says, but she wanted an insurance policy. She turned to the best, persuading Joe Sarno to provide advice and a helping hand where necessary during the five day shoot. The film is an Annie narrative; she plays herself and the authentic sex of its nine scenes bears her stamp. Annie comments that she had a "great time" and experienced "absolute ecstasy" during its production.[35]

In the film's opening minutes Annie shares photos of her early years, no porn star clothes or tattoos, in a segment that humanizes her porn persona. Sexual liberation was in vogue and a "revolutionary spirit about porn" blossomed in those days, she explains. It was imperative to believe in yourself and "what you did" and have "no guilt or shame about it." The movie is brimming with touching, copious amounts of oral sex performed on women and splashed with external cum shots, one of Annie's favorite things. Each scene has a joyous and intimate feel; Annie Sprinkle likes a lot of kissing no matter if it is girl/boy or girl/girl. Real orgasms abound, particularly in her solo masturbation scene. There is only one camera angle and it is straight on so that her self-caressing is in plain view. This is no medical school documentary. Annie's facial expressions and physical intensity visually surround the action on her clitoris.[36]

The occasional stag standby pops up such as the voyeuristic male ogling Annie and another woman pleasuring each other. Aroused he joins in for the usual male centered sexual perfor-mance. Despite this seemingly timeworn narrative, the movie does not celebrate the premise of the phallus; the scenes are a compilation of Annie Sprinkle's reveries in her personal journey. "I didn't act out other people's fantasies," she says, "I wanted my own." Incidentally, Annie's film cops the male gaze and shoots a woman's view of gonzo, a technique destined to become a porn standard by the new century.[37]

At the time of the film "I didn't consider myself a feminist," Annie says. Feminists "were trying to protect me from being abused, exploited, and manipulated," she adds with a smile, but "They had it a little mixed up!" Of course, Annie and her Club 90 sisters would offer another interpretation of feminism within a scant two years at Franklin Furnace.[38]

While Gloria Leonard and Annie Sprinkle created their own cinematic voices, Veronica Hart shaped feminist adult film through producing and directing. In the early 1990s she helped to start the Adam and Eve Channel and joined *VCA*, one of Porn Valley's premier companies, where she produced for famed director Michael Ninn. Within a decade Veronica's directing accomplishments were recognized by *Adult Video News*, the industry's major publication. Proud of her efforts in the feminist genre, the Nevada native created a product that was personally appealing and contained a depiction of sex that was "true to the story." Candida Royalle compliments her friend's work, stating that Veronica's movies have a rawer tone than a *FEMME* film but are clearly "female-centric" with "fleshed out storylines."[39]

One of Veronica Hart's most memorable contributions to feminist filmmaking is her salute to Marilyn Chambers, whom she directed in three comeback films. One in particular, *Still Insatiable* (1999), is about a female legislator and anti-porn crusader who becomes a free speech advocate. In a feminist performance, Marilyn's character watches hardcore videotapes and is spurred to seek out her own sexual encounters. Veronica Hart challenges society's sexual hypocrisy by taking "a woman who's been uptight" and have her evolve, becoming "more human" as the film progresses. The production features cameos by Gloria Leonard and Georgina Spelvin as partygoers who support the early efforts of Marilyn's character to condemn pornography.

When asked about porn and politics Veronica Hart characterizes industry people as "activists" of some variety, whether political or charitable. With a hint of Lena Nyman, Veronica shares her motivation in making pornography: confronting pretense and sanctimony. She is particularly adamant about those who condemn porn. "All these people jerk off to us but would never admit that they watched us," she says, referring to the industry axiom about anti-porn moralists. "They would be putting us down for being in the same movie that gave them so much enjoyment."

Annie Sprinkle joins her Club 90 sister as a political groundbreaker. Her pornography for marginalized sexualities was a daring venture in the 1980s. In 2013 she and her partner of twelve years, Elizabeth Stephens, began the ecosex global movement, which features sexecology, "a new field of research which explores the places where ecology and sexology intersect," Annie says. Through art, film and seminars Annie and Beth want to make environmental concerns "sexy, fun and diverse by switching the metaphor from Earth as mother, to Earth as lover." Carrying an energy that rarely flags, Annie Sprinkle continues to travel internationally. Her performance art remains in demand at conferences, workshops and on college campuses.

* * *

The soul of feminist pornography is as strong today as it was in 1983. The Club 90 women maintain an unyielding devotion to each other with an indefatigable spirit born out of a baby shower. Annie Sprinkle declares they continue to do everything on their "own terms," being their "own bosses." They represent "the feminist shift," she says, showing adult entertainment's younger generation they can grow into "independent business women" if they choose that direction and, as Veronica Harts implies, become as powerful as they want to be.

Chapter 3

My Body, My Rules

"The first thing that gets suppressed is women being able to control their own body for their own purpose, and we can't have that."
Nina Hartley, interview with the author, Las Vegas, January 18, 2012

Upgrading an Image

Club 90 remained East Coast oriented as the New York scene began to wane in the late 1970s. Sunny California stoked new fires of explicit sex that shifted from feature film to video tape. A legendary decade for porn hounds, the 1980s moved adult film to the front page with headlines that painted the industry in stark colors. Drugs were scattered about with cocaine the hot commodity. Georgina Spelvin remembers Sly Stone of the rock group Sly and the Family Stone connecting with porn stars through chemistry. He visited the set of a movie she was doing and "sprinkled nose candy all around. It would have seemed rude to refuse," the diminutive icon recalls. "Bear in mind," Georgina adds, "coke was the 'chewing gum' of the era and was treated like an extra cup of coffee to get your motor running." The fabled John Holmes, who struggled mightily with the white powder, was implicated in the 1981 Wonderland Gang murders in Los Angeles, a saga of drugs, theft and a get-even attitude. By decade's end Holmes, whose performances redefined the male anatomy, was dead of AIDS related complications.[1]

Amid America's conservative retrenchment, the adult industry was hit with accusations of child porn. Traci Lords worked her rumored underage status into a brief career and nearly shut down the industry. With a certainty that women and children are victims of porn's pervasiveness, the Meese Commission, an accommodation of the Reagan Presidency, burned taxpayer dollars in its pursuit of smut merchants. Censorship threats stifled free sexual expression, recalling the chill of McCarthyism in the early Cold War years.

Porn's legality in California was settled as the 1980s closed. Pornographer Hal Freeman beat charges of pimping and pandering, albeit on appeal to the California Supreme Court, over hiring models for a rump filled romp titled *Caught From Behind II: The Sequel* (1983). Legitimate money now flowed unimpeded into San Fernando Valley coffers as smut makers secured filming permits along with their long established kin, Tinseltown's megabudget studios. The hillside sentinel and elusive dream weaver "Hollywood" continued its magical allure. Pretty girls ventured into the cinematic land of milk and honey seduced by stardom. For those with a willingness to spread their legs, the Valley on the far side of the famous block letters became their filming paradise.

Petite blonde Ginger Lynn was a darling of the decade with her girl-next-door perkiness. Anal sex, Hal Freeman's call to arms, crept into shoots and soon bounded past the novelty stage. The 1980s were dominated by "one-day wonders," quickly shot to feed a highly competitive entertainment market held hostage by the VCR. The production of indistinguishable videos in which girls were clones of one another surged. The sex was nudged a little more to attract fan dollars. Anal was one offering and BDSM, although tame and cuddly by current standards, another.

Within this rapidly expanding environment the industry moved to upgrade its image. In 1984 *Adult Video News (AVN)* sponsored a Las Vegas trade show, the *Adult Entertainment Expo (AEE)*, initiating an awards ceremony that featured the Oscars of porn. Another industry group, *The X-Rated Critics Organization (XRCO)*, offered up its own celebration the same year in Los

Angeles. Each event grew into an annual affair. The Valley and Hollywood were quietly connected as the rare adult performer transitioned from doing "it" in Porno Land to making it in Tinseltown. Despite her trail of crocodile tears over a lost adolescence, Traci Lords was the most successful, profiting from a legitimate film and television career.

Moving into the 1990s porn stars appeared occasionally in media outlets such as satellite radio and cable TV shows, a trend that blossomed into the next century. Pop culture shifted to the TV reality show where young women with vacuous personalities marketed themselves through highly sexualized images. A few occupied an entertainment wasteland for no better reason than being paid for being famous. The public ogled the party girls, frowned on their antics and took moralistic potshots at the barely covered models featured annually in *Sports Illustrated*, trotting out the age-old trope of protecting the children. Self-appointed guardians of decency decried the sexual innuendo that crept into a burgeoning sports culture now gleefully riding a runaway money train. Yet the average Joe and Jane rarely withheld entertainment dollars over a trifle such as a bit of almost nakedness.

Through it all, adult film slipped into the outskirts of the mainstream. Upscale sex work flourished with the proliferation of gentlemen's clubs where exotic dancing offered a lucrative sideline for porn talent. Easy money for a handful of appearances made stripping enticing for those performers who wanted a road show of their own. Worries about hardcore penetration under hot lights were pushed to the backburner. In many cases the transition was reversed, start in the clubs and graduate to film. Sometimes dancers with limited on-camera experience journeyed to Porn Valley with the intent of increasing their marketability in the clubs rather than actively seeking a career. On other occasions exotic dancers aggressively sought film shoots, understanding that porn and dancing are portals into each other's respective worlds, crucial gateways that conflate the hardcore and stripping. Adult film legend Nina Hartley, avowed feminist and close friend of Club 90, chose that route. She was no stranger to live sex before she ever walked onto a set.[2]

Nothing Like a Live Audience

"I didn't start stripping until I was twenty-three," Nina Hartley says. On a sunny Las Vegas afternoon we're chatting after a hectic day at the annual porn regalia, the *AEE*. Nina and I had met previously and my memory was not a conversation, but a gesture. She introduced herself with a handshake that commanded immediate attention. I momentarily thought of her on-camera costars and realized it must be quite an experience, having no doubt who orchestrates the action.[3]

When she broke into the sex industry, Nina Hartley was finishing her nursing degree at San Francisco State University, graduating in 1985. Besides her interest in sex and exhibitionism, any money from adult entertainment came in handy to help with tuition. An old high school friend alerted Nina about amateur night for exotic dancers at the Mitchell Brothers' O'Farrell Theater. The proposition sounded irresistible. Since late adolescence, Nina knew sex work with an audience was in her future and she had experience with competition having entered a similar contest earlier at Lowell Pickett's Sutter Street Cinema. On that occasion, she was promised fifty dollars for walking in the door. Nina decided to give it a shot. A neophyte at exhibiting herself for money, the determined Californian felt creeping doubt when she arrived at the Sutter. "I had a cheesy costume and I didn't know anything about anything, but it was San Francisco and I could do a penetration show," Nina says with a gleeful twinkle. That was reason enough. Pickett had introduced live shows and what drove Nina was the prospect of insertion, solo or with another girl. Her natural onstage magnetism secured instant success. "Other than the fifty bucks, I got a hundred dollars and a job," she offers proudly, big money for a girl in college.

The best part of the Sutter gig was a popular set up known as a girl/girl peep show. Customers of both sexes sat in individual booths separated from the performers by mirrors. Nina danced with another girl in a circular white room containing a revolving bed. The one-way mirrors came equipped with a "tip slot." The typical show was twenty to thirty minutes and as it progressed the girls intensified their sexual interactions, edging closer to the mirrors. "I thought this was the best thing since sliced bread!" Nina exclaims.

Nina Hartley found her bliss. A few months later she decided to follow her friend's advice, once again relying on amateur night. The O'Farrell welcomed her fondness for the fairer sex. Willing partners in broader society were scarce, Nina explains. "Back then, before the swing thing and the internet, it was hard to find women who you could even ask to be sexual with." At the O'Farrell there were always three or four girls who would do a set with her. Variety was the heart of the show. "I was doing fisting onstage," Nina explains, strap-ons with other dancers and solo acts with a dildo. Penetration glories unbounded! "As long as I didn't touch a man I could do anything I wanted," she says. "I now know why Mick Jagger is never going to retire because there is nothing like a live audience to give you energy."

The O'Farrell gig was also a fit for Nina's politics. "I was already a feminist," she says, but unlike the mainstream movement, Nina was not out to smash the patriarchy and excoriate porn. Her self-described label was rooted in her intellectual upbringing and a philosophical mantra of "my body, my rules." Nina adored men and the club environment gave her chances to meet them. "I would sit down and show them my body and tell them, 'Here try this with your partner,'" she explains. They were like little boys sitting "in rapt attention," Nina recalls. The nursing student learned she could communicate and combat modern society's premier hang up, a "puritanical sex-negative culture," that claimed both sexes as victims.

The O'Farrell kept her busy. Saturday night sets "with lap dancing in between," Nina fondly remembers. As her college time waned, Nina's next professional move was already at hand. Like many adult performers, exposure to pornography occurred early in her life. She read her first porn book at fourteen and watched her first smutty movie in 1976, sneaking into an adult theater while still in her teens. Though Nina decided early on that filmed sex was a possibility for her, she didn't shoot her first scene until 1984. The time between watching and doing Nina characterizes as "the window." Often asked why she entered adult film, Nina replies with the obvious, "That's where the naked women work!"

Learn the Pleasure

Nina Hartley is a product of middle class liberal parents, a Jewish mother and Lutheran father, who instilled in her a sense of social justice. Protest marches and demonstrations surrounding civil rights and the Vietnam War contributed to Nina's upbringing though religion did not. Nina believes its omission was fortuitous. "I had no issues of heaven, hell, sin, damnation, moral, immoral, when it comes to sexuality," she says. Unfettered from guilt and shame, Nina could go her own way to seek her personal pleasures and sexual enlightenment.[4]

Education is important to Nina Hartley; she is a "third gener-ation feminist" within her family. Nina's grandmother taught English at the University of Alabama. "Her claim to fame was that she taught Bear Bryant [the famed football coach] freshman English," Nina says. In the 1940s her mother studied at the University of California at Davis, majoring in statistics and chemistry, one of the few women to do so. Nina reflects on the dearth of scholastic recognition for women at the time. One day her mother ran into a professor who acknowledged her academic accomplishments, she had reached the top of class. Unfortunately, Nina recalls, her mother's ranking would never be acclaimed. According to the professor, he could not allow her to "lead the grade curve because a woman couldn't be the best in the class."

Looking back Nina believes being raised in Berkeley's West Coast liberalism when people were trying "to make peace with their lives" was her good fortune. She mentions the impact of transcendental meditation and the developmental theories of psychologists Erik Erikson and Abraham Maslow. Though her parents did not always have a presence in her life, Nina understood she had "the right and freedom" to construct her future using her own definitions. Sexuality became its core principle.

Early on Nina Hartley was distinctly aware her sexuality didn't fit society's prescribed norms. At age twelve she felt attracted to both sexes, eventually realizing "bisexual," "voyeur" and "exhibitionist" were words that described her. Being non-judgmental, she never developed negative feelings about herself. By sixteen she had thoughts of "group sex, public sex" and "sex with people who were friendly." Forming love relationships was another more difficult matter. Nina concedes she "struggled" with the idea of settling in with one person in her private life. I had "zero inclination toward monogamy," she explains, not knowing how to say "'I love you' and 'I am not a monogamous person'" in the same breath. Restrictive as this seems any shortcomings, if that's what they were, allowed Nina to formulate a positive attitude about the swinger lifestyle. Her open sexual attitudes that sometimes seem cavalier served her well as a young adult.

Nina Hartley's late adolescence played a role in shaping her future. Popular opinion at the time framed male attitudes as sexist and women as "victims," she says. The second wave of feminism blamed sexism for the ills women suffered. Male sexuality was demonized and "evil," Nina recalls, while women were "soft, gentle creatures." Nina's eventual revelation that men are not "victimizers," nor are women "victims," gave her the intellectual permission to approach sexuality with an uncritical eye. Even today we are primed to view the opposite sex as the source of our relationship problems and end up "talking past each other," she laments. Nina extends this communication breakdown to pornography where men are seen as the "objectifiers" and women the humiliated, at least in the eyes of anti-porn feminists. "People who talk about pornography and what it does and does not mean are strictly theorists," she insists. They know nothing of a sex worker's reality. But even for Nina barriers needed shattering because an intellectual reality does not always bring forth an emotional epiphany. In the end she is forever grateful for her O'Farrell days. "It got me over my fear of men when I realized they're just as clueless as we are," she concludes with a smile.

Getting to know feminists like Susie Bright, Carol Queen and Betty Dodson helped Nina Hartley realize she was not alone in her introspections on sexuality. She vowed to follow a feminist mantra rooted in sex-positivism. "Take responsibility for your orgasm," she proudly asserts, and do not neglect your body. "Learn how to give it pleasure."

The Pink Ladies Social Club

Into the 1990s Nina Hartley was *the* feminist performer in adult film. "I was the only self-identified feminist up until 2000," Nina admits. The upcoming generation was a different story. Anti-porn feminists had usurped what was left of the women's movement, driving any thoughts of feminism from the minds of performers. Because the feminists with "the most press" delivered "the strongest anti-sex, anti-man message," industry women considered feminism awkward or "weird," an anathema,

Nina says.

Nina Hartley's unusual status as a feminist and established star boosted her dancing on the club circuit. She frequently socialized with other porn models who were marketing their names. It was "the height of the feature dancing craze," Nina remembers, when porn performers supplemented their on-screen careers with a dancing income and venturing from one town to the next with little knowledge of what to expect was often troubling. Obviously, communication among touring performers was helpful to everyone. Passing along useful information about working conditions, club owners, money, special events and the like became regular occurrences and eventually a peer-to-peer interaction group developed.

In the beginning girls were just talking to girls: everything from the quality of the dressing rooms to club rules and the ever-present police. The women were friends, Nina says, offering support such as "suggestions for stage shows or swapping costumes." It was professional networking in a time before social media.

The idea of a more coherent industry support group seemed logical and the Pink Ladies Social Club became the brainchild of Nina and her adult film comrades Porsche Lynn, Angel Kelly and Jeanna Fine. In the late 1980s, Pink Ladies emerged as a sounding board on the feature dancing part of their careers. The women would call out the good clubs from the bad in an atmosphere of mutual self-help.

The group established an official logo embroidered on pink satin baseball jackets and distributed a quarterly newsletter. Though these elements suggested a serious effort to bring the performers together, unionization was far from their minds. We were "never about organizing anything" in that regard, Nina remarks, adding that Pink Ladies was "strictly designed to be a support group." Despite good intentions, any real connectedness and consciousness-raising was a struggle in the pre-internet age.

The newsletter was difficult to circulate because traveling the dance circuit made regular distribution impossible. A typewriter, Xerox machine and stamps were necessary, Nina points out, a daunting list for a showgirl.

Although Pink Ladies vehemently denied posing as an association for industry people, film companies did not see it that way. The group drew the immediate disdain of studio moguls. The patriarchy "went crazy," Nina remembers, branding the organizers "dykes" and "a bunch of lesbians" who wanted "to start a performer's union." For a couple of years the women faced a loss of bookings until "the buzz died down." Porsche Lynn was without work for nine months. Studios feared the group would unionize and tell girls what they didn't have to do, particularly non-condom anal sex. The industry wanted women to remain uneducated, Lynn says, quelling any questioning of, or resistance to, certain filming practices. Regardless of how the performers viewed Pink Ladies, it's evident they were feminist in their thinking and empowered with their activism.[5]

While Club 90 and Pink Ladies existed in different porn milieus, their intentions were similar: develop peer support in a forum of shared experiences. Nina claims there was no "official, conscious, or deliberate" relationship between Pink Ladies and Club 90, although the West Coast performers were aware of the Club's existence. In fact, most of the Pink Ladies did not consider themselves feminists so developing a Club 90-like social or political mindset was "pure chance and coincidence," Nina states. Gloria Leonard concurs. "Club 90 existed years before Pink Ladies," she says, "other than knowing one another, there was no organizational connection." Gloria does believe the Club 90 concept was "an inspiration" for the California women and Nina agrees, "The spirits of each were certainly sympathetic to the other." Asked if Club 90 and Pink Ladies were connected in temperament, Veronica Hart is in accord with Nina and Gloria, emphasizing that support groups are needed in the sex industry and both groups are good examples of a filling of that void.[6]

Though links between Pink Ladies and Club 90 may have been tenuous, a feminist disposition lay in both and would influence a new generation of performers within a decade and a half.

A Social Activist Laments

According to feminist scholar Drucilla Cornell, outspoken adult actress Ona Zee believes performers should influence working conditions in their industry. Identified as the "Norma Rae" of porn, Zee advocated unionization in the early 1990s and was predictably blackballed at the time.[7]

The failures of Pink Ladies and Ona Zee reveal formal organization in the adult business remains distant. "Porn will never be unionized," Nina Hartley says. The problem lies within performer ranks. Political solidarity is not of interest to today's talent, Nina claims. They are not well educated (most come into the business with only a high school diploma) and are too young to know or care about the history of the labor movement. Simply put, there is "poor institutional memory" in porn, she says. Current adult film women may be aware of third wave individualism but see it as no real consequence to their current situation. These new century girls assume establishing a porn career and taking pride in their work is "how it's supposed to be and always has been," Nina says. They "accept as fait accompli their freedoms regarding sex, sexual expression and how they choose to make a living." Sold on the popular notion that the feminist sex-negative message is an ivory tower issue, the current generation discards the feminist label. They pay no attention to industry women who identify as sex-positive feminists and take offense at "academic feminists who would dare to call them degraded, [or] deluded," as Nina puts it. Reflecting much of society's attitude about feminism, today's porn models consider it to be the "F" word.

Attempts to organize also fail because of personal disinterest that goes beyond politics. Adult entertainers are "independent creatures," Nina says, "The kind of person who comes to porn is not group minded." Porn models bargain for their work and face cycles of immediate unemployment once their scenes are filmed. To survive in the industry, many performers operate from a three-legged stool of sex work that can create a host of problems. They can supplement a filming and dancing income through booking agents who can get them extra work as escorts. Though the industry mantra is "you don't have sex to get the job, having sex is the job," every woman risks being led to the casting couch, especially if she is a fresh face.

These variances make unionization improbable because bringing performers together is like "herding cats," Nina says. Many are too naive to understand the value of group support and have no interest in meetings and parliamentary procedures. To further render organization unlikely, the circumstances of sex work make it a transitory business. Girls rarely have a long term plan. What is more telling, Nina observes, is that most performers never thought they would "end up" making porn in the first place.

In addition, an important legal issue muddies the organizational waters. Porn performers are independent contractors with an elite few being employees of the studios. Nina comments, "*Wicked* girls are employees" and at one time *Vivid Entertainment* signed girls who "were classified as employees." But there's little else. Legally, unionization requires that workers be employees. Independent contractors have no lawful backing to organize and as long as porn performers are limited to that status unionization and federal protection in the marketplace is problematic.[8]

The organizational ghost remains a topic of discussion, however. During the 2010 *AVN* convention retired performer Sasha Grey, who has crossed over into legitimate Hollywood, gave the keynote address for the "Women in Adult Entertainment" seminar. She recounted her preparation to enter adult film and talked of the film company she owns. During her presentation, Grey mentioned the issue of group support and the lack of solidarity among talent today, unlike the "close knit family" reminiscent of Club 90 and Pink Ladies years ago. Though Sasha Grey does not openly identify as a feminist, her story of empowerment and her concern for talent welfare is an example of feminism's influence in adult film.

Only After They Get Power

Determining how her body will be displayed for the camera is the premier feminist trait. Feminist empowerment shows up each time a performer negotiates her pay and exercises choice. For the handful of feminist directors, giving performers these options is upfront. Performer input concerning costars, "yes and no" lists, hard and soft limits and safer sex precautions are part of a package of respect. This is not to say that male directors ignore these offerings. Some are as assiduous in satisfying them as are women cinematographers. For example, Dan O'Connell of *Girlfriends Films* is among the best. Yet this scenario is not universal. While the patriarchal hand remains influential, issues of value and respect continue to persist.

Feminist writer Wendy McElroy observes that industry men insist they value female performers, though it seems to be more of an "acknowledgement" than "respect." McElroy concludes women need to become more influential industry wide to gain the respect they deserve. The genesis of McElroy's opinion comes from a dinner conversation she had with John Stagliano of *Evil Angel Productions* and performer/director John Leslie at the *Adult Video News* convention two decades ago. During the 2012 gala, I ask about McElroy's remarks. She was referring to comments Leslie made concerning a particular performer, John Stagliano says, and should not be misread as an indictment of the industry.[9]

Clearing up any misconceptions about his late friend, Stagliano explains, "John Leslie was talking 'off the cuff' about his interaction with some women," in particular "some girl with a big ass that he was really interested in." Leslie did not intend to objectify the girl and McElroy's view was an erroneous interpretation of the conversation. The *Evil Angel* mogul backs off a little, however. McElroy believed Leslie did not demonstrate "enough of a feminist outlook," he remembers, and her criticism of Leslie's words in that instance had some validity. Unfortunately, McElroy generalized Leslie's remarks to the whole industry. "John [Leslie] had a huge amount of respect for women," John Stagliano insists, "just look at his movies."

Among industry people John Stagliano is highly regarded. He is feminist oriented in his outlook and actions, though he may not always understand it that way. His support for women he believes are creative in their work, such as directors Belladonna, Tristan Taormino, Dana Vespoli, and Bobbi Starr, bears witness to this. The veteran filmmaker endeavors to produce a top notch product and people are the vital cogs in his machinery. He understands the necessity of creativity and teamwork in an easily maligned industry and he personally *wants* to find value in his hires. "I try to see what's good, what it is they have to offer and treat them with respect. That's the way I prefer to do business." John Stagliano knows his way of interacting with people is not the industry norm. Yet he holds to the belief that "in the long run" doing it his way builds bridges in an environment stoked with "competitive pressure."

Porn's power brokers believe they respect the women they film. Female performers, however, do not universally share that view. Nina Hartley's feminist perspective is not far from Wendy McElroy's. She believes women are "valued for their 'hotness,'" but this does not necessarily translate into respect. Nina talks of female directors who must cope with male egos in the boardroom. There are men who have issues with women and prefer not to deal with them. For some men in the business, Nina indicates, it is challenging to connect emotionally with women.

Veronica Hart supports Nina's interpretation of respect. With a few exceptions, she believes influential women are a work in progress. "I don't see many women affecting the business that much," Veronica says. She mentions director Nica Noelle's "new spin" on shooting realistic sex and Candida Royalle's couples' porn as notable achievements, as are the scripts of director Jacky St. James who presents sex in a female friendly way and Tristan Taormino's breakthrough educational films. Despite these accolades, business success is measured in selling movies and not so much in the artistic accomplishment within them.

Generalizing porn to the corporate world where profit dictates success, Veronica Hart is blunt. "Business is business. It doesn't respect anyone. The only thing it respects is the ability to make money." Having said that, she insists respect has another definition more closely aligned with John Stagliano's: it is personal and built on relationships. Respect depends on "the people you are working with," she says, suggesting it is a viable commodity shared among everyone. As a veteran director and producer, Veronica's success depends on getting the best from her performers, though there are a few who have challenged her efforts in that regard. "Thank God they were fucking because they couldn't do anything else!" she laughs, and "this is coming from a feminist!" She clarifies that merely being in the business does not garner esteem from others. "You earn respect," she insists through a "pattern of being responsible, of standing up for other people, doing and saying the right thing."

The realities of the adult film industry are not a part of Middle America's cultural conversation. People are quick to pass judgment on women involved in the sex trade because perception often dictates opinion. In the public's eye, Veronica Hart says, it is still "commonplace" to demonize porn women as "sluts" though she believes the term "has lost a lot of the stigma" it once had. She turns to opinions voiced about men who are viewed as sexually assertive studs. This is the reality of "who we are" as sex workers, she believes, and like it or not, the smut industry is a "part of society" and cannot be separated from it. On that note, McElroy's assessment may be "more a reflection on society that it is the porn business," Veronica says.

Some industry people, most notably veteran Bill Margold, talk about the adult business in familial terms, the "Family of X" as he calls it. Veronica Hart expands on that thought. "The love in the business comes from the people that make friendships in it," she says. This is what Bill Margold means and what Club 90 illustrates so well. But the picture is hardly complete. Veronica's honesty takes a sudden brutal turn. "We always say 'Oh, the porn family.' Fuck that! It's not a family, it's a business and a business loves nobody, respects nobody except a person's ability to make money. The bottom line is making money," she repeats. We have come full circle.

Veronica Hart and Nina Hartley represent the struggle of an older generation of performers, some of whom have transitioned into working behind the camera. But what of modern superstars like Jesse Jane, Jessa Rhodes, Tasha Reign and Chanel Preston? How are women regarded in their view?[10]

Jesse Jane comments there is some truth in McElroy's statement and agrees with Veronica Hart that some girls are limited to just having sex, being in porn only for the quick money. She cautions them to save their money because options are limited. "Once you step into this career path, it's hard to do something else. You're labeled." Nevertheless, Jesse emphasizes that "there are quite a few of us [women] who know how to run this industry ... There is a reason I've lasted for eleven years, I know how to run my own brand." Women "make the industry," Jesse asserts, and men "know they need us."

Jessa Rhodes disagrees with McElroy. "I think she is completely wrong," the willowy blonde remarks. "There are women in this industry who fight for their [pay] rate and for what they will and will not do," the twenty-year-old says. "Ultimately women have the power they just don't know it" because women *are* the industry. Incidentally, Jessa definitely feels respected, "I wouldn't say that this business is run by men at all. Vagina rules!"

Both Tasha Reign, who is a sex-positive feminist, and five-year veteran Chanel Preston believe they are highly regarded within the business. Tasha suggests the industry has changed over the years and porn is perceived differently than in past generations, especially by women. Today there is a broader acceptance of adult film as part of American culture. "Our minds open up every year, little by little," she concludes.

A more practical Chanel agrees with Veronica Hart about earning the esteem of others. It's "different for everyone because different people demand different amounts of respect," she says, adding that a lack of deferential treatment occurs in any industry not just in adult film. "I think people like to target the porn industry as if it is different and it's not." Chanel mentions Nina Hartley's efforts to enable porn women by example and believes that she contributes likewise. "For me, I feel very empowered doing this" and that brings respect.

Veronica Hart concludes on an up note. Ignored by anti-porn feminists and unrealized by the general public is what adult film can professionally do for women. Porn women are in the unique position of being "in control of their careers," Veronica says, "They've made their own choices [and] have a lot more freedom when they work in pornography than in most other jobs." Referencing her time in the industry, Veronica singles out her successes. "I've been given an opportunity in porn to be anything I want to be. I can hold a camera, I can write, I can direct, I can edit. I can make movies" and that doesn't mean only adult film.

"I can make really good low budget movies," she adds, "whether exploitative sex movies or horror movies or action movies, it's all the same animal. I know how to do that because of this business. I'm very thankful for it."

* * *

Feminist scholar Carol Queen offers that today's porn performer does not realize how feminist-like she is until she understands that there are "multiple feminisms," sex-positive the most formidable example. When porn women narrowly define feminism as sex-negative and anti-porn, the goal of moving women beyond a sexual second class citizenship is lost. Feminism in adult film is about control and choice and many performers exercise both. Nina Hartley illuminates the feminist philosophy with "my body, my rules" which enables her to take responsibility for her own sexual satisfaction, placing her body on film and choosing her partners to suit her tastes.[11]

Nina Hartley projects an overwhelming presence around others. Though she admits she knows nothing of directing or distribution (the corporate part of porn) Nina is one of the most recognized names in adult entertainment. When she appears at industry events, an awaiting crowd presses in. "Nina is very respected in this business," Veronica Hart says.

Success in adult film may come down to money and its reward, influence. In the pornography universe, as in corporate and political America, money translates into power and power brings respect. But those are not its limits. For a porn performer power also means exercising a determination that builds the esteem all women are capable of achieving. The women of Club 90 and Pink Ladies forged a path for themselves that challenged the accepted way of operating in adult film. Women who insist on choice in an industry traditionally built on monetizing male autoeroticism have secured measured successes on both sides of the camera. Feminists in adult film are lending other elements to the money power continuum with a philosophy that expands what it means to be female and express a sexual agency that commands attention. In the final analysis, strong women in filmed pornography are feminist in their actions and in their personal aegis over their careers, though they may not recognize it as such.

Chapter 4

Her Own Amateur Porn Movie

"How easy it is for us to look at the same images and see entirely different things or look on the same experience and draw opposite interpretations ..."
Veronica Vera from "Whoriculture" in Adam Magazine, April 1993

Moving Out of Mayfield

Relying on standard operating procedure, New York City's finest raided a Greenwich Village watering hole anticipating another uneventful roundup of offenders whose major vice was their sexual orientation. The pattern of these forays was predictable: enter the bar, cease all activity and make some arrests. A full paddy wagon headed downtown and later the "usual suspects" were released. The Stonewall Inn sold cheap liquor without a license, condoned frequent drug use and was reputedly Mafia operated. Despite its deficiencies, the bar was the home of the Village's queer population. Couples felt an acceptance, especially since they were permitted to slow dance. Little wonder it remained on the police radar.[1]

On this early morning of June 28, 1969 the club's patrons abandoned their usual pacifism. A crowd gathered inflaming the air with hostility. A police tactical unit was mobilized; anger intensified. A collection of ousted customers and neighborhood residents pushed back against the men in blue. The situation escalated when officers reacted abusively to a gay woman, infuriating those milling around. When hostile spectators rushed the building, the cops retreated inside. Now trapped, the police called for backup.[2]

At the Stonewall, raids were habitual and police violence was commonplace. Getting roughed up often led to a night in jail. Memories of those abuses silenced acquiescence this time; a barrier had been crossed and gays were fed up. The disorder went on for several more nights as protesters and police vied for control of the Stonewall neighborhood.[3]

The ugliness spawned a gay pride parade and a collective sense of organized outrage presaged a movement. In the years to come, gays and lesbians would experience significant changes. "The laws that once criminalized homosexuality have been overturned," *Lesbian News* writer Diane Silver reports, and "[t]he rules that once barred us from federal jobs have been dropped." In time, the LGBT movement would become a reality.[4]

The Stonewall Uprising forced a reordering of attitudes toward marginalized groups whose demand for legitimacy roiled a cultural scene fraught with discontent. Though Stonewall cut its own path, it was not the only embedded element in an age defined by upheaval. A Southeast Asian war and the festering sore of racism primed baby boomers for social change. Youthful rebellion piqued confrontations with society's traditional ethos. The landing of British pop icons, the Beatles followed quickly by the Rolling Stones, altered the music scene, encouraging an atmosphere of mind altering drugs and uninhibited sexuality that separated the Woodstock generation from its parents. All the while the birth control pill appeased the fear of unwanted consequences.

In the bedrooms of suburbia, heteronormative Ward and June Cleavers had their sleep interrupted in ways they never anticipated. Early researchers such as Alfred C. Kinsey, William H. Masters and Virginia E. Johnson investigated the nature of sexual arousal and orgasm. Kinsey, who died in 1956, shockingly suggested that women could participate in intimate pleasure for its own sake, flouting the prescriptive sexuality of the postwar decade. A scant two years after Kinsey's death, research uncovered the clitoral orgasm. In 1966 Masters and Johnson published their stunning assertion that women were capable of repeated vaginal and clitoral orgasms. The National Organization for Women (NOW) was founded the same year as female sexuality entered academic circles and the popular media. If Ward and June wanted little to do with this news their sons and daughters felt otherwise. Abetted by the pill and sexual experimentation, a revolution was underway in a middle class America steeped in conformity. Thanks in part to Kinsey, Masters, Johnson and the counterculture, female sexual behavior was open for discussion. As the meeting came to order, a stubborn Victorian morality remained within the sexual breathing space, haunting women in an environment defined by the quiet domesticity of the Cleavers.[5]

The 1960s represented change. In the years following the Second World War, the workplace liberation women experienced during the conflict was hushed as cultural uniformity threw up barricades to contain the threat of Soviet communism. Donning his gray flannel suit, the returning veteran resumed his bread-winner role and secured his family in suburban Levittowns, the soon-to-be fictionalized "Mayfields" that dotted Middle America. Unfortunately those pesky post-war kids with sex on their minds refused to play within the moral parameters of a homogenized society. The Cold War, racial turbulence, political assassinations, rock music and recreational drugs gave license to new ways of frolicking. Drive-ins offered sexploitation movies where sexual fantasies came alive and nudie cuties, kinkies, roughies and ghoulies fed imaginations resistant to a missionary position ethos. The small town values of Wally and the Beav could not abate the tide of sexual experimentation within a swelling libertine youth. For women the path to sexual freedom remained booby trapped with patriarchal and neo-Victorian conservatism, Janis Joplin, Jane Fonda and Marilyn Chambers notwithstanding.

The anti-establishment counterculture welcomed women poised to fire up their own revolution. Highlighted by "the personal is political," an idea attributed to early feminist thinkers and activists Carol Hanish and Robin Morgan, the agenda for a 1960s feminist ideology emerged. Issues like reproductive rights, daycare facilities and equal pay for equal work gained ground against culturally institutionalized maleness, an oppression feminists came to believe was sustained by pornography and the dominance/submission attitudes it promoted.[6]

Feminist tirades against the sexual were fueled by pornography's chicness. While its exposure across the population sparked curiosity, the cinematic genre remained a turn off for many women, ushering in concerns about rape, domestic violence and prostitution. Feminists indicted smut as male entertainment that objectified, violated and humiliated women. Inevitably academia took notice; pornography energized feminist thought and discussion.

By the late 1970s the nation wearied of New Left liberalism. Feminism was forced into retreat and the American family, tweaked in popular media by the likes of *The Brady Bunch, One Day at a Time* and *The Jeffersons*, withstood a radical makeover. On the broader national scene the right-wing political lion, fed by the diatribes of Archie Bunkers and prowling a jungle perceived to be out of kilter, was ready to pounce. Feminist politics was primed to be cut from the herd for slaughter.

In this pivotal moment women immersed themselves in a contentious debate over the singular issue of pornography. Feminists opposed to pornography became the "establishment" of the women's movement eventually uniting, if ever so briefly, with the government's conservative war on smut. While neither side could uproot the other, those who contested the anti-porn, pro-censorship message triggered a feminist counterculture of their own. By the 1980s pro-porn feminists, BDSM lesbians and others validated a sex-positive point of view. Identifying as pro-sex and anti-censorship, these feminists supported every woman's right to her personal sexual agency (pornography being a part of that totality) and offered women *inside* the adult film industry an empowered voice.

Feminism's second wave began to fracture in the mid- to late-1980s as the flames of a porn-driven internal strife intensified. Into the 1990s the movement became philosophically and politically exhausted with the highest cost paid by anti-porn stalwarts. Fading from the public radar by the end of the decade the once turbulent anti-smut current lingered with some enthusiasm in academia's esoteric environment.[7]

Sex Wars

The emergence of lesbian feminists forced the women's movement to take issue with alternative sexualities. Anti-porn feminists accepted lesbianism as a political statement of feminist freedom, but the eroticism of women who loved women was troublesome. The reform minded National Organization for Women (NOW) found validating lesbianism to be complicated and vexatious. In 1970 the organization came out against gay women, labeling them the "lavender menace." The risk was dealing with a public already suspicious of women's rights. At the time NOW's apprehensions were justified, a creeping backlash against feminism's independent voice was mounting.[8]

Equality as an intellectual and political exercise entered the bedroom. Women could enjoy sex with men as long as males agreed female pleasure was on par with their own. The problem was achieving equality, if it could be accomplished at all. Black Panther Huey Newton, who believed that females in the Panther organization were there to serve men, gave the debate a reality check. Feminist Susie Bright recalls his words. "'Orgasm is pretty easy to achieve cause you can do it solo,'" Newton quipped. "'So I guess that's not the point of sex.'" Parity would prove no easy task.[9]

Lesbian recognition did not progress smoothly. Gay women were encouraged politically but discouraged from expressing their carnal desires. The victims of this awkward accommodation were BDSM lesbians who hovered on the distant margins of acceptance not only in the feminist movement, but in society as a whole. Woman on woman attraction, especially with a sadomasochistic flashpoint, was outré and unequivocally dissuaded. BDSM was deemed patriarchal and demonic along with public sex and pornography.[10]

Despite the post-1960s hedonism of clubbing, sex and drugs, anti-pornography diatribes bubbled to the surface on the West Coast where war drums against smut mobilized feminists. In 1978 WAVPM (Women Against Violence in Pornography and the Media) organized the first national conference in San Francisco to discuss porn's horrors and develop tactics to end its distribution. A "Take Back the Night" March in the city's Tenderloin district ensued; participation reached into the thousands. On the East Coast the following year a splinter group known as Women Against Pornography (WAP) conducted regularly scheduled tours through New York City's Forty-Second street district, exposing the curious to adult bookstores and local grindhouses. The aim was to uncover porn's sleaziness and brutality toward women so they'd become, as anti-porn feminist Laure Lederer says, "better equipped to fight it."[11]

Lesbian estrangement from mainstream anti-porn feminism grew considerably with the rise of WAP. In San Francisco a same sex SM group, Samois, provided a needed voice for disaffected women and held its first open to the public discussion in the Old Wives Tale Bookstore in January 1979. Chief among its concerns were the feminist anti-porn slide shows characterizing SM lesbianism as ugly and undesirable. Over the next two years Samois and anti-porn feminists exchanged fire over the definition of a proper feminist. Lesbians would come to feel bullied by the anti-porn zealots they perceived as unduly heteronormative and puritanical. Today Samois is defunct but its egalitarian spirit survives in the City by the Bay's queer porn community whose art, directors and performers are feted yearly in Toronto's Feminist Porn Awards.[12]

By the early 1980s, the porn wars heated up. A pivotal event occurred in April 1982 with the annual Barnard College conference on feminism, "Toward a Politics of Sexuality." Expanding the discussion of women's sexuality, especially its pleasures and choice, speakers on sadomasochistic practices, roleplaying and pornography were invited. A week prior to the conference WAP feminists swooped in, circulating flyers that claimed sexual degenerates were manipulating the agenda. Organizers criticized WAP tactics as defamatory but the damage was irreparable. Funding was pulled and college officials confiscated the attendee's booklet, "Diary of a Conference on Sexuality." Accusations of censorship flew.[13]

The Barnard Conference became the catalyst for reframing the feminist porn argument by marking the end of the academic phase and the beginnings of the sex wars destined to play out on the public stage. Within a year pornography was reconfigured beyond a First Amendment dialogue into civil discrimination efforts that found fertile soil in the conservative Midwest.[14]

The move into the legal arena occurred with the Minneapolis (1983) and Indianapolis (1984) proposals, the work of anti-porn feminists Andrea Dworkin and Catharine MacKinnon who orchestrated pornography consumption into a civil offense against women. The strategy was to permit individuals (women) who believed they were harmed as a result of pornography to seek financial recompense from those who made, distributed and sold it.[15]

The Minneapolis ordinance failed when Mayor Donald Fraser vetoed it on First Amendment grounds. The Indianapolis effort gained the support of right-wing political groups, introducing

Christian Conservatives and anti-feminist local legislators into the fray. Within minutes after the ordinance was signed into law a "coalition of booksellers, publishers, and others" initiated a court challenge. The law was summarily struck down in every federal court through which it traveled and in 1986 the US Supreme Court offered no opinion on the matter.[16]

Though it was inconsequential the legislative approach reshaped feminist discussion. Anti-porn feminists sacrificed their credibility by recasting the fight as a censorship debate, establishing a directional change that forced sex-positive feminists into a rear guard action to save a woman's right to porn. The pleasures of sexual expression were abandoned. A modern Comstockery now trumped the bedroom though the costliest moment was still a presidential commission away.[17]

The Great Charter?

In the late 1960s the Woodstock generation danced through the Summer of Love befuddling a middle class America rooted in the mythical Mayfields and Mayberrys across the land. Closeted gays and the fetish-minded were rattling the doorknob, if ever so quietly. The Hays Code limped away and filmmakers of every ilk, especially the sexploitation crowd, were pushing the softcore sex and violence envelope as feminist anger at the objectification of women's bodies boiled over. A *new* revolution was reshaping culture in a time of revolution.

Under darkening clouds there was a mounting sense of moral panic. Responding to social conservatives, Congress felt compelled to probe into the business of smut. In 1967 President Lyndon Johnson appointed an investigatory committee whose findings, *The Report of the Commission on Obscenity and Pornography*, were released three years later to a new President and instant astonishment. The committee found no evidence porn fostered sex crimes, caused homosexuality or engendered negative attitudes toward women.[18]

Commission anti-porners were enraged. Charles H. Keating, Jr., founder of the smut fighting Cincinnati based Citizens for Decent Literature (CDL), and his cohorts demonized the Report as a "Magna Carta for the pornographer." For the record, it was Keating and the CDL who had lobbied Congress to create the commission. A late Nixon appointee to the panel, Keating did not actually participate in the commission's work though he led the dissenters in a "belief becomes truth" model that negated academic inquiry in favor of emotional reasoning. The anti-porn panelists declared the nation's virtue to be under siege while, in their view, the committee's liberals relied on scientific inquiry to examine the pornography problem. Mystified by the trust in research, Commissioner Father Morton A. Hill declared pornography to be an abomination before God fueling the view that the nation's religious heritage must be the guardians of society's mores. In the end the conservatives damned the findings as a blatant attempt to legitimize porn and denigrated the panel for being out of touch with America.[19]

President Richard Nixon rejected the report without reading it and declared the fight against pornography was at hand, insisting that "American morality is not to be trifled with." His reaction was indicative of a moral panic: intense and volatile emotionalism surrounding a perceived social evil. Public ire incited by the politics of fear. America was in the throes of emboldening the latest outbreak, this time instigated by a commission.[20]

Predictably labeling the report a product of liberal thinking, Congress followed Nixon's lead. Even diehard traditional feminists, who generated their own mini-version of a moral panic with their demands for reproductive rights, complained that the Commission was too male. The firestorm of faultfinding had little impact because the report quickly became outdated. In 1972 the public was jolted by a seismic shift in acceptability with the coming of Linda Lovelace's oral skills.

Inevitably, the hardcore shock would stir the government again. In the mid-1980s the burgeoning adult film industry would feel the censorship heat, this time with one of the strangest political alliances in recent history. The anti-porn feminists joined forces with the conservative opponents of women's liberation in a titanic self-created struggle against the evils of smut. The vehicle of their union was the next Presidential sortie in the war against porn: the Meese Commission.

Like a prairie dog popping its head out of its lair, another moral panic peeked above the horizon.

A New Road Show

"'These are not friendly people, Veronica. This is not fun and games.'"[21]

Al Goldstein is not kidding. The publisher of *Screw* magazine is a business veteran whose many arrests for peddling porn have given him a nose for the censorship climate. The Feds are once again leaning on the lewd and dirty, this time via a Senate Judiciary Committee investigation, precursor to the upcoming Meese Commission.

Veronica Vera recounts that a "call went out for volunteers to testify on both sides of the issue" concerning porn's harm to women. Club 90 responded. Gloria Leonard volunteered but fell ill, Veronica explains, so she took up the challenge of replacing one of the most eloquent feminist voices in the adult film industry. Veronica appreciated Goldstein's advice and his generosity, the offer of a ride in his limo from New York City. Preferring to fly with Annie Sprinkle, whose camera would document the trip, Veronica declined but did remember his admonition.[22]

Fortified with the bravado and humor necessary to navigate a potentially testy atmosphere, Veronica Vera confesses to Annie the tongue-in-cheek fantasy she has constructed. When it's her turn to address the committee Veronica envisions her best sexual self in an intellectual power play to woo the Senators. Scantily clad and sitting on the table in the committee room, she'll ask the esteemed lawmakers if she incites them to violence. The Club 90 sisters share a girlish giggle before Veronica sets about writing her opening statement. It will be reality, not fantasy.[23]

Adult industry spokespersons are scheduled for the hearing's final day. On this late October morning in 1984, the chamber is not crowded. For the most part Senator Arlen Specter conducts the hearing alone, a solitary figure behind the long wood paneled citadel of Senatorial power. Today's witnesses represent the porn business and most Senators are elsewhere.

Appearing with Veronica Vera is adult performer Seka. The women field questions about their backgrounds and industry experiences. Appropriate for the mood of the committee, Senator Specter wants Veronica's response to retired performer Linda Marchiano (aka Linda Lovelace), whose claims of abuse and coercion during the filming of *Deep Throat* are now legendary. Veronica knows of no one who was forced to perform in adult film. In fact she suggests something else.

"I have met quite a few women who were curious to know how they could go about being in an X-rated film," Veronica states and proceeds to talk about how adult film models are stereotyped with the "myth" of a damaged upbringing.[24]

In her written statement Veronica includes bondage photos of herself. The pictures catch Senator Specter's interest. She explains that the photo session was a safe environment and by delving into the darker side of her imagination, she felt vulnerable and sexy.[25]

The Chairman inquires about the impression of victimization this type of photo creates. She's no victim, Veronica Vera insists and acknowledges a pleasure in acting out imaginative sexual scenarios. The curiosity to give free rein to fantasies is exciting and Veronica tells the Senator that they should be accepted for their erotic value and not be denied. She includes the fantasy of rape that some women claim to have. "I think that that is a part of what the whole field of eroticism is about, exploring our fantasies."[26]

Over lunch with Annie later that day, Veronica Vera believes her Washington experience opened up a new level of understanding about adult film. History will prove otherwise. When the Meese Commission begins its crusade, pro-sex, pro-porn witnesses will be denigrated and feminism feted and condemned by the commission, depending on the witness's attitude and usefulness to the panel.

Basking in their reactionary social ideology, Reaganites celebrated a reenergized American "morning" in which traditional values seemed the proper reaction to 1960s militancy and the resulting social changes it fostered. In particular, a Ronald Reagan second term in 1984 offered an opportunity to extend the culture war against feminism and pornography. Reagan's political acumen persuaded him to repay his election IOU to the Christian Conservatives whose votes he had wooed. He rewarded their loyalty with calculated showmanship by way of a commission.

The aim of this new investigative panel was to rebuff the conspicuously flawed conclusions of the 1970 commission. Reagan's charge to the committee was straightforward: determine the extent of pornography's infiltration into the cultural landscape and contain the menace within constitutional limits. The Chief Executive was pragmatic: attacking pornography resonated with Americans alienated by counterculture radicalism. However, Reagan was satisfied to censure porn as a sop for evangelicals who were now unwaveringly Republican. The President stood against porn by delegation only, never offering any substantive legislation to eradicate adult film.[27]

The commission scheduled a string of hearings to ferret out porn's evils. Borrowing from the old sexploitation peddlers, the government began its road show in the spring of 1985. From June through January 1986, the cross-country tour evolved into a media event adult filmmaker David Jennings characterizes as "part inquisition, part big tent revival, part voyeur's sideshow" and *Time Magazine* remembers as "a kind of surrealist mystery tour of sexual perversity." The hokum of Kroger Babb and David Friedman never travelled with more gusto.[28]

Critics alleged the commissioners were unqualified to analyze adult material. Panelists were selected because their anti-porn views agreed with the Attorney General Ed Meese. When the road show dust settled the nation's chief prosecutor, who never attended any of the hearings, cautiously sidestepped an endorsement of the commission's recommendations and did not call for a ban on pornography. Like his boss, Meese was committed to keep the ball within constitutional bounds by tweaking the commission's expectations. Eventually the Attorney General did initiate federal harassment to contain porn's commercialization, but the panel's findings were of no real consequence other than to offer a political green light for his actions.[29]

An Overly Simplistic Charade

From the beginning, the Meese panel reached conclusions that were overly simplistic and broadly applied. The commissioners tried to establish a link between aggressive behavior, sexual abuse and pornography, with harm to women as its central focus. The panel relied on sensational and anecdotal evidence to produce the sought-after smoking gun. Nowhere was this approach more evident than in Linda Marchiano's testimony at the New York hearing.

Now a popular anti-smut speaker and self-identified pornography victim, the former Linda Lovelace testified to the death threats that supposedly secured her cooperation in *Deep Throat* and being physically abused in her hotel room "for smiling on the set." Verifying her bruises came from a jealous husband, it became clear Linda was a casualty of domestic violence. The former adult star may have felt debased by pornography; but to frame her abuse as a product of her brief time in the business was ill-founded. Nevertheless, her questionable interpretation of events surrounding *Deep Throat* fit the commission's established precedence for seeking anecdotal evidence to support foregone conclusions.[30]

As the hearings progressed, a flurry of opposition surrounded the investigation. Some of the witnesses called to testify spoke decisively by not speaking at all, believing it mattered little what they said and offering their absence as a statement of protest. Women associated with the adult business, Kay Parker of *Cabellero Control Corporation*, Gloria Leonard, publisher of *High Society Magazine* and Candida Royalle were among them.[31]

Such was not the case with Dottie Meyer, former *Penthouse* "Pet of the Year" who braved the New York hearing. Meyer endured a courtroom-like atmosphere in which she was grilled about her preoccupation with sex. Feminist scholar Carol Vance, who attended the hearing, states that Meyer's persona was "on trial" and pilloried because she was "unrepentantly sexual" and did not see herself as a victim. Later Meyer commented she felt demeaned by the commission, verbally punished for her perceived complicity with pornography's malevolence. The former model embodied what the panel disdained, an empowered woman who was the very essence of sex-positive feminism.[32]

Expressing minimal interest in pro-sex feminists, the government ignored their views in the final collated document. Anti-porn women were lionized; Dottie Meyer and Veronica Vera saw their testimony discounted. The witness list was impressively skewed toward censorship and included a menagerie of informants whose testimony was rife with unproven assertions. According to *Playboy* publisher Hugh Hefner, the scene was "a parade of born-again basket-cases, anti-sex feminists and fun-hating fundamentalists." Witnesses of this ilk, in his opinion, would not be taken seriously in a court of law.[33]

Withheld documents, disproportional witness treatment and unproven assertions characterized the government's attempt to build an argument to eradicate smut. The road show was a charade foisted on an apparently disinterested public and a less than enthusiastic Congress.[34]

What They Loathe the Most

Tales of porn's abuse became the gospel with Andrea Dworkin's testimony being the apostle's word. Dworkin alleged pornography condemns women to desperation and misery from which they see no exit. Eventually realizing they enjoy its brutality, they want more. Many are casualties of familial incest and sexual abuse, forced into sex work put on film. Dworkin condemned snuff films as the ultimate end for victims of this horrendous exploitation. Though she charged that women are raped and killed for entertainment and sexual arousal, the snuff film, as it is widely known, is an urban legend.[35]

In the mid-1970s a commercial film called *Snuff* hit the movie scene. According to Professor Whitney Strub, a distributor of low budget fare named Allen Shackleton added the murder of a female in the production crew to an imported Argentine horror movie he renamed *Snuff*. Critics lampooned it as a fraud. On the other hand, Linda Williams credits a 1976 movie titled *Snuff* to "the American husband-and-wife filmmaking team Roberta and Michael Findlay" noted for "their low-budget exploitation violence and horror films." Williams defines *Snuff* as a hybrid slasher film not part of the pornography genre. Wendy McElroy's interviews with John Stagliano and John Leslie reveal that neither man put any faith in the existence of a real snuff film. Leslie claimed no pornographer would be that stupid. On a side note, feminist author Susie Bright recalls gay filmmaker Chris Rage developed the promotional advertisement for the original movie. She told him he had created a "'monster,'" a rumored family secret the adult business would never shake. How right she was.[36]

Andrea Dworkin and Catharine MacKinnon, who delivered a similar message at the Chicago hearings, were embraced as expedient allies in the commission's effort to "snuff out" pornography. To what extent the panel agreed with the anti-porn feminists is questionable, but the convenience of their views was invaluable. The religious right's moral agenda of defining proper sexuality was served.

Linda Williams points out that though the commissioners never defined pornography, the panel scoured adult film for the most egregious images to contrive a standard to evaluate all adult film, thus establishing a government benchmark for "normal" sexuality. The commission disparaged sexual practices considered to be perverse, asserting that acceptable sexuality avoids all displays of violence even if they are concocted fantasies. In their collective view permissible sexual expression lay within a range of narrowly formulated behaviors. What is agreed upon as *not* acceptable permits easy condemnation of those who huddle among the minority: openly sexual women, gays, lesbians, transgendered persons and BDSMers. In legitimizing a sexual criterion, the panel validated pre-determined behavioral standards, in effect putting a government face on a sociological issue.[37]

Ed Meese and the anti-porn feminists agreed that pornography illustrated and instigated male violence against women. However, such a broad assertion was problematic. For example, the BDSM film genre does not always display women as the gagged and beaten and men as malefactors of harm; the reverse also has its audience. Additionally, the sexual practices of gays and lesbians muddy the waters. Gay porn is frequently BDSM oriented, illustrating female-on-female rough sex when the genre features all-girl shoots. Generalizing porn's manifestations as violence against women was flawed. In its shortsightedness the government ignored sexual depictions as fantasy, deliberately negating Veronica Vera's testimony before the Specter committee. The commissioners policed the imagination and silenced the erotic, censoring both in the process.[38]

In the years to come, confronting such a restrictive view within the women's movement fell to sex-positive feminists. Pro-sex, anti-censorship women faced two arduous tasks. First, defend the right to view and consume pornography and second, insist that sexual minorities be recognized as major components of society's erotic panoply. Their efforts became the harbingers of a new regard for the explicit.

The 1970 and 1986 government-induced moral panics are reminders that rights and freedoms are at risk when culturally defined virtues are perceived to be in danger. By defining the normal, abnormal, bizarre and violent, the Meese panel appropriated the role of America's social scientist and moral censor. In the end, the government accepted partial victory, condemned sexual violence and inadvertently went into the porn distribution business by putting commercial samples of sexually graphic descriptions in the Final Report. Incidentally, Andrea Dworkin and Catharine MacKinnon produce anti-porn writings that contain highly descriptive sexualized passages bordering on the prurient in ways not much different from Meese's extracted examples. Perhaps in the end the zeal to censor landed both the anti-porn feminists and the government in a position to become what they loathed the most: pornographers.

Implosion

Feminism shifted internally to the right in the 1980s, compartmentalizing a woman's sexuality as submissive and chaste, bathed in domesticity and child rearing. Sexual satisfaction and orgasm were male-identified behaviors which good girls avoided. Ellen Willis defines this change as "neo-Victorianism," an anti-porn feminist creation that insists men are focused on penetration and unconcerned about nurturing relationships while female erotic needs are tender, caring and non-orgasmic. Pro-sex feminist Gayle Rubin agrees, declaring that anti-porn feminists believe women occupy a moral higher ground by virtue of birthing children, thus affirming a docile, tender female sexuality that is apart from the carnality of men.[39] As the sex wars dragged on, the rhetoric between pro-sex feminists and anti-porn feminists escalated the levels of nastiness. Writers Kathleen Currie and Art Levine state that each side condemned the other as traitors to the feminist cause. The anti-porn feminists accused their sex-positive opponents of being a "front for pimps and pornographers." The pro-sexers retaliated by slapping the moniker "'sex cops'" on anti-porners who were unsympathetic to sexual minorities and the right to free expression.[40]

The feminist movement was imploding, leading Gayle Rubin to predict that feminism would deteriorate into ongoing crusades against "recreational sex" and pornography. The Meese investigation confirmed her foreboding. The government hearings also revealed the politics of feminism and pornography would become saturated in censorship/free speech debates with female pleasure a forgotten issue.[41]

In the heat of the sex wars Catharine MacKinnon and Andrea Dworkin refused to debate other feminists who confronted their pronouncements. Like the Meese panel's singular view of American morality, the anti-porn feminist interpretation of sexuality was a non-assailable monologue. However, the threat of civil action such as Indianapolis and Minneapolis could not go unchallenged. Pro-sex feminists organized the Feminist Anti-censorship Taskforce (FACT) to push back against legal efforts to stymie sexual expression. Anti-porn feminists denounced FACT as a tool of the pro-sex, pro-porn crowd. The organization was no friend of women, they insisted, because it encouraged the oppressive patriarchal system. More troubling was FACTs support of sexual expression deemed undesirable with fetishes, BDSM and pornography topping the list.[42]

FACT's transitory existence highlighted the need for a companion group. Led by feminist academic Marcia Pally, a group of women met in a New York Law School classroom on the evening of January 29, 1992. A variety of occupations were repre-sented from businesswomen to filmmakers to sex workers, reminiscent of the 1970s when women with common interests came into the feminist movement. Joan Kennedy Taylor recalls opinions on pornography differed, but supporting "the rights of those who produced it" was unanimous. Out of this meeting came Feminists for Free Expression (FFE), an organization that believed sexual images cannot be defined by any "feminist code" because the open "marketplace of ideas" promises all women choice. Simply put, FFE vowed to fight censorship and sexism.[43]

For the record, Club 90's Candida Royalle, Annie Sprinkle, Gloria Leonard and Veronica Vera joined FFE's activism, volun-teering to speak at seminars, college campuses, and wherever else they were called. Despite the challenges of the early 1990s, FFE prevailed in its efforts.

The years 1984-1992 were the most combative of the sex wars. The feminist worldview on porn was morphing into an "us versus them" issue. While the battle over porn continued, the backlash of the Reagan years held firm in its condemnation of feminism. Feminist writer Naomi Wolfe describes the late 1980s as a conflation of conservative politics and its accompanying anti-feminist rhetoric. In short, "Feminism had become 'the f-word.'"[44]

The MacDworkinites were fated to see their cause slip away out of simple disinterest. The women's movement questioned its future as pornography's financial boom encouraged American capitalism to sexualize commercial images. Advertising, reality TV shows, music television and online websites saturated the public with suggestive sexual overtones. For anti-smut feminists the new porn reality was devastating. Young women entered the adult industry to finance a glamorous lifestyle, revel in fan accolades and simply have fun. They were now more self-absorbed than ever, exercising their own feelings of empow-erment with a "do-it-yourself" attitude that did not always recognize its debt to the second wave.

Little energy remained in the sex wars after a 1992 University of Michigan confrontation over a sexually charged exhibit. Characterized as a "fracas," the dustup demonstrated the tensions gripping both sides. Student planned and organized, the conference on prostitution and activism invited an art exhibit, "Porn Imagery: Picturing Prostitutes," to campus. Opening the week preceding the conference, the exhibition included documentary film, photo essays and interviews with sex workers.[45]

Learning of the subject matter wrapped around the art, Catharine MacKinnon, Michigan law professor and the event's keynote speaker, quickly reacted to complaints the exhibit was offensive. Her sense of fairness as an educator was scuttled over personal prejudices. Within hours of the opening, a tape produced by Veronica Vera, "Portrait of a Sexual Revolutionary," was removed due to its pro-porn stance. Autobiographical in content, the tape covered Veronica's history as a porn model, film producer and activist for sex worker rights. Also included was footage of her testimony before Senator Arlen Specter's committee. Though the presentation was designed to spark academic discussion, student organizers were persuaded to tell the curator, Carol Jacobsen, to remove the exhibit because of safety concerns. Symposium attendee Andrea Dworkin claimed men who viewed such material had bullied her in the past. Suddenly an exhibit devolved into an issue of self-protection.[46]

Though MacKinnon denied any role in withdrawing the material, she supported the student action. For their part the students admitted to Jacobsen that the forum's intent was skewed toward an anti-sex worker statement. In response the curator announced forbidding a portion of the show was equivalent to censoring the entire presentation because, Veronica Vera remembers, the real issue was stifling "dissent." "Carol Jacobsen was passionate in her commitment not to let censorship go unprotested," Veronica adds. The students then decided the exhibit should be removed.[47]

Some Michigan students remained convinced the situation was a safety threat. In what way was not clear. The law students who organized the event later conceded pulling the tape was a hasty decision that muted freedom of expression and offered no suggestion for improving security. The dispute escalated. MacKinnon characterized negative reactions to the episode as mudslinging by "First Amendment fundamentalists" who scurrilously portrayed Andrea Dworkin and her as free speech opponents. The ACLU's Marjorie Heins countered by questioning the constitutionality of the action, pointing out the university was a state-supported institution. More egregious in her view was the First Amendment problem that moves to center stage when silencing views some people find distasteful. Simply stated, Michigan turned its back on a university's mission to be a free marketplace of ideas.[48]

This unfortunate episode offered another message. If the combatants listened closely they would have heard the faint death rattles of feminism's second wave. Some of the students felt "manipulated" by prostitution's opponents who refused to participate if the other side was represented. As a result of this intransigence and bickering, the students became disheartened. Reevaluating how they felt about feminism, some commented that instead of working for the common good of all women, the proceedings deteriorated into political infighting. "This is not women uniting to solve problems," a female student remarked, "this is just women fighting amongst each other."[49]

The issue was finally resolved in October 1993. The ACLU assisted in a lawsuit against the university over the exhibit and judgment was rendered in favor of the petitioners. The presentation was reinstated in mid-October accompanied by a "public forum" examining feminism, free speech and sexually oriented art.[50]

As the sex wars dissipated and the new century opened, a little-noticed feminist culture grew within the adult film business. These outspoken women did not seek to dismantle pornography's traditional patriarchal culture; rather, they demanded a say in how women are depicted on film and treated on both sides of the camera.

On society's broader front transitioning into the 2000s confirmed tides of change favored the pro-sex crowd. Today's young women are the children of a highly sexualized media environment in which pornography is an accepted reality. The modern woman can fantasize about and create her own amateur porn movie if she so desires and feel personally invested in real sexual outcomes in her life, confirming that the doors to the Secret Museum will never be completely resealed.

PART TWO

"I was always told as a child, when you grow up just do what makes you happy. As I got older, I was drawn to rock bands with female singers and art by female artists because I could feel their power. When I got to college, I started to find out about feminism. I've read a lot of feminist literature. It makes me feel good about myself and has molded my actions today."

Bobbi Starr on how she came to feminism as told to the author on January 8, 2010.

Chapter 5

An Attitude, Not a Movement

"Feminist porn is porn made by women and treats women, and men, as positive sexually empowered beings."
Jamye Waxman, feminist author and educator, as told to the author on January 8, 2009

Awareness

The *Feminist Porn Awards* is Toronto's springtime gala for adult film feminists and their fans. The joyous atmosphere is far removed from the glitz and glam of Porn Valley. The adult film performers and directors who gather in the Canadian city could be any and every woman plucked from Middle America's farms, towns and cities. They are the Dorothys of feminist porn, celebrating their art and politics with an exhilaration best described as riding Auntie Em's house up the funnel cloud stairway into the Land of Oz, Judy Garland in tow.

Prior to the April 2010 ceremonies I sat down with feminist producer/director Courtney Trouble and feminist performers Tina Horn, Jiz Lee and Dylan Ryan at Toronto's Gladstone Hotel, a cultural hotbed in the city's arts district. Over dinner an open discussion evolved. The answer to my central question would not be easy or unanimous.[1]

"How would you describe feminist porn?"

Dylan Ryan suggests it's an individual experience. Her on-screen sexual expression is authentic and she hopes her audience can relate to her performance that way. Realism is important in feminist pornography and her efforts are singular, Dylan insists, highly personal and self-satisfying.

"I'm representing myself. It's not, 'I'm a feminist and I'm

making feminist porn,'" she says. The context and content of her film work has little to do with any type of *collective* action as defined in feminism's second wave or its succeeding third.

"It's not about a movement. It's kind of about me."

Jiz Lee offers another interpretation. A "feminist perspective" in porn, Jiz says, means the film is open to individual interpretation and, recalling Justice Potter Stewart's oft quoted insight, Jiz knows feminist porn when Jiz sees it. Genuine sex is an ingredient, Jiz insists, but there's more. The movie must have "gender equality," a condition Jiz defines as an individual's sexual agency. The model must be personally invested in the performance being filmed.

From the director's chair Courtney Trouble mentions objectification and how feminist porn handles that vexing issue. A feminist oriented scene seeks to remove objectification from female and male performers, she says, elevating the men beyond "dicks" in the corner ready to penetrate on cue. A worthy goal, but difficult to achieve. Both sexes will always be "objectified" to a degree, she concedes, because film is art and the director is creating a product to be marketed and sold. Courtney's intention is to alter the meaning of objectification as it is argued in the anti-porn pronouncement of harm to women. She stresses that it was not "objectification" but "exploitation" that presented problems for the old second wave feminists.

Expanding on Courtney's thoughts Dylan mentions the confusion of pleasure and objectification. She structures a scenario in which the director is male and the female performer is "being totally smacked around" and poses the question, can that be feminist? "Yes!" Dylan insists, assuming the female performer is present in the situation and has an "awareness" of what is being filmed. The model must acknowledge the intention of the scene and be cognizant of "who's having sex" and if "they're comfortable." Dylan stresses personal responsibility and consent. Is everyone there "of their own volition" and having a good time? Her best scenes are "over the moon" when these things fall into place, she says.

All things considered, Dylan Ryan admits she has difficulty describing feminist porn because it is "in the eye of the beholder," in effect supporting Jiz. Dylan does insist the feminist product *is* different from mainstream porn and she wants the table to know feminist adult film has "an energy" sometimes lacking in a Porn Valley shoot. The roundtable represents the San Francisco porn community of small independent film companies where money is sometimes in short supply. Standards of attractiveness are far more inclusive than in Southern California studios where male definitions of "hotness" hold sway. Mainstream also refers to product distribution over larger and more profitable networks that deal with wide consumer demand. For the most part feminist porn is artistically self-reliant, individualistic and self-contained, giving it a special energy to be personally satisfying for everyone involved. Simply put, feminist porn throws a light on the collective notion that sexual orientation, behavior and gender preference is a kaleidoscope of possibilities protected within an intimate framework of devotees. The feminist porn audience is smaller, enthusiastic and highly devoted to the product they treasure, much like fans of the indie music scene where bands tour to make ends meet and remain true to the art they create.

After much discussion, the roundtable presents four broad conclusions. First, feminism in adult film is not a collective effort, but a personalization transformed into a sustaining attitude. These adult film performers have redefined feminism. Their roots are in the movement's sex-positive past but they are operating in a unique environment they have forged for themselves, one that highlights the individualism so vital in Dylan Ryan's assessments. This is not to deny they are mutually supportive of each other because their intimacies drive their work.

Modern adult film feminism also presents scenes in which

consent blurs the lines between exploitation and objectification. These new filmmakers are the children of a sexualized society. They give themselves permission to be objectified as long as they are relishing the sex and controlling the director's chair, as Dylan and Courtney illustrate. Converting object into subject, the feminist performer simultaneously becomes the pleasured and the source of pleasure. Above all, consent is essential. Adult film feminism is about choice and if these women are not offered it they will claim it for themselves.

In addition, adult film feminism gives women the permission to take on traditional male "identification" while reinforcing their own sexual agency. Today's feminists no longer rely exclusively on the female lens long associated with couples' erotica. They have co-opted the male gaze into their personal agenda, converting it into a "female-identified" moment if it suits their cinematic needs. They use the old stag formulas to establish a female agenda, honoring the aggressive woman of a Russ Meyer sexploitation film and Lena Nyman's early feminist politics. In the manner of Fifi Watson, Georgina Spelvin, Marilyn Chambers, and the *Deep Inside* concept of Annie Sprinkle and Gloria Leonard, they call their own shots, never forgetting the "my body" and "my rules" that define the legendary Nina Hartley.

Lastly, marginalized sexualities, shut out for decades, now tout their specific versions of explicit sex. The roundtable's repertoire includes a variety of fetishes, BDSM, transgendered and gay filming. By rewriting the pornographic image, queer directors such as Courtney Trouble and Shine Louise Houston take ownership of gonzo scenes shot from a female perspective while performers like Dylan Ryan and genderqueer Jiz Lee express a cornucopia of gender and sexual preferences.

This feminist evolution has altered the way modern women regard pornography, a change feminist producer/director Erika Lust calls the "New Wave" movement. Today's young woman is more porn friendly and doesn't feel shamed or debased by it.

Reflecting this evolving view, modern adult film feminists represent a concept I identify as *pornography feminism*. They blend porn's maleness with feminism's sex-positive roots that honor empowerment. Their sexuality takes on a third wave/post-feminist flavor, an individual expression that moves past the circumscription of softer erotica, includes marginal sexualities, and wants little to do with consciousness-raising or group movements. Their filming is open to all behaviors as long as performers demonstrate awareness and total consent with female pleasure being the central message.[2]

The new century solidified other elements that are necessary to pornography feminism. The reality porn of the 1980s and 1990s is now part of the broader feminist genre. Alternative (Alt) porn features tattooed and pierced performers of all sexual orientations in hardcore scenes with extreme sex play. The work of performer/director Belladonna and feminist Joanna Angel have added an outré flavor to the female filming perspective. Included in the mix are fetishes illustrated in the BDSM work of *Kink.com* and internet sites like Courtney Trouble's *QueerPorn.tv.* Pornography feminism is all inclusive of sexual and gender orientations, offering marginalized communities their own adult film voice.

This does not mean pornography feminists have abandoned the ideals of Club 90 and its pioneering commitment to female erotica. In fact pornography feminists embrace them. Feminist leaning studios like the long standing *Wicked Pictures* and *New Sensations* offer couples erotica for a woman's eye. *Girlfriends Films,* a company that advertises authentic lesbian sex and *Hard Candy/Girl Candy Films,* the feminist rich operation of Nica Noelle, are the heirs of Candida Royalle's *FEMME Productions.* Pornography feminists shoot the sex they take as their own while maintaining an unabashed right to make choices and honor those of others.

Pornography feminism is artistic and political, the ascendancy of women within a space they have been clearing for a generation. In her award acceptance speech at the 2010 Toronto show, Courtney Trouble gleefully shouted, "We all belong here!" Truly the big tent of female generated adult film is now open to everyone. In a post-feminist era of individualism, preserving the institutional memory of women in porn is easily lost in a transitory business; a tragedy because pornography's past is always the undercurrent of its present.

A Part of and Apart From

"Second wave feminism seemed to be all about equaling the score," says feminist director Ilana Rothman, whereas third wavers abandoned "the point system entirely." Now post-feminists are asking a simpler question. "Why bother keeping score. Let's just play." Rothman's comment recalls the third wave "do me" feminism coined by *Esquire Magazine*'s Tad Friend in his 1994 article on pro-sex feminism. A woman can make her own sexual choices of where, when and with whom, a carnal menu fed with the desserts of sexual fluidity and diversity.[3]

Third wavers are products of a social media age. Their vehicle is the blog, internet consciousness-raising where women construct their own online community. At home in cyberspace, third wavers are transitional. Though they might speak at times of feminist descriptors, their desire is to abandon old identifiers, shedding the "wave terminology." Feminism is now about individual expression and contradiction and less about a patriarchal culture. Feminist Melissa Klein credits punk's emergence within the music community as defining where third wavers position themselves. These girls want little to do with the second wave movement perspective and more with embracing their differences. Pornography, the old bastion of maleness, is part of that difference and its resulting contradiction.[4]

Young women now have permission to feel comfortable with

their choices, a self-controlled sexual independence with the inclusion of sexual minorities as part of their standard. Three pivotal developments: the *Riot Grrrl* Movement, Madonna's enduring evolution and the illumination of urban queer communities, shape their attitudes. These changes coincide with pornography's rising cultural acceptance and the resulting sexualization that facilitates experimentation with sex work.

Originating in the 1990s' punk music scene, the *Riot Grrrl* movement is a rebellion against a male fixated music culture that expresses female resentment and animosity with all-girl music shows and "women-only mosh pits to draw attention to the problem of sexual abuse." According to feminist editor Andi Zeisler, displaying an ill temper that's raw, rarely pretty and very realistic, young women deliberately shun conventional thought and flaunt their sexuality at a society contemptuous of women who step on accepted traditions. It is somewhat reminiscent of New Left individualism.[5]

Riot Grrrl ideology carries over to another feminist issue: sex work. The 1990s woman abandons the morality lens of her predecessors. Accepting porn as a cultural norm, she regards the adult industry as a kind of "subversive glamour" that is an extension of her individualism. Becoming an exotic dancer or a professional dominatrix is no longer dismissed as deviant and finding the occasional college student who finances her education via the sex trade is not unimaginable. This young woman sees "no theoretical inconsistency" in her professional decisions and how she conducts her personal life.[6]

The legacy of *Riot Grrrl* is contradiction, women needed to be "'sexy, powerful, and angry at the same time.'" In its brief time on the cultural scene, the movement liberated and validated individual choices. Feminist writer and adult film critic Alison Lee emphasizes *Riot Grrrl* as the impetus for young women to initiate a discussion on sex work and sex-positive possibilities in their private lives. Girls alienated by culture and boyfriend and inclined to explore alternate sexualities can find a space in the *Riot Grrrl* fold. In its attitudes and sexual images, *Riot Grrrl* leaves its footprints from college campuses to urban queer communities to the internet universe of fetish porn.[7]

Though more personally provocative than *Riot Grrrl*, Madonna also uses sexuality as liberation. Her own version of contradiction, images of sexual alterability queer oriented with a BDSM taste, highlights The Material Girl's ongoing reinvention of herself and her commercial appeal. Madonna's popularity resonates across the sexual landscape because she never suppresses her kinks for any audience. Her magic lay in her image, carefully formulating herself as the object of desire and its subject. Using her unabashed sensuality to market female presence, Madonna's message to young girls is do what you want and be what you want. Her self-commoditization allows Madonna's flash to play closer to the margins of broader mainstream than does *Riot Grrrl*.[8]

Madonna shrewdly masters her own empowerment and seduction, reminding the audience she pushes the show as far as it can go. Whenever she drifts near the irrelevance dictated by commercial culture's short attention span, Madonna reappears for another round of marketing, keeping her sexual edge on the public radar. Though she lacks the defiance of *Riot Grrrl*, Madonna's brazen carnality remains linked to punkers in spirit. While her teenybopper groupies become sexual overnight, *Riot Grrrls's* jaded rebels act out their sexuality in an ostentatious response to male dominance. Both reinforce their status through their physical appearance, tattoos and piercings always among the options.

Riot Grrrl and Madonna provide third wavers with sexual equality and an exposure, as they desire, to pornography/erotica. The 1990s cultural scene licenses young women to do more than abide the pornographic; it can now be "celebrated, written, theorized, produced and performed." Modern women anticipate erotic pleasure and recognize fantasy fulfillment as a part of what they desire. A personal definition of what is sexual and the choices it offers, writes feminist scholar Molly Merryman, leads them to the premier expectation: orgasms.[9]

Third wave sexuality is a movable feast, promoting social tolerance and acknowledging changeable definitions of sex and gender. In time the "identity politics" of gay, lesbian and bisexual persons transitions into the "queer movement," and its role in "current sex-positive feminism," says Alison Lee. She adds that queer theory and "activism from the early 1990s," particularly in "gay male culture," is its driving force. Madonna is a part of this evolution in which lesbian and gay identifiers are not the only alternatives to definitions of straight. She facilitates the shift by being "unapologetically pro-sex." According to feminist author Carol Queen, Madonna's most powerful message lay outside the commercialization of her image, it is her insistence that we "look squarely at sex."[10]

For pornography feminists, the LGTBQQKI community is re-visioning feminist pornography in ways that showcase consent and choice. Expressing sexuality contradictory to society's predominant and traditional values, this energized alternative community is part of San Francisco's Queer Porn Mafia (QPM), independent film companies, internet websites and the emerging BDSM genre. *Riot Grrrl* and Madonna facilitate and encourage this emerging revolution.

Empowered Sexuality of Self

At this point, the Toronto roundtable turns to a discussion of where feminism is today. Courtney Trouble mentions a sex-positive attitude did not gain traction with her generation because second wave feminism was regarded as sex-negative, "very anti-sex work, anti-porn, and anti-men," she says. Women of her college generation seeking feminist ideas often ended up in the wrong camp. They began their journey with anti-porn feminists "instead of Annie Sprinkle, Carol Queen, and Scarlot Harlot," and were quickly misguided. Jiz Lee agrees: some young women are still not aware of second wave sex-positive feminism's contribution to culture and film.[11]

Courtney gives credit to third wavers who pushed female sexuality forward with conversations about the "empowered sexuality of self." She explains third wavers wanted to own their sexuality in the ways they experienced it, which included "do me" feminism and a rougher sexual play. Attitudes were in flux and sex-positivism spilled over into art, Courtney remembers. Erotic art was creating its own cultural scene; artists were "opening the doors for more interesting things," she says, nurturing her film production and its feminism. Other changes played a role. "Sex work activism and advocacy awareness popped up" as her generation was forming a more complete picture of feminism. But the pathways are not unhindered. Though the young director credits Annie Sprinkle and Candida Royalle for "putting the freedom of sexuality into the feminist ideal," she grants that sexual expression in film remains under fire because "anti-porn feminists are still around today."

That said, Courtney retains her cultural memory and respects the past, mentioning again Annie Sprinkle, Carol Queen, and Scarlot Harlot as advocates for "sexual choice." Her generation would not be the expressive feminists they are, she claims, had these older women not fought for their beliefs.

Reflecting the individualism of modern feminists, Courtney Trouble does not see herself connected to any wave or movement, leaving the impression the new century is indeed an era of post-feminism. Yet she praises Dylan Ryan's appearance in a "mainstream" movie in which she ends a scene with "cum all over her face," noting that it's "feminist in the third wave sense" because Dylan is "embracing sex" in her own way. The willowy brunette responds with a tinge of pride. Prior to entering the industry, Dylan explains, she would view porn and think, "I guess kind of arrogantly, 'I could do better.'"

In fact so did other women. They went to work creating their own niche and challenged the male oriented market for a greater share in film distribution and profits. The result was the steady growth of feminist pornography into a recognized product with directors in the Southern California scene like Tristan Taormino, Belladonna, Bobbi Starr, Nica Noelle, Jacky St. James, Joanna Angel, and Dana Vespoli. They have taken male identification and artistically colored it feminist.

A handful of feminist directors represent the zenith of queer filming, Courtney Trouble, Shine Louise Houston, Madison Young and Princess Donna are prominent names. Joining the group is feminist performer April Flores' husband and soul mate, the incomparable Los Angeles based artist and director Carlos Batts. Feminist porn is sometimes designed in an educational format, evidenced by selected work from Tristan Taormino and Jaiya who produce instructionally oriented products for a wide audience. Of course, feminist production companies are not limited stateside. Two Europeans, Spain's Erika Lust and England's Anna Span, are major stakeholders in the foreign film market, along with Australia's Anna Brownfield. Nor is the feminist identifier limited to women. The previously mentioned Dan O'Connell of *Girlfriends Films* comes immediately to mind as a maker of feminist porn. Coming from a largely hetero environment, Dan's mainstream company supports and nourishes female sexuality.

Mirroring cultural changes that have allowed women to become as aggressive and sexual as men, these adult film feminists want their own space in the pornography mosh pit while blending the desire to be a part of with an independence to be apart from. In this evolutionary story, the sex-positive attitude of Club 90 and Nina Hartley is a constant presence, reminding everyone that an institutional memory is part of the feminist package.

The Feminist Alternative

Whether independent or mainstream, home grown or foreign born, feminist directors are a distinct group of filmmakers. They are not uniform on what passes for good sex and their personal tastes dictate the content of their product. Feminist film is a menagerie of approaches with an erotica flavor, a gonzo direction or an alternative fetish that is all-inclusive. Joanna Angel, whose alt product comes straight out of the glaring punk rock scene, summarizes what pornography feminists inherently understand: making adult film and being a "real, honest-to-god, hardcore feminist" is a blend of creative expression that empowers the woman in front of and behind the camera.[12]

A brief look at four directors illustrates how being a pornography feminist offers more than one path to success.

A graduate of Connecticut's Wesleyan University with a degree in American Studies, Tristan Taormino abandoned a planned career path in law to write about sex. Her resume is impressive: former editor of *On Our Backs*; author of *Opening up: A Guide to Creating and Sustaining Open Relationships* and *The Ultimate Guide to Anal Sex for Women*: and creator of a sex education video series honored by *Adult Video News (AVN)* and the *Feminist Porn Awards*. Tristan also manages her own company, *Smart Ass Productions*. She is a dominating feminist presence in adult entertainment.[13]

The Long Islander entered feminist porn in the late 1990s. With a little prodding from women who found her book based seminars instructive, Tristan ventured into film. Her desire was to make an educational movie informing women they are entitled to their own personal fantasies illustrated in a safe and respectful way. Knowing the film was a risk, Tristan decided against the independent route, opting for a strategy to reach the masses, the "non-converted" as she describes them. She shopped the idea to major porn companies believing they were the best avenue to reach a mainstream audience. Rejected at every turn, Tristan finally got a call back from *Evil Angel's* John Stagliano, who offered to fund the project and was on hand to help her through each stage of the filming process.[14]

Admitting that she knew nothing of movie making, Tristan was not "prepared to jump in feet first." Nevertheless, she is proud of her efforts. The budding director had never picked up a camera or taken a film class but she knew what she wanted. She assembled a reliable cast and took her first stand on what would *not* happen in a Tristan Taormino film, ejaculating on a woman's face. Tristan believes porn's formulaic acts contribute to its lack of creativity. Facials were an adult film "cliché," in her mind. "It's the one on-screen moment when most women look bored, turned off or downright miserable," she says.[15]

To address her inner sense of playfulness, Tristan wanted her performers to take part in a ten person all-anal gangbang in which she was the chief participant. Then she gave herself over to the talent and their professional skills. It was the "ultimate feminist gangbang," Tristan notes proudly, emphasizing that she, like everyone else, is entitled to her fantasies. In reaching for a wider audience, Tristan thinks of herself as the embodiment of the proverbial girl next door showing the viewer sex can be delightful and energizing. Her porn is a teaching tool: what is on the screen can be imitated in a safe and informative way.[16]

The movie elevated Tristan's status in the adult business. Joining a handful of feminist directors whose artistic sense addresses what a segment of female viewers desire to see, Tristan compares her philosophy to Candida Royalle's, no facials or extreme genital close ups and a limit on the external "pop shots."

The business side of adult film was in a state of flux at the time of her first film, Tristan says. By the 2000s the industry believed porn for women was mired in the romance novel genre popular in the 1980s, a stereotypical view of female tastes. The new century brought the reality show concept and many couples demanded porn that was more carnal and less romantic. However, by the century's second decade, Candida Royalle's story based work reappeared with a darker twist. The popularity of the printed trilogy, *Fifty Shades of Grey*, romanticized BDSM for women and couples looking for a sharper taste to flavor their mutually shared affections. As for Tristan, she remained true to her own direction that keeps her on that cutting edge. The fetish oriented second film in her "Rough Sex" series won the "Hottest Kink Movie" in the 2011 *Feminist Porn Awards*.

Though Tristan Taormino maintains clear boundaries of what she will put on film, she understands no particular sex act can be labeled anti-feminist. She encourages her performers to establish their own preferences, realizing today's young women sometime desire a harsher sexuality, blurring the objectification/exploitation lines once again. In that way her work encapsulates what it means to carry the pornography feminist label, reclaiming nasty and bawdy as descriptors of female empowerment and weaving them within feminism's sex-positive space. However the feminist product is reframed, the woman who chucked a law degree to make pornography believes adult film feminism has an instructional mission to promote fantasy and encourage women to enjoy the adult product.[17]

Beginning sex work as exotic dancer, Nica Noelle eventually found her way into the adult industry. Armed with feminist ideas, her timing was not fortuitous. She was quickly disaffected by the anti-porn rants of Andrea Dworkin. "Women like me were considered bad for the cause," Nica says, catering to men and "sleeping with the enemy." In her mind, feminists like Dworkin were "sour-puss women" who dictated to others what they should and should not be doing.[18]

Despite her discontent Nica was willing to give feminism a second chance. She discovered "The Feminist Stripper" website whose founder, Alysabeth Clements, was "the first pro-sex work feminist I had ever met," Nica says. Realizing that feminism comes with "many faces," Nica's attitudes were transformed. Shedding feminism's anti-sex disposition her career as a performer and director was energized. At the 2010 Toronto festival her company, *Sweet Sinner Studios*, won the "Sexiest Straight Movie" honor, a reflection of her "mainstream" porn roots. As of 2012 her newest adventure is *Hard Candy Films* and its partner *Candy Girl Films*, an all-girl studio.[19]

The New York City native believes individual choice is the centerpiece of feminist porn though criticisms linger, especially from women whose belief system is in the shadow of sex-negativism. If a model chooses to do a scene in which she is "slapped or choked or spat upon by a male," Nica explains, she is "immediately suspect" in the eyes of anti-porn feminists. Assumptions follow. The performer must be "inherently damaged," plagued with self-esteem issues and incapable of lucid decisions. Mental problems or drug habits produce "diminished cognition" and the performer must be protected from harming herself. This attitude is "the same intolerant, narrow-minded ideology" predominant in the sex wars. Discrediting choice or denying a woman the space to select her personal experiences is anti-feminist, Nica declares.

Adult film is "an extraordinary place" where a woman can explore her personal preferences and boundaries, Nica says, and learn to negotiate "power and gender themes." Nica cites biological factors that are rarely considered when viewing pornography. Women have "powerful urges" to comprehend and define their "roles as mating creatures." Pornography takes on these issues. Feminist pornography speaks directly to women, she believes, highlighting a raw sexuality that ventures beyond eroticism. For example some women prefer a submissive sexual role, opening the door to reconciling feminism with the "power play" dynamics of BDSM, though submissiveness does not necessarily define her relationships outside roleplaying venues. Nica stresses a woman expects to be treated as an equal. Adult film is equipped to explore her sexual awareness in ways that encourage her to experiment with her preferences. "Not understanding your sexuality can deeply confuse you about yourself," Nica asserts, including who and what "makes you happy." Once self-understanding takes place, a woman commands her own intimacy in a way that is "life changing."

Nica Noelle concludes sex is a kaleidoscope of complications and desires. No one can judge what any person needs or wants. To suggest a particular sexual expression is "wrong" or experiencing sex a certain way is "bad," is inexcusable. Nica believes attempts to control this strongest of human cravings are misplaced, especially if they come from a position of "fear and apprehension." Through her work as a director, she puts all these entanglements and intimacies into a cauldron and extracts her version of feminist porn. Club 90's Veronica Hart is an admirer of Nica Noelle's style and content, verifying that the feminist director's filmed sex is realistic with every shoot she produces.

"A man fucked up his butt is feminist, but a women fucked up her butt is not? Come on!"[20]

These are the words of European pornography feminist Erika Lust whose product is internationally recognized as art and sex with an urban rhythm. Born into a cultural environment amicable to sexual expression and egalitarian ideas about women, Erika's middle class background sparked an intellectual curiosity about politics and social history. A degree from Sweden's prestigious Lund University suggested a career pursuing injustices toward women. In 2000 an opportunity to promote cultural diversity led Erika to Barcelona and an unexpected detour in her plans. Realizing media and politics are inseparable, Erika started her own audiovisual company, *LUST FILMS*, to produce a "feminist" approach to her media interests. Pornography is a division of its business.

Erika was troubled by how male driven porn depicted sex. Women were not seeking pleasure or satisfaction. The industry paraded women as "character stereotypes," such as horny teens and hot nurses, that were "just plain offensive," she says. Knowing porn could be better, Erika went to work eliminating its clichés. Sex for women, she believed, could be shown in a more realistic way so the transplanted Swede opted to construct her narratives to present intimacy as she personally experienced it. As a result, a Lust film is widely recognized for its innovative cinematic techniques and its pro-woman message.

Erika Lust believes that pornography communicates attitudes about masculinity and femininity. If women do not participate in the process of making porn then the male view, the way the "fantasy sees us," she says, will prevail. Erika wants feminist pornographers to reclaim the social construct that fuels the fantasy. They can dismantle, rebuild and reenergize masculine stereotypes on *their* terms based on *their* desires. Women can present their intimacies "in an explicit and graphic way" to help men understand what they "just don't get," like the patience to orally arouse a woman's passions.

A woman filmmaker approaches sex differently from her male counterpart, Erika asserts. She escorts the viewer into a highly sexualized pulsating urban world. Mixing her scenes with MTV "cool," Erika offers a cosmopolitan pornography for a social media age. Her narratives are designed for the way women want sex and feature intelligent and communicative males with a sense of humor. Erika maintains an upbeat pace with an illicit hint that permits the viewer to meld respectful voyeurism and cathartic participation. Anne G. Sabo describes a Lust film as fluent and smooth, awash in lighting and color with technical skill that's precise, sharp and driven by an "indie-style pop-rock soundtrack." Her movies generate the "tension and heat" of a youthful, urban sexual rhythm. Linda Williams compliments the Spanish filmmaker's ability to construct an emotional tautness around sexual interplay while honoring a woman's take on sex. Erika Lust dispenses with pornography's repetitive feel, Williams believes, by fashioning various ways to engage explicit sex.[21]

Feminism is a state of mind, not a specific practice, and Erika Lust considers herself to be a feminist "no matter" how she personally engages in sex. "A woman can be a strong feminist," she says, and still have the desire to "be taken" and have her lover's "cum all over her face." Like Dylan Ryan, Erika speaks of awareness and presence, keys to feminist porn and female pleasure. Yet she concedes Victorian sexual orthodoxy is the replay of the well-worn good girl/bad girl disconnect that keeps women oppressed. Within the bad girl or "whore" scenario, she believes female sexuality is "often expressed very powerfully" but in ways inimical to all women. Unfortunately sexually desirable female images are often limited to "slutty women, prostitutes and lap-dancers," an attitude that devalues the intimate feelings of average women like mothers, sisters and girlfriends. Erika's feminist approach affirms all women are sexual. Wanting to be carnally desired and fulfilled is not limited to the sex worker image.

Nowhere is the Erika Lust philosophy more beautifully portrayed than in her award winning movie, *Five Hot Stories for Her* (2007), a series of vignettes that includes a feminist remake of the oldest of stag film plots: the delivery man. Erika's spin on the formula is titled "The Good Girl." It is a joyful experience. The female protagonist orders a pizza on a sunny afternoon. The guy shows up. Attracted to him she is painfully short of the courage to communicate her desires and when he leaves her face wears the exasperation and disappointment of a lost opportunity. The viewer's heart sinks with hers before good fortune intervenes. He has forgotten his motorcycle helmet! Given a second chance our heroine makes the move. The sex is passionate with definitive romantic elements. Before leaving the second time he writes his phone number on the pizza box, assuring that passion's doorway remains open. The viewer is emotionally drawn into the film, rooting for the girl and delighted she revels in an opportunity most women would never experience. She achieves her desires in a film that crushes the tedium of formulaic sex.[22]

A *LUST FILMS* production presents a mutuality of respect. Men and women are equals in Erika's projects. She does not want her actresses trapped in repetitive gonzo, making the required eye contact with the camera, pointing their toes nicely and enduring the acrobatics of double penetrations (DPs). In actuality, Erika doesn't shoot DPs. They are unnatural and require performers to have a healthy dose of athleticism to twist and frame their bodies to the camera's demands. In her opinion most women wouldn't consider them in their private lives. There is little sensuality in the act and certainly no intimacy. This does not mean Erika Lust ignores rough sex in her products. Admiring Belladonna's fetish films as powerful and edgy with BDSM suggestiveness, Erika concedes gonzo is preferred by some feminist directors.

Like so many of her feminist sisters, Erika Lust saves her highest veneration for Candida Royalle, the first woman "to step away from the mainstream male porn" and do something different, smashing the barriers to porn's ole boy network. The Swede who found her career in Spain is following Candida into the adult film boardroom and encourages other pornography feminists to do likewise.

"Femi-nazi" described the popular view of feminism when she was growing up, Jacky St. James says. The women's movement represented an extremism not to her liking. Acting, not politics, was her forte and steeping herself in the leftovers of the feminist sex wars was off the table. After college the young scholar drifted away from the arts for a brief interlude, burning a handful of post-college years managing ad campaigns for a Fortune 500 company. Aware the theater was the muse that would not sit still, Jacky migrated from the East Coast to California in 2004. Within a short time of her relocation, a new career guided her to couple's oriented pornography and a forthright expression of what she once avoided: feminism.[23]

Pornography is Jacky's corporation and her employer, *New Sensations*, gives the talented thirty-something a broad swath of creative latitude. "The films I direct and write are absolutely feminist because I have a hand in their creation," Jacky says, elaborating she takes "great care" in cultivating her performers, seeking those who fit the story and respond to her guidance on the set. Female talent is most dear to her creative process and she demands more than simply walking through a script. She wants actresses who can play strong independent characters "who aren't solely defined by their relationships with men, but by their own values and desires." In selecting talent, Jacky seeks acting ability over physical beauty. "I've never even thought about a performer's looks when I cast people," she says, because everyone can "exude sexuality." It's up to the director to "showcase" it.

Feminism is critical to the pornography genre because it embraces a woman's ability to produce, write and direct. From Jacky's perspective female sexuality resists pigeon holing. A woman's "sexual interest" is as diverse as a man's, she asserts, but with a uniquely female style. Sometimes Jacky steps back from the traditional "story-driven" romance for a dose of raw biting sex she considers to be feminist because it mirrors what turns her on personally.

Putting aside the varying styles and diverse content produced by "a new influx of feminist pornographers," Jacky St. James believes there is a singular element in good porn: visual equality. "I always stress the importance of seeing two people on screen during a sex scene," she says. Minimizing gonzo type close ups, Jacky St. James expands carnal by turning it cerebral. Sexuality is mental, Jacky believes, far beyond mechanical penetration. "It's a thought. It's a look. It's the way a person catches their breath, or holds it," she says. But she also acknowledges outré themes. "I want to normalize sexuality in all forms," she declares, and that means "taboo" subjects like BDSM and anal sex. In one of her pivotal films, *The Submission of Emma Marx* (2012), Jacky includes an anal scene that avoids the "crazy, insane thrusting" characteristic of a rougher gonzo porn. Realizing that women viewers are not universally aroused by anal sex, Jacky frames it to be "less intimidating and more connected and beautiful," emphasizing there is "nothing wrong with romantic anal."

The Washington, D.C. native believes her acting background sets her apart from other directors in porn. She tries to fit her performers with the style that best suits them. Jacky varies her approach depending on the moment. Sometimes she relies on the performer's physical presence "to carry the scene." Other occasions require taking actors to "dark places" and "using emotional memory" or getting them to "live within the space of the characters." Referring to *Emma Marx*, Jacky explains, "Emma begins as this insecure, uncertain young woman who is just beginning to own her sexuality." The story progresses and so does Emma, evolving from "tentative to confident and trusting." The young woman confronts and conquers her inner need to redefine normal as it applies to her sexuality, fully embracing the sexual submissiveness of BDSM and sealing the film with a feminist statement. Incidentally, Emma is played by bondage model Penny Pax who credits her award-winning performance to Jacky's skill in bringing the best out of her cast. She was "amazing and helped me nail the delivery of lines and emotions," Penny says.[24]

Jacky's choreographed sex scenes are the raison d'etre of her films, they must "enhance the story," she insists. Characters poorly fleshed out result in a sexual component that lacks the "intensity, connection, and passion." And that, Jacky St. James asserts, is a waste of time, money and creative effort.

Loves Her Experience

Feminist pornography is about respecting performers for their skills and directors strive to bring out the best in each without a sense of repetition or ennui. Nica Noelle and Tristan Taormino want models to explore their eroticism, to do what turns them on. Tristan Taormino gives her talent latitude to choose what they want to do, "share a piece" of their sexual selves and explore real pleasure. And, they do not always have to listen to her direction. Sexual compatibility is all important, of course. Nica Noelle directs her performers to open up and become "vulnerable" to achieve the true eroticism she seeks.

Erika Lust and Jacky St. James regard performers as actors. A *LUST* film is role specific and casting mirrors a mainstream production. Erika shares the screenplay with the actors so they have a sense of the character they are expected to portray. She solicits their ideas and the sex is decided upon before filming begins. Jacky's drama training dictates that her hires must be "in tune with their emotions" and those of the other cast members. Her performers are more than line readers; they are expected to be the characters that develop with the story. She lets them loose for a bit, but reins them in when necessary. "I never let them take over the scene or change the scene's intention or the character's motivations."

Performer consent is *first priority* for feminist pornographers. Sexual predilections can elevate a scene if carefully planned. Nica Noelle explains what pornographers learn but don't necessarily observe: pre-film discussions are requisite in establishing sexual parameters. A fundamental rule centers on performer limits expressed by "yes and no" lists. Feminist directors are adamant that nudging a performer to do a sex act not previously agreed upon is taboo. In turn, performers have certain responsibilities. Controlled substances are forbidden and any model not in command of his/her faculties is sent home. "No drugs are tolerated, period" because impaired judgment inhibits "proper consent," Nica warns. She remembers killing a scene because a popular actress, who now publicly speaks about her substance abuse and "the perils of porn," showed up under the influence. Similar stories from others indicate that in feminist pornography, at least, sobriety is the watchword.

Pornography feminists do their best to accommodate performer needs. Set cleanliness is appreciated and because everyone gets hungry, food is a priority. Crews often work a twelve-hour day and for talent the old tagline "they don't pay us for the sex, they pay us to wait" has not changed. Making the long hours less taxing is the aim of a conscientious director. On Erika Lust's sets scenes are carefully choreographed because she is a stickler, scheduling "time for lunch, rest, make-up," she says. At *LUST FILMS* the shooting day starts early in the morning and finishes on time for another reason. Dinner with the family and sleeping at home is a personal priority for the Swedish director.

In the final analysis, the Toronto roundtable cites a collection of characteristics that describe feminist porn and a look at directors indicates how feminist ideas are used in producing film. There are other elements that shape feminist porn as Carlyle Jansen, the sponsor of the *Feminist Porn Awards,* elucidates. In her mind, empowerment, respect, choice and diversity constitute the genre. Choice must extend to all parties, actors, directors and consumers, with diversity the major point of inclusion. All bodies, colors and ethnicities have space in feminist porn.

Beyond those parameters, Carlyle reduces the discussion to a single question. "Do the women get their fair share of the pleasure?" If the sex is "positive" and the performer's enjoyment is evident, Carlyle holds, it is the tipping point that defines a "feminist" evaluation of porn. As sex-positive feminist performer, Tasha Reign, declares, feminist porn demonstrates that a woman "loves her sexual experience" no matter how it is illustrated.[25]

Chapter 6

Space for Everyone

"Feminist porn or sex-positive porn has connection. It's documenting real sex, real exchange of energy and real pleasure."
Madison Young, interview with the author, Las Vegas, January 8, 2010

Context of Fantasy

"When watching porn I would sometimes say, 'She's not into what's happening to her.'" Dylan Ryan sparks nods of agreement from the roundtable as our talk continues.[1]

Dylan explains. A disinterested or uncomfortable performer is "obviously not present" in what she is doing and certainly not experiencing "erotic enjoyment." The shoot comes alive when the girl is enthusiastic instead of bored or mechanical. Dylan contemplates how that same narrative would affect her if she "climbed into" it. Watching the scene unfold in her mind, she predicts, "If I were her, I would be having a wicked great time!"

Commenting on Dylan's imaginary rough sex scene, Tina Horn mentions her sexual preferences sometimes reflect a similar scenario, clearly a break from the softer stereotypical eroticism for women. There are times, Tina says, when she wants "carnal images" so that after moments of self-guided pleasure, she can get on with her day. Porn is fantasy and Tina encourages the female porn consumer to address her desires up front, doing it solo if necessary. If that means hardcore spiced with rough sex, the "option" to see it should be available. Nowadays, Tina says, no one should be "shocked" because in porn "anything goes."

Of course, anything leads to the ever-present criticisms of

humiliation and degradation. The problem with pornography is the way it is interpreted, Tina Horn points out, and cautions the viewer to never lose the "context of fantasy." Though the scene may appear to be a non-consensual situation or become "explicitly degrading" in its storyline, professional actors are exercising their consent and their skills in filming the sex, offering the audience the chance to experience its eroticism in a safe way. Believing "a fantasy of degradation can be hot because it's taboo," Tina understands the average female viewer is hesitant if faced with such a scenario in her personal life. The film's narrative serves to relieve any sexual tension surrounding private desires she prefers to keep to herself. Having the "right to portray those kinds of dynamics in film" is a significant role for porn, Tina insists, and "feminist pornographers are very vocal about putting it there."

John Stagliano, whose production company offers a voice for feminist directors, believes pornography can be an emotional release for women. Some adult film models "have a fantasy of being sluts," he mentions. They want to "give in" and shoot a scene that may be interpreted as abusive, but is nevertheless enjoyable for them. They can enact their fantasies in a safe, personally acceptable and comfortable way. His views are more widespread than might be expected. For example, models who film for *Kink.com* frequently return because the action is on a film set where possible real harm is forestalled by the watchful eye of director, crew and fellow performers.[2]

What of the charge that pornography is damaging to women, promoting violence and harm? Dylan Ryan regards the indictment as "completely fallacious," pointing out there is no research to confirm that allegation. Though the argument is outdated, she admits it remains an interpretation anti-porn feminists "continue to utilize" as a censorship weapon. Dylan does concede when she kneels in front of male performers who are going to ejaculate on her face, her submissiveness disturbs some viewers. "Am I the object and they [the male performers] are the ones in power?" she asks. "Sure, in theory, but I placed myself there." Her performance is consensual and by choice.

To see degradation through the eyes of an anti-porn feminist means decoding film from only one direction, Dylan suggests, an interpretation that steals a woman's sexual voice. Such an attitude, she insists, reinforces a sexist imbalance, saddling women with the collective status of "lower class citizens." Whatever role pornography plays in today's attitude toward women is inconsequential, Dylan concludes, because the anti-porn feminist degradation argument "has absolutely nothing to do with sex." The real problem is political, the power differential between men and women. Out of this debate porn becomes the scapegoat.

Sexual politics and sexism still dictate a woman's role in a patriarchal culture and Dylan believes anti-porn feminists paint the adult industry as the overarching villain, blaming it for "the undoing of female empowerment." This is offensive, she believes, because sexually assertive women, like those in adult film, suffer unfair criticism. Passionate about her career, Dylan speaks with an intense rhythm, accentuating her personal pronouns in a fist-pounding manner.

"*I* show up and do this. That is all *me*. I'm there because *I* want to be. *I* signed up for what I'm doing. I'm getting paid to do it. *I* leave happy, and *I* feel good about *my* choice!"

Dylan Ryan's final comment strikes at the heart of what matters most to all of us, our identity. She knows her critics will insist her attitude is destructive to women, though she categorically rejects the allegation. But there is something deeper. She feels her detractors have "lost sight" of her and have little understanding that her sexual reality is also an option for them.

"They've almost looked past you, haven't they?" I ask.

"Yeah," Dylan responds, her voice inflected with a hint of anger. She has a message for those who decry porn while insisting women become more powerful to fight oppression. "Don't overlook me!" she declares. "It's my agency and empowerment to be doing what I'm doing." Dylan urges her critics to be open minded. She wants them to realize *what* she films and *how* she films it might just be a "good, positive thing for people."

Above all, Dylan Ryan wants fairness and recognition. "There has to be space for everyone," she says, calmly and with conviction.

She Knows She's Good at It

Filmed pornography has its allure. Fan adoration, parties and quick money are irresistible and for elite models, expensive clothes and flirtations with high rent neighborhoods become reality. Careers are short, a few months the widely accepted average and most girls never become A-listers or walk the industry's red carpet. For models who survive a handful of years, income will slow when popularity fades and bodies lose their resilience. Knowing how to cope is the first step to longevity and learning the self-control to manage finances is the second. Success is built on personal responsibility, something many girls find more elusive than Indiana Jones's quest for the Holy Grail.

A small number of women are invested with confidence and self-assurance before they shoot their first scene. Describing porn as a "chapter" in her life that she is experiencing in the "safest way possible," Bobbi Starr considered the ramifications of adult film before stepping in front of the camera. Crediting feminism with providing the tools to guide her decision making, Bobbi composes her "own script" of what appeals to her. Above all, she is a pragmatist. Her present situation is temporary and she will move on when she is finished with the pornographer's lens.[3]

Confident exterior notwithstanding, Bobbi admits moments in her career have been daunting but her self-reliance allays her doubts. "If you act like you know what you're doing," she says, "people believe that you know what you're doing." Her personal take on what it means to be a feminist allows her to manage her career with a deliberation and intent uncharacteristic of most industry women.

Nurtured in a "female powerful family," Bobbi's self-assurance comes from her mother who, Bobbi comments, "doesn't go around saying she's a feminist, but she is." Mentioning the influence of two aunts and a grandmother, Bobbi's early adolescence programmed her to be confident with her choices, especially if she is passionate for what she wants. Family brings up a question many people have for adult film women, "Do they know what you do?" Bobbi's is "okay" with whatever makes her happy, she says. They respect her drive to start her own business within adult entertainment's greater framework. The Northern California lass is quick to admit with a smile that no mother wants her daughter taking off her clothes for pornographers and concedes hers would "prefer that I was doing something else!"

Bobbi Starr is representative of today's feminist attitude. For her, as it is for the others, feminism is a personal experience that does not necessarily connect with a movement. "I am the person that I am and I'm going to do what I want, when I want to do it," Bobbi says with conviction. She is not beholden to anyone's opinion and refuses to allow others to render judgments that might limit her behaviors or preferences. Yet Bobbi is thoughtful in her perspective on her career, believing she has grown as a person. She ventured into hardcore because she was "curious," but unexpected revelations shaped her personal certainties regarding sex. Treasuring the "value of intimacy" in her personal life is foremost to her now, Bobbi says, and she clearly distinguishes it from "sex for work."

Bobbi Starr's ability to call her shots is widely esteemed in the adult community, illustrating that strength of mind and will is an acknowledged and powerful trait among the most admired of industry women. "[Bobbi's] all about it," Dylan says in her staccato style. "She's making that choice. She loves what she does. She's good at it. She knows she's good at it." Dylan Ryan and Bobbi Starr reflect each other attitudinally and philosophically. They do not consider themselves to be negatively objectified and express a confidence devoid of arrogance and clearly rooted in personal responsibility.

"Third wave, sex-positive, porn-friendly, sex-friendly, and non-man hating" is how Dana DeArmond describes her blend of feminisms, though she admits that some people tell her, "'you're not my kind of feminist.'" No matter, Dana knows her way through a complex business that can rip the soul from the weak. We're sitting in the *Girlfriends Films* booth at the 2013 *Adult Entertainment Expo* in Las Vegas.[4]

A self-described "army brat," Dana was raised by liberal parents, unusual for the military. "I don't have the traditional football watching dad and the housewife mom," she laughs. Her mother entered the service to pay for college. Dana's father is gay, HIV positive and noted for his cooking skills. He's a "pastry chef" who can turn out "crepes and glaze," Dana interjects with noticeable affection.

Her parents' child rearing wisdom stands out in their oft-repeated aphorism, "If you act like an adult, we'll treat you like an adult." Good advice for a budding teenager who found little purpose in high school. After securing her GED (General Educational Development) certification, Dana tried community college, but "structured education" once again bored her. Relying on her determination to "think outside the box," Dana marketed herself in the entertainment world, forging a career path built on responsibility and caring about others.

Dana defines her image as "a humanized porn star," a persona that encourages her fans to do "what they are interested in sexually," she says, and not be shamed by it. Studios like

Girlfriends Films and *Kink.com* give Dana particular satisfaction in communicating her message. She comments that shooting for Dan O'Connell is especially exciting because she can incorporate her wit and her "acting chops." Dana likes improvising on the set. "It's a fun exercise and good for your brain," she says.

Though Dana may lack the credentials of formal learning, she is intelligent in ways that enhance credibility and survival in a demanding industry. I suggest she is a skilled businesswoman. Dana smiles and offers her philosophy, "Stand out, be unique, market yourself and be nice to everyone."

Raised in Orlando, Florida, Dana DeArmond discovered early on entertaining was her forte. She began as a dancer for *Universal Studios* and worked parades for the Disney resort complex before another kind of dancing seduced her. After turning eighteen Dana appeared in gentleman's clubs while keeping her day job at *Universal*. Both gigs offered zestful pleasure. Nightly twenty-dollar lap dances wedged between minimum wage choreography became her employment reality.

A porn career eventually knocked but not until Dana was into her twenties. In February 2004 she peeked through a door ajar. "I didn't think I was going to be a porn star when I walked into *Kink.com*," she says. Years later, the respected industry personality shoots in both the Los Angeles and San Francisco markets. A self-described artist taking a "sexual journey," Dana relies on feminist empowerment to guide her professional decisions and her private life. In particular Dana cherishes her relationship with her "porn wives," as she calls them, for whom she feels a special affinity: Joanna Angel, Princess Donna and Aiden Starr.

Now in her early thirties, Dana DeArmond listens to her maturity, a radar that picks up scenes no longer a fit for her. "I am not a new girl," she says, "I've been around the block. I know what I'm doing." Commenting on gangbangs for instance, Dana insists that she doesn't want "a bunch of idiots who don't know what they're doing" all over her. "It's miserable." Chemistry on the set is important because some performers don't "mesh personality-wise or sex-wise." Over time a girl selects her scenes judiciously because the pleasure of being on camera is a reward in itself. Making adult film has its dicey moments and for Dana to be uncomfortable isn't her style or how she approaches her art.

Carrying a feminist-like dignity, the ex-Floridian stands her ground in the face of criticism. Pornography is a stigmatized business and icy disapproval is of no consequence to Dana. "My parents don't judge me and I don't let people make me feel weird," she declares. Her determination to do what she wants under circumstances she selects has honed her longevity skills. Behind her veteran exterior is an intuitive understanding of the people in adult film and a desire to protect them. Dana mentors other girls. In her mind it is part of being a feminist. "I don't know if there is a word for my kind of feminism," she adds, it's all about how "people should treat each other."

Dana DeArmond understands being there for friends, "to stick up for other girls," as she phrases it. The downside for new models, naiveté and inexperience, can be crushing. "There are girls who lock themselves in the bathroom crying," Dana explains of breakdowns on the set, "they're so young and clueless." Jumping into porn too early can become a nightmare. "You're eighteen. You're still a baby." She is emphatic, "Try something, anything, other than porn."

Tara Lynn Foxx entered adult film in 2009, putting her body in front of the camera at the earliest acceptable age. She started with web cam work, posing for thrills and some money before heading to Southern California.[5]

A touch of regret creeps into Tara's voice when she recounts her past. The Bay Area native grew up on the self-confessed wild side and admits she deviated from her family's expectations. Realizing an adult film career would always be there if that's what interested her, Tara could have furthered her education and "experienced normal stuff" while those opportunities were unblemished by porn. "I'm not going to lie to you," Tara says, in describing her first year in the business as "a rough patch." She was unprepared to negotiate industry pitfalls, specifically agents and directors who can ensnare a new girl into an off camera world of free sex. Remorse haunted her. "I felt like I degraded myself," she confesses, and "let my family down." Facing periods of introspection and self-imposed isolation, "time alone," she calls it, Tara eventually conquered her malaise with a renewed sense of purpose. The brown-eyed blonde rationalized she had an opportunity to cultivate her own self-permission and enablement. Within time, "I realized how powerful my job is," Tara says.[6]

Tara Lynn Foxx learned about feminism through family while her contemporaries were exposed to its ideas in the college classroom. Feminism arrived via her sister, Tara says, who is "a huge feminist" and decidedly not anti-porn. Tara remembers her sister and mother pooled their resources to purchase books as holiday gifts, including one on feminism. Though her feminism is self-taught, Tara garnered a working knowledge of the "new wave," as she identifies it, and how it is more empowering than the "old style." In clarifying her views, Tara knows that many feminists are disdainful of her because some of her scenes can be interpreted as demeaning and objectifying to women. The Northern California native believes her film work demonstrates personal empowerment, illustrating choice in a way that portrays her as contradictorily submissive, "I like to be vulnerable on screen. That's more powerful to me." Tara does not see her work as objectification and like Bobbi, Dylan and Dana, markets herself as a bondage model among her other professional offerings.

When asked how feminism grants her a sense of command over her professional life, Tara is unhesitating. I'm "pro-active," she declares, "in choosing what I do on camera." Tara believes adult film is constructive and instructive, especially as a form of sex education, something she has learned from her fans. Is she rationalizing decisions that cannot be reversed? Is she buffering a young woman who, by her own admission, has grown up too fast? Perhaps, but it is feminist in its intention, nonetheless.

Tara Lynn Foxx is representative of attitudes emanating from sex-positive feminism and third wave individualism. Despite jumping into the porn cauldron too soon, she perseveres. Like Dana and Bobbi, her success is built on an understanding of how to market herself. During our talk in San Francisco Tara emphasizes she is her own corporation. "I am an adult film actress on camera doing something that is for pleasure and for entertainment," she says, with all the gusto of a twenty-year-old going on thirty.

"I'm a kinky girl who sacrifices her fetishes to make vanilla porn."[7]

Casey Calvert is a stunning twenty-four-year-old relatively new to porn, having entered in 2011 after completing her telecommunications degree at the University of Florida. An East Coast native, Casey pursued adult film as the consummation of a career experiment that began with nude modeling. Prompted to describe herself, the former national champion rock climber says, "I'm nerdy, intelligent, athletic, creative, shy, and extremely sexual."

Though she cannot remember why or when the feminist light switched on, Casey says, "I have always been a feminist before I ever knew the word. To me, it means the woman's right to choice." Though she lacks specifics about her personal feminist history, Casey is adamant about her fetishes. Her innate exhibitionism slowly evolved over years of sexual self-exploration while her intuitive submissiveness became its bedfellow. "I knew from a very early age that my fantasies were different," the dark-haired beauty says, emphasizing that visions of domination and spanking were most arousing. "I never once fantasized about just sex," she comments. Now in young adulthood Casey charms the phantom that shines a light on her sexual happiness: masochism. She embraces adult film because it provides a safe and sane environment for the extreme BDSM scenes she loves; likewise, her feminism's right to choice licenses her desire to act upon them.

As a vulnerable twelve-year old, Casey miscalculated a risk with her sexual feelings. She revealed her carnal thoughts to a school friend and the admission quickly turned on her. The girl "told all our friends and I was mortified," Casey amusingly remembers. Like any adolescent exposed and embarrassed, Casey withdrew her sexuality from her social persona, wrapping it in a blanket of secrecy. Not an unexpected reaction from a girl who was, by her own admission, "always the shy kid." "I had friends," Casey says, "but I was never popular."

At twenty-one her sexual breakout occurred. Casey met famed rigger and bondage enthusiast Lew Ruben who revealed the BDSM world to her, helping her unveil her excitement about physical pain. The epiphanic play session she experienced that memorable night in Orlando brought Casey unexpected joy. She was consensually whipped and experienced an explosive orgasm. Impressed with the perky brunette, Rubens, who once mentored a youthful Bobbi Starr, suggested Casey give modeling a try. Shooting topless led to bottomless and the early pavement in the road to porn stardom was mixed and set.

"When I met [Lew] I just wanted to get tied up," Casey recalls. When the bondage master promoted modeling, she was befuddled. "I didn't feel like I was cute, let alone model material."

That same year, Casey lost her virginity in a planned tryst with her much older boyfriend. "It was just some rope, a hotel room, and us." Her world was soaring at light speed. Moving to the West Coast, the sultry newcomer called on her feminist determination and made a seamless transition into adult film. Truth be known, it was hardly haphazard. "In my personal life progression, doing porn felt like the natural next step. I had been thinking about it for a very long time," she declares.

Casey's advantage in porn is a ready-made audience. She's not just another adult actress. "I love getting tied up, that will always be pleasurable to me. I also love pain, I can cum from pain," Casey says, using her submissive brown eyes to enhance her point. "The fetish arouses more than the actual sex," she claims, because "my orgasms are in my head." Those in the BDSM community would nod their affirmation. Casey Calvert makes a living with vanilla shoots, working the Porn Valley scene. She does the standard formulas, interracial, DPs, anal, girl/girl and the like, to go along with her bondage preferences. When she can get a booking, Casey flies to San Francisco's BDSM paradise to film in its secure and well-monitored environment. She considers herself lucky. "I am very concerned with my safety and well-being, and honestly, if I didn't do porn, I would have a lot of unfulfilled fantasies."

A well-respected and sought out professional, Casey Calvert knows what drives her to improve her craft, a good performance is in her "perfectionist nature." "I want every scene I do to be perfect, to be better than the last. I want to give the best product I can give."

Oh yes, Casey Calvert's family supports her career. She has a solid relationship with her parents and her little brother even touched up one of her earliest model photos.

Queer

Feminist porn performers such as Bobbi, Dana, Tara and Casey, and feminist directors like Nica Noelle and Jacky St. James are based in the Los Angeles area where the bulk of the adult industry resides. In Northern California, San Francisco has its own porn business that is smaller in scope and includes a greater emphasis on diversity. For the record, performers from both cities make film in each environment.

The roundtable participants are representative of San Francisco's queer porn community and its adult film product. Queer porn offers sexual expression for those whose sexuality is fluid, a feminist creation "true" to the performers and their values. There is a "major shift happening in the mainstream adult industry," Jiz Lee declares, and "increased queer visibility" is a part of that change. An intellectual voice for a minority community, Jiz defines what it means to be queer and a respected porn star.[8]

A native of Hawaii, Jiz tried a variety of professional endeavors that included athletic coaching and working for nonprofits before meeting queer porn director Shine Louise Houston. Jiz's natural "sexual exhibitionism" seduced the camera, creating an erotic composition that commingled Jiz's physical talents with a flair for theatrical performance. Jiz hints at what it means to be in queer porn. "[We] have our own choice of what acts we want to do and how we want to do them," and Houston's company, *Pink & White Productions* with its famed *Crash Pad Series,* endorses that opportunity. At the 2010 *Feminist Porn Awards,* Jiz's talent received the coveted "Boundary Breaker" of the year award. In winning the honor, Jiz cites its purpose, "to welcome new, honest, desired, or curious exhibitions of sexuality."[9]

Queer porn is about validating a performer's natural eroticism coupled with sexual and gender choices. Jiz envisions queer porn as a critical teaching tool to broaden the horizons of a heteronormative culture. Growing up in a sexually restrictive atmosphere, Jiz was not educated about physical and emotional attraction and how sexual identities can shift and be reshaped. Ultimately, Jiz learned queer porn introduces different avenues that give performers "authentic" sexual agency no matter their gender, sexual preferences or orientations.[10]

Jiz Lee believes the political is fundamental to adult film. Asked which came first, porn or politics, Jiz has no doubt. "Porn" because porn is personal and the "personal is political." A 2003 Mills College graduate, Jiz discovered a brand of feminism on the all-female Oakland, California campus where second wave sex-negativism was not the predominant thought. Workshops and discussions on safer sex and queer sex and the annual "Fetish Ball" enriched Jiz's student life. Today, Jiz's feminist political voice permeates a Jiz Lee shoot. It's a pro-sex statement built on Jiz's activism in San Francisco's genderqueer population.[11]

Refusing recognition as either male or female, Jiz Lee remains true to an identity that is "genderqueer," a personal definition that embodies gender bending and blending. Jiz self-interprets Jiz as a compilation of "marginalized identities" who are able to engage the world from a unique synthesis of minority and majority views. In the past, Jiz self-identified "as a bisexual dyke and as transgender male" but was not satisfied with either because of their implications in the male/female binary. Jiz mentions Jiz has never identified as a lesbian because queer, which indicates "sexual orientation," includes a broad spectrum of lovers and gender possibilities. Jiz settled on "'queer,'" Jiz says, because in present day society "sexualities are presumably determined through the gender of oneself and lovers" which for Jiz is too confining. In other words, Jiz's partners are dissimilar in their sexual orientation and this inhibits Jiz from selecting a definitive label for Jiz's sexuality, so "'queer'" seems most appropriate. In this respect Jiz is *not* a "her" or a "him" but a "they" because Jiz is comfortable with an identity that can be reframed when Jiz feels the necessity.[12]

Though Jiz describes Jiz as female bodied, Jiz requests the use of "gender-neutral pronouns" (such as they and them) be used when referencing Jiz, or if this is a grammatical problem with editors or writers, that pronouns be abandoned entirely. My preference here is to avoid pronouns when referencing Jiz's queer identification.[13]

Jiz Lee's personhood transcends the use of a single pronoun to linguistically reference individual attributions continually redefined by emotion, experimentation and personal growth and reminds everyone that "We can't tell how someone identifies by just looking at them." This is the heart of queer porn's visual representations. Jiz Lee is at once male, female, androgynous and maybe something not yet defined. Options are open. Jiz can be trussed up in a fetish scene with lipstick, unshaven legs, heels and a boy's cap rakishly tilted to one side, a kaleidoscope of images. Or Jiz can appear in a still photo clean shaven, pierced nipple exposed, ejaculating for the camera.

Annie and the Queer Porn Mafia

Annie Sprinkle always believed that sex is about diversity. Possessing an open and loving attitude for all people regardless of their sexuality or sexual proclivities, Annie enjoyed relationships with men, women and transgendered persons. Dylan Ryan's self-description, "[M]y queer identity is pansexual ... I have sex with people of all genders and sexualities," could have been Annie's words a generation ago.[14]

Annie Sprinkle is a pioneering activist in supporting the transgendered community. Male-to-female transpersons were cautiously wading into the adult entertainment waters years ago with Jill Monroe being the first TS (transsexual) magazine centerfold. In 1988 Annie attended her first female-to-male (FTM) support group meeting. Her heart went out to "these women who were becoming men," she says. They faced a myriad of difficulties and Annie, in her characteristic style, decided to "love them up just the way they were." In those early days transpersons were "hard on themselves," she explains, sometimes enduring poorly done surgeries to free the identity they felt inside. Their most stressful issue, "wanting to pass and not passing," spurred Annie's desire to eroticize the FTM experience. According to Annie, there is no evidence that porn for this community existed before her film, *Linda/Les and Annie: A Female-to-Male Transsexual Love Story.* The narrative reveals Les Nichols' personal history and the anatomical changes Les bravely endures. Included is an explanation of his genital reconstruction using photos and drawings similar to medical journal fare. Annie addresses Les's "androgyny," the excitement, as she puts it, about his being both male and female. She describes performing oral sex on Les as "wild and strange" because of his penis and vagina. There is true affection in the film, especially when Annie is overcome by Les's "optimism and good humor" that mutes his "emotional pain."[15]

Unfortunately the production did not play well with San Francisco's FTM community. Because of uncertain public reaction, the community was cautiously restrained. "They didn't want F2M porn." she says. "Some of the San Francisco F2Ms thought it was too out there, because Les was pretty eccentric." Annie remembers Les as sexy and romantic, but also an "extreme masochist," which she plays down in the film.

Annie Sprinkle is accustomed to being censured for her work. Because she "interacted" with Les's vagina on camera, Annie received a harsh letter of criticism from the FTM community for creating the impression the trans population was "weird." They did not appreciate a pornographic narrative with an FTM transperson though Annie is adamant that Les was "totally into" making the movie. Today's queer porn owes a debt to Annie Sprinkle. "We were ahead of our time," she proclaims, "it was controversial."[16]

Linda/Les and Annie was released on videotape in 1989, playing many LGBT film festivals. Another Annie Sprinkle film, *Sluts and Goddesses* (1992), featured both drag queens and kings. Annie mentions that the first drag king workshops were in her

New York apartment, the Sprinkle Salon, where piercing parties and Tantra classes flourished. This part of her sexual history was the "punky, edgy, sort of dark and grungy" New York scene, very different from San Francisco where she eventually relocated, an area she describes as "more pagan-ish, holistic and spiritual."

A bridge between second wave sex-positivism and third wave sexual diversity, Annie Sprinkle has philosophical residence in both. She transitions biological sex and gender definitions, validating new interpretations of feminism. Feminist writer Chris Straayer proclaims Annie's talents lie in conflating sexuality, politics and queer into an all-inclusive home for an array of differences that welcomes gays, trans people, BDSMers and other marginalized sexualities. Annie's enlightenment reflects third wave inclusion and egalitarianism, ushering in those who went unnoticed in the old days of feminism's sex wars. As Straayer puts it, "Annie Sprinkle puts queer theory into practice."[17]

Pornography feminism, San Francisco style, is a blend of art, politics and the queer porn community. Jiz Lee suggests that queer productions are panoplies of sexuality reinforced by "emotional connection[s]" among performers and directors. Each shoot is valued and each experience honored. Out of this environment emerges a camaraderie seldom found in the Southern California porn scene where paychecks, agents, and bookings drive the business.[18]

Inevitably artistic commonality nurtures friendships. The Queer Porn Mafia (QPM), an informal support group loosely akin to Club 90 and Pink Ladies, is something borrowed and something new. It is creating a new century of pornography whose genesis is Candida Royalle's feminist vision, Annie Sprinkle's celebration of diversity and Gloria Leonard's and Nina Hartley's political feminism.

The origins of the QPM came out of a self-identified group at the 2009 *Feminist Porn Awards* that included Jiz Lee, Dylan Ryan,

Syd Blakovich, Shine Louise Houston, Courtney Trouble, Madison Young and Ken Rowe of *Trannywood Pictures*, a gay male porn company. Known early on as the "San Francisco Porn Posse," this cadre took on a new name, the Queer Porn Mafia, at the *AVN* awards in 2010. What began as a "joke," according to Jiz Lee, "ran on." Shine Louise Houston became the group's "'Don,'" Jiz says, with veterans Tina Horn and April Flores and trans newcomer Drew Deveaux joining later as a result of doing scenes with each other. The performer exception was director Carlos Batts who entered the group via his own "special ritual."[19]

In our 2012 interview in Los Angeles, April Flores acknowledges that husband Carlos and she were indeed late arrivals to the QPM. They did not become involved in the San Francisco scene until 2009-2010 when they filmed for *Good Vibrations*. From there "we became friends with them [the queer porn community] and started shooting with them," April explains, noting that San Francisco was a new experience for Carlos and her. The City by the Bay is a different environment, April observes, comparatively small when stacked against Los Angeles's population and sprawl, yet its "sexual presence" far surpasses Southern California.[20]

The QPM has a communal perspective about casting and filming that is "very different" from Porn Valley. We're artists with "like-minded ideas" about how to present our personal expressions, April explains. Confirming the QPM sees itself apart from the Southern California scene, she insists the gang is "sticking together, we are going to continue moving forward."

Carlos is impressed with the QPM's uniqueness. It's "a select group," he says, which makes developing and sharing an artistic vision exciting. "I respect them and their work ethic," he says, they're independent women with a collective "spirit and energy" far exceeding the norm in pornography.

The QPM is part of a broader movement rooted in the

"creative erotica" of Annie Sprinkle, Carlos believes, and uses a political interpretation of queer to illustrate his point. "Queer to me seems more like an ideology, where fetishism is more of an aesthetic." Queer is about "individual taste," he says, which means there can be "many different kinds of queer." Carlos offers an insightful comparison. "Fifty percent of the sexual population is vanilla and the other fifty percent is filled with thirty-one flavors." Most everyone thinks sexual desire must reflect that of one's parents, he says, but this century is culturally and politically debunking that assumption with new ways of interpreting the erotic. Vanilla sexuality is becoming less important, Carlos states, and cites the Washington DC environment as an example of "a champion for transgender behavior."

"Our movement," as Carlos identifies the queer phenomenon, "has been cooking since the nineties." It's a product of Generation X which spawned "a broader understanding [of society] whether it be sexuality or color or culture." This is modern feminism's "biggest secret" and what is little understood about it: the creativity, the "consciousness of freedom" and the self-expression that naturally follows. Carlos is not suggesting there is an underlying organization at work here. The movement has evolved spontaneously. The African American director sees today's queer generation inspiring others in the future, whether they be women, people of color or individuals in search of their political and creative voice. For him, it is "consciousness" and "being different" expressed in all ways that are good.

Carlos accedes to my desire to categorize and catalogue and my notion of time as a factor in establishing a movement. "You are a historian," he acknowledges, "You know that in time things do fall into compartments." But he insists, "I do think movements start with attitudes." Carlos demonstrates a social scientist's perspective pointing out change is happening now but recognizes his generation is too "close to it." "Maybe in twenty years we can see it as a movement," he says. Carlos insists that no one is "purposely or consciously trying to be different" in shaping this current tide. "People are just expressing themselves in a very bold way and not everyone is on the same page," suggesting a little chaos is part of every political and artistic endeavor. Nevertheless, Carlos, like his wife, knows "the like-minded crew will stick together." A new movement may be in progress that will solidify with the next generation of feminist pornographers and queers. Time and history will be the benchmark.

Though they seem most comfortable in their own self-interpreted world, pornography feminists have a universality that constructs a loose sisterhood apart from the broader social movements of the past. They are very much post-feminist in that respect. However, they retain the ever-elusive institutional memory that Nina Hartley longs to see. Pornography feminists remain allied to second wave sex-positivism in spirit and the aggressive individual attitude of the third. To suggest they are part of a new movement, as Carlos Batts predicts, is not yet evident; to recognize they possess a collective vision is appropriate. Is modern adult film feminism still "about me and my choices" as we have seen in the remarks of the performers presented here? No doubt. But these introspective persons cannot shake their commonality. They are at once conforming and diverse, expanding boundaries by smashing boundaries while occupying an individual inner space called feminism.

Chapter 7

Real People *are* the Medium

"I wanted a place for women who would not feel comfortable going anywhere else [to] feel comfortable here."
Carlyle Jansen, interview with the author, Toronto, April 15, 2011

"We'd Had Drinks Together"

Though an informal sex toy presentation at a bridal shower may be out of the ordinary, Toronto's Carlyle Jansen took advantage of such an opportunity. Her personal enthusiasm and engaging affability impressed the gathering and soon Canadian women were showing up at Carlyle's workshops to learn more. Ultimately, Carlyle realized that something more intimate was needed: an accepting space for women to examine products designed especially for them. Using her business acumen, Carlyle opened *Good For Her*, a retail shop located a short distance west of the University of Toronto campus. The store became *the* destination for women, where seminars and conversation cooked up a heady brew of sexual recipes with the personal touch.[1]

* * *

Braving a chilly mid-April day, I've finally arrived at *Good For Her*, a quaint narrow building that could step into a Dickens novel disguised as a London merchant shop. The small establishment is tucked away among other storefronts aligned like a bed full of Victorian children all dressed alike and awaiting good night kisses. In fact *Good For Her* is hardly noticed, even by locals. My frustrated cab driver drops me off to walk Harbord Street and inquire where the business might be. After a little nudging here and there, I finally spot the *Good For Her* sign hanging over the sidewalk. Intrigued by the shop's inconspicuous exterior, I'm ready to investigate this enticing charmer.

The interior is compact; well-stocked shelves display a collection of videos, toys, books and the like. A smiling Carlyle Jansen offers a quick tour and explains that getting past the door is not easy for some newcomers. Facilitating this transition means putting visitors immediately at ease. A single salesperson, on this day a dark-haired young woman, politely greets everyone then quietly slips behind the counter, giving shoppers access to the merchandise sans the slightest sales pressure.

The atmosphere is hushed; conversation whispered. Products are gently examined like antique books quietly removed from the shelves of a venerated library. A college-age woman browses the merchandise, her interest focused on a double penetration toy. In deference to the customer's privacy, Carlyle suggests we move upstairs to the offices. Negotiating creaky steps to an equally small second level whose wooden floors carry an old world ambiance, I renew acquaintances with store manager Alison Lee. Carlyle settles in and gives me an overview of the business. *Good for Her* is the essence of the personal, she explains, a discreet setting where individual choices are respected. The store's philosophy is to ease a woman's reticence in shopping for sexually based products and assisting anyone who feels awkward. Carlyle's goal is "a place where people who want to see tons of edgy sex and the biggest dildo they can have is celebrated and supported."

Good For Her's mission statement takes a revolutionary step toward unfettering a female sexuality that has been circumscribed and conforming far too long. "Women and marginalized communities need access to information and products that are not always easy to find or easy to talk about," the statement begins. "[There is] nothing shameful about an open, honest dialogue about sex and sexuality." The business's emphasis is on an atmosphere that is deferential to everyone's right to investigate sexuality in ways agreeable to them. Accept the term *everyone* literally because awareness of gender fluidity and sexual self-identity highlights *Good For Her*. To accommodate diverse sexualities, the shop maintains some scheduling limitations; hours are arranged to give everyone discreet opportunities to visit uninhibited. The heart of the matter is "courage" because Carlyle Jansen knows that "to simply walk into our store" is no small task and *Good For Her* wants everyone to feel welcomed.[2]

The commercialization of women's sexual enjoyment has its prototype: San Francisco's *Good Vibrations*. Opening its doors in 1977, a time when feminism's anti-porn/anti-sex message was gaining momentum, *Good Vibrations* nurtured an idea: all women can entertain their personal desires. Sex educator and therapist Joani Blank realized her clients and the public in general lacked information about a woman's intimate pleasures. Material from mainstream bookstores was inadequate; the information gap that forever hamstrung women's knowledge of their bodies and desires remained. Blank's solution was *Down There Press* launched in 1975 to publish books for women. Within two years, she opened the original *Good Vibrations*, "a friendly, 'clean, well-lighted' alternative to conventional 'adult' bookstores," in San Francisco's Mission District. Met with "enthusiasm and appreciation" from both sexes, *Good Vibrations* grew, adding a mail order business into its storefront. Over the years *Good Vibrations* opened a shop in Berkeley and expanded to the East Coast with one in Brookline, Massachusetts.[3]

The *Good Vibrations* business ethic reflects its mission to provide and promote attitudes that reinforce "sexual health and pleasure," among them safer sex. The store takes care to support programs benefiting sex educators. *Good Vibrations* also sets the standard for gender policy, stating that "gender and sex are subjective notions" involving "diversity and difference."

Understanding sexual fluidity and discarding outdated Victorian ideas are the philosophical commonalities of *Good Vibrations* and *Good For Her*. All sexual communities have an accepting space to deconstruct and redefine sexuality however they please. Both stores offer a marketplace of ideas and become, as feminist professor Lynn Comella states, "a platform for sex activism and education."[4]

In time women-oriented businesses moved forward with the next leap in female sexual expression, recognition of pornography as a film genre women can claim as their own, thus creating a subjective interpretation of explicit sex and celebrating it if they choose to do so. By offering critical ingredients in the modern potpourri of human sexuality, Toronto's *Feminist Porn Awards* is part of that platform.

* * *

Carlyle Jansen originated the *Feminist Porn Awards* in 2005 and two years later welcomed Alison Lee to the event team. Hired to fill the position of *Good For Her* store manager, Alison channeled her feminist efforts into the annual celebration with unbounded zeal.

Alison Lee came to feminism as a teenager but with contradictions that were more than typical teenage angst. A *Riot Grrrl* follower, she took an interest in the women's movement, wanting to understand its history and attitudes, particularly those about pornography. Unfortunately Alison's local library was limited in its feminist literature; reading choices were mired in the bygone days of porn as violence against women. Alison realized her generation was awkwardly positioned between feminism's second and third waves without a foothold in either. Dissatisfied, Alison shaped her own feminist views, accepting pornography and beginning a cultural journey to understand its impact.[5]

In the early stages of her odyssey Alison discovered what

many connected to the industry quickly learn: porn is quite fascinating though at times dull and disinteresting. Performers have a typecast look; their names are hackneyed with sameness glaringly repeatable from girl to girl. Content is likewise overly predictable. Shoots stick to formulaic sex scenes sold in different box covers. Simply put, there is good and bad porn. Epiphanies do occur and Alison's attitudes, fostered by culture, research and intellectual thought, were shockingly personalized when she came across some photos displaying the face and nude body of a woman she knew. "We'd had drinks together," Alison exclaimed, over discussions on feminism and politics. An "aha" moment, a sudden insight illuminating what seems obvious but remains elusive, hit home. *Real* people *are* the medium and they *are* more than pictures and fantasy. Porn *is* culturally significant; those who make it literally expose their most private realms, giving pornography the power to fascinate, anger, disgust, amaze, arouse and even bore.[6]

Alison Lee now wanted to know how porn could be more authentic and attractively packaged with a woman's fantasy in mind. The question became her compass with the *Feminist Porn Awards* the final destination. Results are impressive. New age filmmakers are quieting the anti-woman indictment traditionally leveled at the industry while celebrating an artistic quality that is the foundation of feminist porn.[7]

As *Good for Her* is not original to women's shopping choices, the *Feminist Porn Awards* has predecessors, among them the Oscars of Porn bestowed annually in Las Vegas.

A Cacophony of Hipness

Sponsored by the Los Angeles based trade magazine *Adult Video News (AVN)*, the porn Oscars began their run in 1984. Adult stars emulate Hollywood's panache and swagger for a treasured moment in the limelight. Gallery tickets for the Saturday night event are pricey and floor tables reserved for industry moguls go for thousands. The marketing of porn glitz drives this annual Las Vegas celebration, a flashy display that defines its undeniable "cool."[8]

The days that precede the show are filled with an all-industry convention which I first attended when the gala was in its swan song at the Sands Convention Center. By 2012 the January week relocated to The Hard Rock Hotel, a smaller venue off the Vegas Strip. The story, as told here, begins with my initial visit to the Sands in 2010.

The *Adult Entertainment Expo* (*AEE*) as it is officially known, is a carnival of provocatively clad women available for fan photos and small talk, knowing a brief pose will convert their image into a screensaver back home and office conversation on Monday morning. The mammoth convention floor greets the visitor with a phalanx of studios, *Wicked Pictures*, *Adam and Eve*, *Evil Angel*, *Digital Playground*, *Hustler* and *Vivid* among the most prominent. Their flamboyancy echoes the upscale Moulin Rouges of urban exotica that have come to dominate the sex industry. Big screens and booming club music compliment the stars available under the company banners if one has the patience to queue up properly.

Some models cultivate a bit of tawdriness that contrasts remarkably with their softer, air brushed seductiveness displayed on gigantic posters scattered about the arena. Resembling coveted box covers, the billboard-like advertisements dwarf the real woman putting in her time signing one sheets (mini posters) a few feet away, a reminder her persona as much as the flesh beckons the faithful and the curious. The mystery of her body evaporates once she is put on film, leaving only her skills, cloned from shoot to shoot, to distinguish her from a hundred others. An inkling of the woman behind the poster is the best that can be expected. Offering a smile and an autograph finessed to blend fantasy and reality, the "porn star" remains alluring and elusive. Every girl under this big top is an entertainer, a smidgen of salesmanship and an occasional dose of down home neighborliness. For performers who develop a flair for this demanding task, profit and fame are enhanced.

The floor's circus-like atmosphere is a snapshot of the hustle and hucksterism of the desert community that is its host. The three ring wonderland of activity competes for the attention of wandering onlookers, just as tourists on the Vegas Strip are wowed by its faux opulence. Though reminiscent of the traveling carnivals generations ago, the porn convention cannot escape its modernity. Kiosks, booths and exhibition stages are eclipsed by the massive sterility of concrete and steel, while technology, porn's lifeline, promises faster images in sharper pixels.

Narrow aisles snake around the floor, verifying what I was told to expect by an industry insider. Product displays, pole dancers and mini stage shows are ever present, reinforcing the loud brassy atmosphere that is the fan's elbow-to-elbow experience. Girls mill about at every turn, striking well rehearsed and provocative poses whenever cameras pass. Indeed the convention is rooted in the old carnival midway that lured the small town curiosity of my youth. This updated version, populated with mythical barkers hawking sex in the imagination of every attendee, resurrects images of country rubes and the old "see it all now" promise.

A repetitive look prevails even among nonperformers. Attractive young women seductively packaged greet passersby and promote the studio or the company product. Men with earrings, buzz cuts and t-shirts a shade too small hang around to deflect any customer interest beyond the commercial. Both sexes are complimented with the ubiquitous tattoos. The culturally sexy is socially constructed. The sideshow, the house of mirrors and the cacophony of hipness are hyped with a contemporary flare that might blunt the senses of David Friedman, Kroger Babb and Russ Meyer but the old road show deans surely would admire its flash and flesh.

Behind the Sands' frontline of branded names are the lesser ranks of the pecking order. Smaller kiosks buried within the bowels of the convention center are like rows of adult storefronts relegated to an urban district zoned for the sex trade. In this arena backwater pole dancers clad in the legal minimum entice fans while vendors promote their video wares and sex toys. Adult performers also represent other businesses such as *The Mustang Ranch*, a high-end Nevada brothel that employs some industry women. An arm around the waist, the automatic "flashbulb smile" and a seductive pose are instantly offered. Weariness sometimes looms here but geniality is rarely at a premium.

The presence of Christian groups softens their floor space though the hustle is still prevalent, "when in Rome" as the old saying goes. Clean-cut young people looking very much like the kids next door quietly offer their literature with a smile and the gentle firmness expected of the devout. Their most popular booklet is aimed at that nagging sense of guilt that trails some fans. The glossy little paperback insists adult film is addictive and offers the age-old promise of something better to conquer sin. It carries the amusingly deceptive title, *Jesus Loves Porn Stars*.

To be honest, the convention is hard work. Fatigue appears as the event lengthens and performers are bound to tight schedules. Over a period that includes the initial day for industry affiliates, performers obligingly dedicate floor hours to cultivate their fan base. It *is* draining but consumer dollars grease the porn machine. Bobbi Starr appreciates her fans, taking care she responds positively to them. Always smiling, Tara Lynn Foxx's amiability brands her name with each autograph. The lines to see Dana DeArmond are lengthy and she maintains her mantra to be nice to everyone. These women represent the best of the Vegas show, as does Nina Hartley whose floor time is swamped with admirers eager for a moment of her attention.

There is a sense of hurry in Vegas because the porn machine never stops. Interviews, photo ops, appearances with the clubbing crowd and late night parties to entertain industry folk occupy a performer's schedule. The girls are always selling: videos, personalized trading cards, website memberships, personally endorsed sex toys among the list. Other financial opportunities are also available. Film shoots can be booked around floor time.

Everyone comes and goes cognizant of time ticking away to the Saturday night awards show. It's a countdown that this "Alternative Hollywood," where futures are limited to the next booking and paydays are by the shoot, regards as its own. No million dollar contracts and no dedicated fans lining up overnight for a seat at a theater premier; but there is still the dream. The "stars" arrive in limos, walk a red carpet and pose for industry paparazzi. If nominated for honors such as best actor, best sex scene (a huge variety), best production and a sundry of technical awards, pride is everywhere and is no less than that of mainstream Tinseltown.

The 2011 show is more upbeat due to the reconfiguration of the hall and everyone's awareness of the state of the industry. Internet regulations and product piracy are hot topics once again and the continuing battle over mandatory condoms is pressing frayed nerves in every corner. Attendance is down though the space reduction minimizes its impact. The *AEE* that includes the girls, videos companies large and small, and support groups such as Protecting Adult Welfare, is limited to one part of the hall. The other section of the floor is the home for the *AVN Novelty Expo*, the mecca of sex toys, clothes, lubes, condoms and the like. The concrete desert of the previous year is gone, minimizing the Sands' hollowness. Friendliness among performers is enthusiastic, though there are fewer models in attendance. Curiously, the presence of Christian groups is hardly noticed.

Over dinner an industry friend remarks next year's show is to be moved for reasons that are unclear. The recession is the best guess. One performer hints that her shoots have dropped to the lowest level in her career, a mere three per month compared with fifteen in 2008.

With 2012 the *AEE* settles into its new home. The Hard Rock maintains the spirit of the Sands though the carnival midway is replaced with chaotic intimacy. Kiosks are cramped; aisle traffic reaches an urban rush hour standstill. Performer receptiveness remains energetic, though some models come only for two days (Friday and Saturday) with the once Sunday hours now just a memory. A shorter week produces a less tired performer and an added benefit, reduced expenses because many attend on their own dime. Incidentally, for people connected with the industry, a girl asking to share hotel space wherever she can find it is not unusual.

By the way, when I passed out my business card and scouted for interviews in my first year, I sometimes got the notion I was being simultaneously entertained and politely dismissed. Not surprising, I was an unknown. As an industry writer, I now have an insider's perspective. Yet, my initial impressions remain. Las Vegas is a downloaded imitation of the Playboy Mansion bringing together all aspects of the business with the offer of a good time. It's the old hustle of the road showmen except the woman on the screen is in person and very real. The people of adult film are most congenial and I admire those who can survive the stress of the Vegas week. The music is still too loud and the crowds are off putting, but my appreciation for its place in our cultural heritage grows as my little boy fascination with the carnival midway fades.

A Complementary Tale of Two Cities

Pornography feminists move between two worlds. They glam it

up in Vegas and become sister-like in Toronto. The Hollywoodesque Porn Valley is far removed from the queer porn alt community rooted in San Francisco's diverse culture. Brash and ostentatious characterize Vegas while Toronto presents a different feel, smaller and raucous but also more political. Symbolic of this intermingling is Toronto as the "crossroads of two porn cultures." In 2011 Bobbi Starr and Jiz Lee attend the Canadian event together. According to Jiz, the *Feminist Porn Awards* is increasing its industry presence; Toronto and Las Vegas now "'go hand in hand.'" A celebration of ethical and sex-positive "'feminist-minded'" porn is Toronto's niche, the diminutive San Franciscan notes. Bobbi is grateful that her mainstream Porn Valley work is considered a part of the awards presentation. By the way, Bobbi and Jiz share a hotel room for the event, further underscoring a melding of the feminist adult film geography.[9]

Many Toronto honorees and fans are queer identified and fetish oriented with a style that maintains an international film flavor. Audiences are smaller and mostly female bodied; the Vegas show is heavily male, primarily hetero and vanilla driven. The two environs are evidence porn is anything but monolithic.

Though awards shows tend to be repetitive, Alison Lee stresses that Toronto fosters a "feel good" approach in which everyone supports all nominees with enthusiasm. Being there generates the magic, winning is secondary. The film screenings and awards program are open to anyone who wants to drop by and share the energy. The price of admission is reasonable with tickets sold at the door, unlike Vegas where admission is purchased prior to the ceremonies and can be cost prohibitive for many fans. Most important, Alison believes the *Feminist Porn Awards* represents a jubilation that the event happens at all![10]

Toronto carries the message of inclusion. By supporting the sexual art of marginalized communities, the *Feminist Porn Awards* is a vanguard of political change, serving notice to old anti-porn second wavers that diversity moves beyond their narrowly defined sexuality. Lauding a variety of sexual tastes, Toronto confirms that to see porn as degrading, humiliating and physically harmful has little merit. Directors take careful steps to ensure working conditions establish a credible standard and models choose their sexual preferences. The essence of the awards, Alison Lee asserts, is to celebrate a woman's empowerment no matter if her sexual predilections are "rough and raunchy" or "tender and sweet."[11]

Springtime in Toronto has no convention-like expanse where models and companies set up shop. The Vegas hustle is replaced with an intimacy that makes Toronto into a community. Quaint and close quartered, the Gladstone Hotel, the Victorian charmer located in the city's arts district, is the hotspot for directors and performers. Movie screenings are held at the nearby Bloor Cinema, a historic movie palace that is now an arts venue. Built in 1905 the Bloor is a vestige of yesteryear. Its vintage seats hug the moviegoer with a well-worn texture that retains the musty smell of Saturday afternoons spiced with black and white double features. Fans queue up around the block for seats in an electric atmosphere. After nominated films are sampled and the sex applauded for its rowdy authenticity, a brief seminar takes the stage. Feminist directors and performers discuss their artistic style before entertaining inquiries from a vocal audience.

The awards ceremony the following evening is held at Berkeley Church, a nineteenth-century landmark converted into an all-purpose space. A mixture of theater and ballroom, its double-tiered expanse is suitable for a variety of events including a festival showcasing a community rising above its marginality. A large wrap-around gallery enables fans to gaze down onto the stage. Church pews have long been removed; seating on both levels is portable. Informality reigns, including the unisex restroom.

Before the show a VIP gathering in the gallery entertains fans and industry people who chat like neighbors at a block party. There is no sense of rush and no separation between performer and fan because they are often one and the same in spirit and actuality. Industry merchants, moguls and agents are noticeably absent.

The *Feminist Porn Awards* is a double bill of its own, a mixture of feminism and queerness. Carlyle Jansen notes that the alternative community is increasing its visibility. Benefiting from the exposure of "queer themes" in music and the media, she believes "people aren't hiding" their preferences anymore. The community is getting accustomed to its "social power," authentically presenting its lifestyle and taking control of how its sexuality is portrayed. For people who "normally aren't represented" in the media and on film, Carlyle explains, it's "exciting" to see their sexual images played out on the big screen.

The evening is a boisterous party that toasts feminist pornographers responding to a public hunger for a different product, asserts writer Dusty Horn. Commonality runs through the program, an insistence that feminist sexual representations recognize a healthy diversity presented with artistic "pride." Horn's observation separates Toronto from Vegas. The *Feminist Porn Awards* will undoubtedly never approach the glamour of the *AVN* soiree and it should not, its inclusion message lies elsewhere. Berkeley Church brims over with a big tent feel that underscores the egalitarianism of feminist porn.[12]

The tale of Toronto is a Dionysian urban flair set in a historic city. It's cerebral with a slower feel. Performers and directors are willing to relax in a quiet spot and explore ideas in the manner of a university seminar. They take pride in an artistic expression produced by a handful of apostles in a huge pornography kingdom. Dylan Ryan is quite correct when she asserts that art and sex are intertwined in the expression of what it means to be human. Toronto is a celebration of "us," a collective community. When honors are handed out, everyone's sexuality is loudly applauded. Though the *Feminist Porn Awards* ceremony is steeped in a boisterous atmosphere, the event is an artist's palette: colors brilliantly interwoven into a mosaic of film, definitely not corporate, no big money in sight.

As adult entertainment expands, women now patronize their own retail shops and consume their own pornography however they wish. Toronto's message is direct and simple. Women and diverse sexualities are producing and celebrating pornography/erotica their way because, as Carlyle Jansen sums it up, "it's all about where you sit and what you feel is normal, healthy, sexual desire."

In the final analysis, Vegas and Toronto are as distinct as a big box store and the neighborhood merchant. Their milieus are a continent apart, a desert playground and a historic international city. There is a sense of separating the beautiful people of Southern California from the every "body" and any "body" of feminist porn San Francisco/Toronto style. Each city is complementary of the other and each is worthy of the other because neither can claim superiority.

Chapter 8

My Porn-Art Daughter

"The habit of explaining away sexual variation by putting it down needs to be broken."
Gayle Rubin, Cultural Anthropologist from "The Leather Menace: Comments on Politics and S/M," in *Coming to Power: Writings and Graphics on Lesbian S/M* (1987)

Wet Should be a Color

A winsome redhead with a petite body, Madison Young loves rope and a good flogging. Sexual masochist and feminist artist, Madison cherishes the BDSM play space where her fantasies come alive. On this day she is doing a scene for San Francisco's *Kink.com* that will flash through cyberspace for *Kink's* paying members. Director James Mogul, dressed in his Gestapo style boots and all black attire, walks onto a dungeon-like set, one among several within the illusory underground of *Kink's* medieval-like facility.

A naked Madison is curled up in a suspended cage. She smiles slightly at James in a way known to lovers who are about to play. Madison's eyes are muted vulnerability and her submissive demeanor follows James' lead without a hint of resistance.

Released from her confinement Madison kneels in front of James. He attaches a chain he identifies as a "training collar" around her neck and reviews a list of instructions she must complete. Her eyes are obedient and fawning. James' voice cracks almost imperceptibly. He is "training" his partner for all to see; it's the realism of their sexual interplay that sells the shoot. It cannot be any more personal.

James orders Madison to stand and spread her legs. He works quickly sorting through an array of bondage gear as if a handyman looking for just the right gadget. Madison is shackled spread-eagled. Passive and quiet, she lifts her heels as the bar to which her wrists are secured is hoisted.

Properly suspended in the best of BDSM rigging, Madison Young is displayed crucifixion-like in the manner that ignites her arousal. Madison's half-closed eyes and faintly parted lips drift in their pursuit of fantasy as the drug of heavy sensuality comes over her. Her ability to absorb pain is surreal in its expressive pleasure, transforming a chained woman into a goddess of submission. As the shoot heats up, Madison nears the edge of that special place called subspace where her desires and orgasms will float and dance together under James' command.[1]

Madison seduces James with a persuasion that satisfies her fetishes and stretches his BDSM persona as a dominant. Her destination is another realm where their sexual play becomes an expression of their shared affection for bondage, pain and eroticism.

The Rope Called My Name

Born near Cincinnati in Loveland, Ohio, Madison Young was raised in the heartland of conservatism. Educated in a performance art high school, she later attended the socially and intellectually liberal Antioch College. Virginal through her high school years, Madison's earliest sexual fantasies were about women. Her journal entries describe dominating female figures, sometimes comic book super heroines, who erotically torment and arouse her. Visions of kidnapping, blindfolds and bondage consumed Madison's secret adolescent world where submission dreams of rough sex with the same sex became an integral part of her accumulated fetishes. She was "educated" sexually as a college student and not surprisingly by a woman. Opening like a tender orchid, Madison ventured deeper into her sensuality, exploring her exhibitionist urges through the reality of public sex, fisting and light bondage.[2]

Madison Young's early life was wrapped in overachievement. For young women nurtured in a social construct that teaches them to please, self-imposed perfectionism can exacerbate stress and self-esteem issues, complicating developmental years already troubled by the demons of conformity and acceptance. Madison minimized these adversaries and bargained her intellectual inclinations into a successful scholastic record. Establishing priorities and sustaining academic excellence are daunting tasks, but the diminutive Ohioan proved equal as she graduated in the top ten percent of her class. Psychoanalytical theory postulates that who we become is the product of who we once were and Madison's adolescence reveals that negotiating childhood anxieties creates a thoughtful adult. In the twenty-first century, her artistic and political vision serves a respected feminist who is revolutionizing attitudes in art, pornography, and alternative sexualities.

Floating in a pure white background, a rope bound typewriter turns carelessly in random circles. Likewise a nude and suspended Madison gently sways back and forth, around and around, moving within reach of the machine, then away from it. Close-ups focus on her body, hands secured behind her back, rope binding her genitalia and breasts, feet wiggling against the restraints. A paddle smacks her backside with resounding whacks. Next a Hitachi Magic Wand massages her clitoris. She moans.

A male voice asks, "How do you feel, Madison?"

"I feel like I can take on the world," she responds in a voice over. The pounding of typewriter keys clicks in the background.

With one hand freed Madison reaches out to finger the typewriter as if it were a lover, probing around its keys, trying to take control. The evasive machine drifts away and back again. Her body and the

typewriter are contradictorily fluid and constrained. Madison's
voice over describes frustration and speaks of a female lover's hands
on her body.

"Wet should be a color," the voice over says, "deep, dark and
wet." Madison licks the typewriter, smearing her lipstick as the
voice over yearns for her phantom lovers' hands inside her. In search
of her love, Madison's forefinger caresses a single key.

So opens Madison Young's filmed memoir, "Tail of a Bondage
Model," the story of how a profession and a passion lead to love lost
and a future reconsidered.[3]

During her teenage years, Madison Young worked with her
father's tree service where a rendezvous with suspension and a
fondness for rope would hallmark her future. These early experiences served her later in college when she suffered anxiety
attacks. Retreating into what comforted her, Madison sought
relief through rope and immobility, drifting into a self-defined
nirvana of harmony and bliss. Calmness enveloped her; anxiety
was blanketed and fears ameliorated in an "acceding to" process
that evaporated tension. Giving one's self freely and peacefully is
often cited as *the* characteristic of sexual submission, releasing
tautly drawn emotions and animating a fantasy that brings
solitude. For Madison Young it became therapy, a transcendental
experience that soothed and aroused, recollecting the magical
hush of a teenager suspended by rope gently floating in the
trees.[4]

Madison came to appreciate Japanese Shibari, a rope bondage
art highlighting geometric patterns on the human body. It
celebrates the female form as a serene breathing sculpture,
belying the initial interpretation of restraint as physical or
mental discomfort. The model is intoxicatingly submissive,
bound but not uncomfortable. As a performance artist,
Madison's interpretation of the Japanese rope mastery is a
spiritual connection with her audience. She is the "material" in

an animated "work of art," she says, with an added benefit. The oxymoron of immobilization accentuated by natural movement is personally liberating and emotionally reenergizing.[5]

Shibari is an erotic expression and each performance artist has variances in her interpretation of the bondage experience. For Madison the Japanese art is a sexual meditation that harvests the enchantment of her girlhood fantasies. Her submissiveness finds joy in homage to something greater than itself, a feeling Madison identifies as grounded in Buddhist philosophy.[6]

The fantasy of flight offers an escape from adolescent anxieties. Floating and flying is the stuff of dreams. The ancient Greeks whispered of Icarus soaring too close to the sun; the Victorians amused their children with the adventures of Peter Pan. Madison's adolescence, wafting in the trees, symbolically and literally flying, was a rare preparation for adulthood. She went where few are privileged and discovered moments of ecstasy every child desires: retreat into internal solace. The little girl breathing within Madison cherishes the bondage experience and reorients it into a consummate sublimity where pain turns into pleasure and a suspended restraint gives way to an exemption from restraint. Her film odysseys take Madison's psyche into places of extraordinary liberation, dimensions where peace is attained and pleasure assured, something many lovers, vanilla and fetish, can only imagine.

Madison is on the road again this time doing a bondage shoot with her close friend, rigger and actress Clair Adams. The scene is a play within a play; photo stills are intermingled with live action. Madison is suspended, face slapped and lovingly hugged by Adams. This section of Madison's memoir is titled "NYC: The Cold Winter, The Pleasure of Pain" and reinforces her love of her fetish. The voice over is steeped in desire as the scene fades and the camera moves once again to a floating, rope bound Madison reaching and longing to gain control of the ever elusive typewriter.

"The rope called my name. She had a sweet voice. She started out with a whisper in my ear and a firm yet gentle bite to my skin ... My hunger grew for her to be inside of me ... I was hers, completely and utterly ... riding the wave of pleasure she produces."
    The rope has a sex and is sex.[7]

Impact Point

Madison's masochism releases her fears, driving away her anxieties. When she is whipped, flogged or caned she feels "invincible." Following a *Kink.com* shoot with Princess Donna, Madison compliments the pain Donna inflicted as exhilarating, surging through her body in a scene steeped in intensity. Channeling it to her arousal points, Madison transforms the stinging and biting into carnal sensations, converting the physically distressful into orgasmic pleasure caressed by rope suspension.[8]

Though BDSM scenes can induce erotic rewards, reaching them is a process of collected experiences. Spanking or flogging can be off putting for novice submissives, Madison explains, who often react with tension, confining the pain. On the other hand, circulating the flogger's sensation through the body creates a sexual heat that is metaphysical. Bobbi Starr amplifies Madison's view. At *Kink.com* she canes performers who want it as part of their shooting experience. The implement's flexible striking ability produces a "quick, fast, really sharp pain" with an acute "impact point" that spreads out quickly, Bobbi says, going deep into the flesh to linger much longer than a spanking. A successful scene requires the model to relax her muscles. Madison's ability to do so is a testament to her command of her body and her erotic pleasure.[9]

The BDSM scene is play space, not the Inquisition, and it serves erotic preferences that differ from "a vanilla girl" who wants to be softly and gently caressed. BDSM has its own sensuality not easily understood by the uninitiated, but one that brings immense satisfaction to its devotees.[10]

In a Madison Young shoot the bondage often involves penetrative sex, once a self-imposed taboo in the porn industry. Though distasteful and confusing to many, the combination has its followers. Candida Royalle summarizes the hard edge. Erotic thoughts of "forced sex" can be therapeutic for a woman because she can alleviate the dual burdens of personal accountability and self-reproach that can quell her desires. Madison's lifestyle and her performance art unwraps a female passion some consider over the top. Nevertheless, she insists all possibilities exist for every woman if she is willing to delve into her imagination and communicate with her partners. The message is simple. By understanding and embracing her fantasies, a woman is empowered to gain her own erotic gratification. It is a feminist statement.[11]

Madison Young also knows her sexuality reaches beyond the bounds of some participants in the BDSM community. Describing erotic pain as "warmth and colors and different sensations," she recognizes she processes it in ways others might not. BDSMers have a variety of activity preferences, Madison says, and hers are extreme, "intense" and "very transcendental." Her favorite "punishments" do not mean her BDSM experiences are more or less than those of others within the community. They are just different.[12]

In the opening scene of "Tail of a Bondage Model" Madison is pleasured by longtime friend Jiz Lee who performs under the name Gauge. Madison is caressed while bent over the kitchen table. There is a window just above the table and the camera moves outside as Madison pushes her face, eyes closed and lips pursed, against the glass.

Later punishment will replace penetration. Madison's lover is exasperated, weary of Madison's time away from home.

"When am I going to have my girlfriend back?" Gauge snaps.

Ready to leave once again, Madison reassures her partner that she is hers always.

"So what?" is the sharp response, "You're never here!"

Angrily indicted for spending time with photographers and her rope fetish, Madison begs for patience, pleading she must work to make the rent payments. Stockings in disarray, she holds her hastily packed suitcase. The camera moves to a cat's scratching post. Once again Madison is off to scratch an itch, reluctantly abandoning a lover's scratch while hoping for enough scratch to keep the household going.

The camera shifts quickly to payback time. Madison is standing, hands bound behind her back; two large plastic jugs are attached to her labia with clothespins. Madison's lover holds a container of water with "years of tears" taped on it. Madison begs for forgiveness but retribution is inescapable. She must suffer; the pain is sweet arousal buried in a scolding. The jugs are filled; Madison grimaces and moans before the liquid's weight overcomes the clothespins. The motif is revisited later when clothespins on Madison's breasts are ripped away with painful gasps punctuating the scene's masochism.[13]

Madison Young maintains a hectic schedule, traveling extensively to model, lecture and conduct workshops. Journalist Brian Alexander describes her as a "cute, tiny, farm-bred girl," an endearing image that offers Madison a distinct niche in adult film. Primarily a fetish model, Madison also crosses over into mainstream porn where her shooting history includes major production companies like *Digital Playground* and *Evil Angel*.[14]

Time away from home is an issue explored in *Tail of a Bondage Model*. Madison explains leaving San Francisco on a fifteen-day shoot a few years ago affected her immeasurably. Her girlfriend moved out. "I lost someone that I really loved," she says. "That really woke me up to the whirlwind of travel my life had become."[15]

During that melancholic period the unexpected filled the void. "James happened," Madison remembers. James Mogul is a director, rigger and photographer whose specialty is fetish porn. Coping with their own respective breakups, the two became close. Maintaining a personal relationship within the adult industry is fraught with problems but Madison and James keep their balance. The director is more than a lover; he is also a business partner, working with Madison to maintain her website. In turn Madison performs for James in the larger arena of *Kink.com*'s *The Training of O* website. Incidentally, Madison remembers shooting for *Kink* was her "first taste of a whip or rope [and she] fell in love with both instantly"[16]

> *In the final scene Madison is bound to a medical table, feet in stirrups. The examining doctor is played by another close friend and sister feminist, Lorelei Lee. The doctor places suction cups on Madison's nipples before applying medical forceps to open her vagina. Suddenly astonished, the physician tells Madison she is pregnant, chastises her and pulls rope from Madison, tossing the hemp on her face. Caressing the rope and taking in its aroma, Madison smiles. Her fetish is exceedingly personal and privately borne, a fantasy lover who first appeared in her adolescent sexual reveries.*[17]

After she directed and performed in *Tail of a Bondage Model*, Madison welcomed another irreplaceable love, daughter Emma, an "aroma" born in 2011 she could not have found anywhere else.

"Powerful Woman"

Art is a conduit for activism and Madison Young, steeped in her feminist beliefs, knows this well. Her brand of political engagement supports *Femina Potens (FP)*, a nonprofit arts space that breathes the spirit of San Francisco's queer population. Translated as "powerful woman," *FP* is Madison's vision and the embodiment of Madison herself. Beyond her role as the gallery's curator, she utilizes its workshops to give voice to a community. Madison has several loves, James and Emma being the most personal, but *FP* is her feminist passion.

Femina Potens reflects Madison's personal dedication to "melding and deconstructing art, sex, and gender" and "being aggressive about female sexuality." *FP* seeks to dismantle restrictive political barriers between art's makers and patrons, encouraging artists to work for social change by questioning "preconceived boundaries." Offering innovative opportunities for female and transgendered talent, the gallery advocates social consciousness. Inclusion and visibility for all sexual identities and orientations construct *FP*'s centrality.[18]

Founded by Ohioan Tina Butcher, *Femina Potens* originated in Cincinnati in 2000 as a theater company for local female playwrights, actors and directors. Venturing to San Francisco to work with an all-female Shakespearean theater troupe, *FP* transitioned into an art venue for women. The gallery eventually set up shop in the Castro, San Francisco's internationally known gay neighborhood, where it resided until 2011.

Femina Potens' community involvement is multifaceted. Its health and wellness efforts support causes involving homophobia, transphobia and censorship. *FP* provides events targeting "body image," an issue directly linked to sexuality and gender identification. It also functions as an outreach by sponsoring events to validate alternative sexualities and offering services to the city's feminist, sex worker, kink and sex-positive communities.[19]

The gallery does not rely on public money because government oversight accompanies public funding. Artists are free to voice their politics without fear of sanction as happened with the NEA in the 1980s. *FP*'s "Art of Restraint" events, for example, celebrate the kink and performance art communities and highlight well-known rope artists.

Madison's primary income is generated by adult film, a respected career that has given her iconic status. Having finished a college internship, Madison saw an ad for nude modeling, took the plunge into erotic photography, and eventually succumbed to the allure of film. "Even before I was in the industry I used to beg my girlfriends and boyfriends to tape us having sex," she recalls. Her first porn shoot was for *Good Vibrations*, a "g-spot" educational film shot with her girlfriend at the time. Madison filmed for about a year before accelerating her career with *Kink.com* in early 2003, breaking in with a *Hogtied* shoot. Her porn popularity moved at light speed and Madison seized the opportunity before her. Commercializing her body and fetishes closely paralleled the ascension of *Femina Potens*. When the gallery needed money she regarded her modeling with urgency; the quickest way to support the gallery was through the immediate payout generated by adult videos. Asked how many anal scenes were needed to create the art space, Madison is amusingly honest, ten for starters but that did not cover the physical construction to get it open and functioning. Part of the project required ten more in short order. A lot of penetration expended even for an adult film veteran, but good paydays nonetheless.[20]

Because she wants to validate the sexuality of San Francisco's queer community, Madison Young also operates her own film company, *Madison Young Productions*. Her movie work is a hybrid of traditional sex-positive feminism and her personal commitments. She says,

> Performing in videos in a sex-positive way, being aggressive around my sexuality, giving and receiving genuine orgasms on film, and letting the viewer into an intimate and honest part of my sexual self is a form of activism that can change the face of porn and the way that it affects the viewer.

Madison's affection for fetish studios runs deep. They are female friendly and sex-positive. The mainstream porn world is less so, Madison says, nevertheless she carries a positive mood and sexual energy onto their sets. Madison believes performers should step beyond the mechanics of formulaic sex and indulge the authentic sensuality pornography feminists regard so highly. Sensitive to the interpersonal relationships of porn talent, she insists that performer chemistry makes her scenes stronger and visually more engaging. By creating well thought out scripts that complement all sexualities, Madison's shoots are an educational experience and a documentation of the sex of queers and kinksters.[21]

Madison Young's professional endeavors play a role in how women and the queer community perceive their sexual selves. She is a revolutionary at a time when sexuality influences cultural mores via the media, be it late night talk shows, prime time programing or consumer products. Her effort is honest and addresses the needs of a community that will, as the century deepens, gain the recognition it rightly deserves. For her part Madison's feminism is a meaningful political expression and a sexual insurgency for women. It is firm, but not militant, and done with an artistic flair that supports the larger portrait of pornography feminism.

In one of her declarative moments, Madison defines herself, her art and her politics. "I choose to make waves in feminism one orgasm at a time."[22]

A Feisty 5'2"

Although cognizant of second wave feminism, Madison's arrival into the feminist fold was not shaped by it or by third wave messengers like Madonna and *Riot Grrrl*. Madison's feminism was a personal odyssey of self-discovery. She connected with her desires and aspirations and created an artistic platform to explore her sexuality. The former Midwesterner takes particular care to remain close with pro-sex feminists Carol Queen, Annie Sprinkle and Nina Hartley who advocated early on that feminism and pornography are quite compatible. Their efforts taught Madison that porn allows a woman to express her sexual agency in powerful and natural ways.

Annie and Madison have a unique personal relationship. "She's my porn-art daughter," Annie says with warm affection during our 2010 interview. Madison characterizes Annie and Annie's partner, Beth Stephens, as her "chosen family," her "mother figures." Annie and Beth are also dear friends, "the two women that I truly look up to in regards to art, activism, and love," Madison says. Though separated by a generation, Annie and Madison are political animals in their own right. Madison's activism pays tribute to Annie who endured jeers over her performance art. The history of anti-porn feminism and right-wing politics reveals that "censorship has always been on our backs," Madison notes, citing photographer Robert Mapplethorpe and her beloved Annie as targets. Waves of change continue, nonetheless, and Madison is categorical: erotic art is growing in popularity.[23]

Over drinks in a San Francisco wine bar, I asked Carol Queen to define Madison Young. Historians always revere original source material and on this particular evening it happens to be a bar napkin. Dated "9/29/10" and signed by Dr. Queen, the napkin reads: "Madison is at the forefront of integrating porn and its performative aspects of the arts, especially the edgy/radical alt world." Madison flavors that definition when she talks of her fans, many of whom delight in sexual activities far beyond vanilla.

A lot of my fans become invested in who I am. They ask me about my gallery, about what I'm doing. They say it inspires them and that makes a big difference to me. I'm giving pleasure and connections to couples that admire me as a person.

As porn settles into a place near the mainstream of American society, its feminist vanguard is unfolding a political statement that encourages future generations of young women to reject silence and shame regarding their sexuality. *Femina Potens* is part of that expression and stands as the feminist vision of "two" women who are singular in statement and person. Tina Butcher is the transplanted Ohioan who broke into nude modeling while Madison Young is the San Francisco actor, producer, performance artist and member of the Queer Porn Mafia. Together they meld into a feisty 5'2" package that exudes confidence, courage and a political commitment to marginalized sexualities and free expression.

Sexography

Madison Young believes western culture should document sex in ways that promote understanding. Using the "visibility of queer sex, aggressive female sexuality, [and] empowered submission," Madison seeks greater acceptance for alternative sexual expressions. As performer and director she validates everyone's experiences on the set, hers included. With these dimensions in mind, Madison contends the long accepted interpretation of "pornography" is inadequate and too limiting in describing her work. She prefers to redefine pornography as sexography to emphasize its authenticity and educational function.

Madison's sexography is a new spin on an old concept. Socialist feminist scholar Lynn Chancer proposed such a reinterpretation in 1988. The patriarchal adult film business creates a product in which females satisfy masculine fantasies, Chancer believes, leaving women with little means to illustrate their erotic ideas or sexual feelings in ways they wish. Sexography is not a "sanitized version" of female sexuality nor does it censure commercially defined pornography. Rather, sexual narratives are cultural and women can present them in their own style. By reconstructing sexuality's images and gaze, sexography becomes a political tool to combat what Chancer interprets as a sexist society.[24]

Madison's sexography alternative is rooted in Chancer's second wave sex-positivism. Both women suggest society's male based porn can be modified, though in Chancer's opinion, traditional adult fare will never be entirely liberated from a sexist culture. Nevertheless, invalidating the long standing definition of porn as the depiction of whores is doable because sexography changes the lens through which explicit sexuality is viewed, offering a version that is more woman centered and positive.[25]

Madison Young recognizes that many feminists and much of the general public remain sex-negative, believing porn humiliates women. Female models are paid more than male performers, Madison reminds critics, and that translates into power. She does concede degradation and money do go hand in hand in some people's minds though anyone who hastens to describe porn talent as degraded may want to take a second look. Madison and other pornography feminists do not feel devalued or coerced and do not perceive themselves as abused. Business opportunities proliferate with income generated by film, websites, personal appearances and even the occasional book deal. In the end degradation, like pornography itself, is in the "eye of the beholder."[26]

From Madison's standpoint adult film supports a woman's acceptance of her body image and the exploration of her personal sexuality, teaching her to release her inhibitions and relish her orgasms. For consenting adults, viewing pornography can be an affirming experience. Feminist Wendy McElroy argues porn has purpose for women. It provides information, relieves emotional confusion, breaks down stereotypes and acts as sexual therapy.

The value of Madison's film work is the inclusion of queer and BDSM themes. Marginal sexual expressions are deconstructed and legitimized, reminding us that everyone's humanity should be respected including the women who choose to put their sexuality on film and the women who want to watch. This is the new sexography. Women *are* consuming more porn than ever before and the demographics will continue to expand. As women begin to realize their personal options, the influence of feminist adult film professionals like Madison Young are destined to broaden our sexual horizons.[27]

Moving into her thirties, Madison Young is formulating her next decade. Her agenda is varied. She envisions taking part in film festivals along with an expanded involvement in writing and the academic discussion of sex. Madison is an activist in the New Left sense, not in a glaring upfront way but in a consciousness-raising one. She is indicative of a new sexual revolution, a pansexual multiculturalism struggling for legitimacy beyond liberal urban communities. Will she continue to perform? Absolutely, "as long as there is an audience out there that wants to watch," Madison declares, because her quest to film "honest sexual explorations" continues. Madison is blunt, "When a woman is embracing her orgasms and pushing her sexual self to new dimensions, [t]hat is a feminist act."[28]

Madison's natural body beckons to be cuddled in ways suggestive of those sassy stories about the farmer's daughter. Yet she was never destined to remain entirely Tina Butcher, a small town Ohio wife in waiting. Madison Young is now international in her art, attitude and film work. She is at once artist and art, the maker of film and the film itself. Her accumulated statuses support all women in spirit, including those who may never have watched a pornographic film.

Chapter 9

Too Much Gray

"We don't say 'safe sex', we say 'safer sex' because no sex is completely safe ... nothing is completely safe."
Jiz Lee, interview with author, Toronto, April 8, 2010

Latex Averse

By the late 1990s on-screen sexual antics swept away boundaries and anal queens became the hot commodity. Customers demanded more so pornographers filled the three female orifices with a variety of penetrations. Inevitably HIV, the peril of gay filming, crept in through the back door.

Anne Marie Ballowe, "nom de porn" Brooke Ashley, contracted HIV during a shoot in Chatsworth, California sending shock waves through the industry. In a March 1998 escapade billed as the *World's Biggest Anal Gangbang*, Ballowe handled a cobbled together collection of males that included a few industry professionals and several locally recruited fans. According to the director Cash Markman, Ballowe wanted condoms on the men she did not know personally. No one insisted she accommodate anyone unfamiliar to her though her contract did call for some bareback penetrations. The cute brunette was upbeat early on, Markman remembers, before flagging as time lengthened. Distrustful of strangers, she became more insistent on protective barriers. By day's end a fatigued Ballowe was wary of the chances she had taken.[1]

At the time the industry was well aware of the STI danger but felt protected and for good reason. Adult film is a small closed community whose population works together frequently. Performers must have updated blood tests before they step onto a set. Though test accuracy is vital to the industry, breakdowns can occur. Among the males Ballowe trusted that day was Marc Goldberg (Marc Wallice in the porn world), who apparently infected her. She commented later they were long time acquaintances and she expected working with Goldberg was safe. Coincidently, four other actresses tested HIV positive around the time of Ballowe's incident. Goldberg was implicated in their cases.[2]

Marc Goldberg's alleged irresponsibility, he presented outdated test results, fueled industry-wide anxiety. Rumors and speculation spread, a performer boycott was in the air. Producer nervousness grew and shooting agendas were interrupted. Club 90's Gloria Leonard, President of the Free Speech Coalition (FSC), observed that performers would not film without condoms. Though a meaningful work stoppage might have changed the industry, the situation could not endure. Quite simply "monetary needs outstripped any sense of life and death danger," Gloria remembers. Within a short period of time the "so-called boycott" was over.[3]

The FSC did not want the issue to slip away. In a meeting at the Sportsman's Lodge in San Fernando Valley, Gloria Leonard urged industry personnel to address their responsibility to protect the talent, even if that meant a condom policy. Ignoring condoms was unwise, she warned. Producers and directors could be held legally responsible should an infection be traced to a specific shoot. Retired performer Sharon Mitchell brought "the room to silence," according to director Ira Levine, when she explained the possible effects of Goldberg's actions. Performers three times removed who "had sex with someone who had sex with him" amounted to just about everybody in the industry, she said.[4]

Studio honchos took a positive stand. *Vivid Video*, *Wicked Pictures* and *VCA* (now a subsidiary of Larry Flynt's *Hustler* conglomerate) were among the companies that came to a safer sex consensus. David Schlesinger, spokesman for the Los Angeles based *Vivid*, called for total compliance until AIDS was eradicated.[5]

Gloria Leonard was less optimistic because she knew what porn moguls quietly understood: the possibility of an HIV infection was remote despite the daily abundance of shoots. She also recognized the renegade nature of the business. Independent minded people tend to be rebellious in spirit and action, taking orders and organizing is not part of their makeup. Hoping all studios might join ranks to support condoms, the FSC realized an agreement over safer sex would never become uniform. Several cinematographers were "on board with a 'condom only' policy" at the beginning, Gloria said, but others simply laughed, insisting condoms were not what consumers wanted to see. Her caution was well founded. With the exception of Steve Orenstein's *Wicked Pictures*, the safer sex promise was abandoned and the industry predictably retreated to its "old ways."[6]

In the new century, Porn Valley continues to gun sling in its film content. Limits are pushed; the "Age of Gonzo" remains entrenched though erotica is making a comeback in some quarters. Across the land a heavily sexualized reality TV poses as legitimate entertainment, real hardcore is a mouse click away while sexting technology makes the graphic more commonplace. All the while, the industry pressures itself to keep the lid on health risks. To its credit the system works... as long as performer responsibility holds its ground.

In a billion-dollar industry that profits off "the new girl," studios and agents always welcome fresh faces despite an ample supply of existing talent. At a naive eighteen or nineteen, many girls are unequipped to deal with porn's harsh realities. Saddled with a propensity for first shoot jitters and an eagerness to please, they can be persuaded to take chances that may have disastrous consequences.

With anal penetrations and deep oral thrusting, behaviors unthinkable in the porno chic era, female performers face infection risks and potential health consequences later in life. Shoots last several hours. Overly endowed males have access to Viagra and Caverject (self-injected directly into the penis) to maintain "wood," wearing out a girl's body with multiple penetrations. Vaginal and anal fisting is on the upswing with more girls doing ATM (ass-to-mouth) than ever before. Through it all, adult film companies remain convinced consumers are condom averse.

As the media glamorizes the porn star image and more newcomers seek a Porn Valley identity, concern for performer welfare has never been far away. A former actor, William Margold, established Protecting Adult Welfare (PAW) on July 12, 1994, the day following the tragic death of Savannah, a contract girl for *Vivid*. Her career was plagued by drug and alcohol problems and a supercilious attitude that concealed the pain of a lost soul. After a round of partying, Savannah plowed her Corvette into a fence. Sustaining minor injuries, a broken nose and facial lacerations, she walked the short distance home. The impact of potential disfigurement, her sensitive mental state and substance abuse apparently caught her in a riptide of despondency. Within minutes of entering her house, Savannah located the Berretta she may have kept for personal protection. Unable to end her life quickly with a single shot to the head, she lingered for several hours.[7]

With performer validation the overarching goal, the nonprofit PAW offered informal counseling and conducted some STI testing early on. The necessity for a wider reach led to a new FSC funded organization. Adult Industry Medical Healthcare Foundation (AIM) began in 1998.

Under the direction of Dr. Sharon Mitchell (PhD in Human Sexuality) AIM established a centralized testing facility. Like Bill Margold, Mitchell was an industry veteran and performer friendly, a benefit to AIM's credibility. Naturally distrustful of attempts to monitor their activities, performers needed to feel comfortable with the clinical setting to shore up AIM's message of "community based health care." As a result, the organization became "a shirt-sleeve operation," Ira Levine says. Though not an official member of Club 90, Mitchell was close to the group and supported their feminist leanings, especially choice concerning safer sex. Her friendship with Gloria Leonard encouraged the FSC to assist in the funding of the nonprofit clinic.[8]

Establishing testing for blood borne pathogens, AIM evolved as the industry health monitor. A single HIV-positive test initiated an immediate quarantine, as happened with another brief crisis in 2004. After AIM established its foothold, testing virtually eliminated HIV and minimized other STIs. Unfortunately, the non-profit did not survive. In the spring of 2011 AIM financially collapsed and shut its doors, the victim of pressure from the Los Angeles County Department of Public Health and the AIDS Health Foundation (AHF). Privacy issues concerning performer health records and AHF's uncompromising demand for industry-wide condom use became the tipping point. In the end, performer well-being was sacrificed in a political dispute steeped in emotionalism, legal wrangling and misinformation.[9]

How Safe is This?

A look at the safer sex issue reaches two conclusions. First, a blood testing protocol works if performers are conscientious about updating their health status and second, industry health statistics are always debatable. Neither dismisses risk and performers recognize the gamble they take but consider it a tradeoff for steady employment. The sheer volume of anal, vaginal, and oral penetrations suggests STIs are in the waiting. To complicate the picture, the porn community is contradictory in its makeup. In one respect, it's an ever-changing circle of participants with many women lasting only a few weeks or months. On the other hand, much of the filmed sex is limited to the same performers who work regularly with each other, minimizing the turnover rate.[10]

Most models work without condoms and are cognizant of exposure risk but have minimal knowledge of the *extent* of that risk. Not surprisingly, statistical studies are few, performer samples small and results disputed. Understandably most performers will not, and should not, personally reveal their infection history. In fact only three performers I know did so to me and then almost as an afterthought. The threat of gonorrhea, chlamydia, HPV (human papillomavirus) and herpes is ever present, but probably no more or less than with the sexually active civilian population.[11]

Some neophytes come into the business with safer sex practices in mind, but for the majority getting hired means forgoing condoms. Researcher Cristina Rodriguez-Hart summarizes the typical reaction. A performer she interviewed was not going to "jeopardize" her chances of working by taking a firm stand on latex. Models seem little concerned about infection consequences, at least on the surface, Rodriguez-Hart believes, because many are vigilant in self-medicating as if adhering to a magical elixir that wards off potential demons.[12]

In some cases condoms may be available on set but not made known to talent. When Bobbi Starr entered the business, she remembers she did not know she could have requested condoms, believing no protection was her only option. Of course, asking is generally not encouraged as most studios prefer bareback scenes.[13]

In gay male pornography, "no condom, no HIV test, no audience" is the historically recognized mantra though bareback shooting is making a comeback. While gay studios know a condom-only policy requires adjustments by the consumer, they doubt safer sex shoots would cause the financial collapse hetero powerbrokers predict. Incidentally, the option of protective barriers offered by feminist directors supports the gay industry's point of view.[14]

With anal a permanent resident in straight porn, performers are aware of the toll exacted upon them. To complicate the issue, anal sex is not always penile. Sex toys and fisting can expand the rectum, leading to eventual infections if protective barriers are ignored. Shoots specializing in anal only gangbangs, such as the Ballowe incident, intensify the danger.

Bobbi Starr, an eight-year veteran, a lifetime by porn standards, comments that her specialty is anal. She cautions anal is "very unsafe without a condom" and understands any object inserted into the rectum can create anal tears, opening portals for infection. Latex and friction can also create anal abrasions which leaves her "at a higher risk" for a variety of STIs. Bobbi also has a latex allergy which prevents shooting the next day if she uses condoms. Should she be hired for a condom-only scene, Bobbi brings non-latex as a precaution.

Finally, penetration *with* a condom is uncomfortable for Bobbi, requiring more lubricant. So her choice is to go bareback with the hope of minimizing risk. Because her shoots frequently involve rough sex and multiple partners, Bobbi works only with people she trusts. Yet her words belie an understandable concern: she takes a chance every time she allows her body to create a visual fantasy for someone else's entertainment.

Nina Hartley and Dana DeArmond rely exclusively on testing. Condoms negatively affect the way she interacts with her male costars, Nina says, because latex is a "'physical barrier to the free flow of sensation." Intimacy is muted, making her job more difficult. Latex is also physically irritating. "In real life the average length of intercourse is ten minutes," Nina mentions, in porn it's much longer with males who outsize the average man.

No matter how much lube is used, the friction is enough for Nina to conclude that she and latex "don't get along anymore." Dana's story is similar. "It's uncomfortable to use condoms, I don't enjoy it," she says. But Dana takes the condom issue up a notch. Putting aside the health picture, she feels condoms are a political statement. It's about free expression and her right to choose to go bareback.[15]

Some performers who don't like condoms prefer their sex to be industry only because anything outside the closed community requires condoms to keep the working population safe. Like Bobbi Starr, African American performer Imani Rose has allergy issues and in porn she can be sexually active without latex, though it is not foolproof. Monogamous in her personal life with a regularly tested partner, Casey Calvert has little faith in condoms. "They break," she says. Her philosophy is to refuse sex with anyone who does not have "a clean test," adding, "I would gladly have sex with both forms of protection, but never just with a condom."[16]

Every performer negotiates a path that works for her and sometimes the lessons are difficult. When Tara Lynn Foxx confessed she was skipping college to enter the adult industry, her mother's initial concern hit home. "'Can you use condoms?'" and "'How safe is this?'" Eighteen at the time, Tara admits had she been smarter and said "'I'm not doing any porn unless I can use a condom,'" her adult film career would have been smoother. "But, it's too late for that now," she says. Asked about that moment of doubt when an unwrapped penis is about to work its way into her backside, Tara is honest. "When you're doing a scene your concern shows." For a time she vowed to stop accepting bareback anal shoots but her resolve weakened and Tara returned to filming without protective barriers. Though zealous models grow up fast, Tara's concession is less an indictment of her personal strength as it is a yielding to the realities of a powerful billion dollar industry.[17]

De-prioritization

In "They Shoot Porn Stars Don't They," Susannah Breslin writes about Ryan Hunter who has returned to adult film after a time away at the behest of a boyfriend. She's now back sans sweetheart and in need of money. Today is a solo performance, sort of. Her costar is a machine with an extended arm that will move a dildo in and out of her vagina. Hunter is suspended spread-eagled in a harness attached to the ceiling. An afternoon's booking offers her immediate cash, though she laments the shoot is not to her liking. After all, a machine doesn't sag from exhaustion. When the director suggests an anal scene, Hunter is reluctant, but yields after some light cajoling. Breslin reflects on the girl's decision. If she decides to not continue, this may be the end of her comeback. So she caves.[18]

De-prioritization, the hidden pressure that drives Ryan Hunter's decision, also haunts performers who insist on condoms. Not getting work is far more threatening than the possibility of infection. During the Toronto roundtable, Dylan Ryan is blunt in her assessment of the situation. If a performer requests a condom, Dylan says, it's likely she "will be deprioritized below women who do not." Dylan compares the circumstances to a prostitute's dilemma when she insists a client use protection. If he refuses, she may lose business to another girl. Performers describe de-prioritization as a "blacklist," a kiss of porn death. To recover, a girl who once insisted on protective barriers may resort to changing her name or her agent.[19]

On the other hand, a performer's status in the industry may matter. An established veteran, Dylan Ryan claims no one challenged her whenever she insisted on condoms. She cannot recall ever hearing, "We're never going to hire you again." Though Dylan insists that "no one's forcing me to do anything," she does emphasize that having latex available is a good thing. A quick sampling of Dylan's shoots from online promos reveals most of her work is without condoms.

Agents are often up front about condoms, letting their clients know safer sex insistence may hinder future bookings. Some representatives are openly receptive to a model's preferences and will support her accordingly. Bobbi Starr is one such example. She tells her agent what she wants, though she is cognizant the porn road is littered with the career carcasses of women whose mental toughness fell far short of hers.

With their A-list status, it is doubtful Bobbi or Dylan would be deprioritized. They learned to play the game early on, developing an acumen that finesses situations as needed, perhaps holding their collective breath as the bareback cylinder is spun one more time. Clearly, lessons learned do not quell anxiety. "I've been very fortunate," Bobbi says. "The worry for me comes with hindsight. I think what could have been ... I guess you could say the more knowledge I've gained the more paranoid I've gotten."

In a final assessment, Steve Nelson, editor of *Adult Industry News*, offers a definitive view. Shooting without condoms is the expectation, he says, and girls who insist on latex get fewer calls because cinematographers won't hire them. Safer sex is a personal call for each model, Steve insists, but the "pressure to go non-condom" is certainly great. Nina Hartley agrees. "Ninety-five percent of all performers prefer bareback," she says.[20]

Opportunity to Choose

Pressed to offer solutions for the safer sex issue, what do those who take the risks say? Bobbi Starr responds that she can envision a condom-only business, though under present circumstances that's unlikely. "The industry will not yield to condom-only, most production will move or go underground," she says. As a result, non-condom products will inundate the market and negatively affect "mainstream condom-only sales." Bobbi understands the dilemma and doesn't blame the studios, conceding that the industry may have done everything it can to deal with the issue. Fearing the government may decide to intervene, her solution is to look at present regulations and urge Cal/OSHA (California Division of Occupational and Safety Health Administration) to establish specific safeguards for adult workers. Separate procedures for condom friendly companies and those who prefer to shoot without them might be workable, Bobbi believes, giving studios "the opportunity to choose" what suits their production codes.

Dylan Ryan believes mandatory condoms would shift responsibility from the performer to the studio and enforcement would serve as "a good example for young people," including anyone who is considering entering the industry. But Dylan is conflicted. Government interference is troubling and she doesn't believe federal or state agencies should dictate sexual practices, including condom use.

Recognizing Dylan is of two minds on the issue, director Courtney Trouble maintains that the studios should have a uniform condom use policy because a united industry benefits everyone. If the government steps in, Courtney believes a safer sex regulation that is anti-discriminatory, addresses unfair practices based on gender or sexual orientation and restrains any prejudices "against a performer who chooses to use safer sex" should be considered.[21]

Nina Hartley endorses choice, but comments that the number of cinematographers who film with protective barriers is small. Safer sex policies may reflect the size of the studio and its marketed audience, Nina believes, mentioning Courtney and Shine Louise Houston as examples. Their businesses represent indie studios whose overhead costs are lower. "They don't have to produce so much," Nina asserts, because they have a "niche market."

Imani Rose's view bypasses setting examples and underlines

the purpose of porn, the fantasy which condoms dilute. "Nobody wants to see that [condoms]" on film, she says. Although her position follows the studios' long held belief, Imani does insist "the law should be the girl has a choice."

Candida Royalle offers a historical perspective. In the mid-1980s FEMME adopted a condom option while the industry as a whole ignored the issue. She survived the years when the feds tried to push porn "out of existence." Regulations like the 1988 laws against child pornography (known in the industry as "2257") are not far away if porn companies continue to resist self-monitoring procedures. The studios are being warned, she believes. If they do not "police" themselves and safeguard the talent, intervention is likely. Such action is not necessarily negative, Candida insists, if it has the "genuine interest" of the performers at its core.[22]

I do not believe anyone at the time of our conversations thought their warnings and apprehensions would ever become reality. In the fall of 2011, the Los Angeles City Council voted to require condom use on adult film sets. In the general election a year later, a ballot proposition to enforce condom use industry wide became law.

Before the election, the industry rallied in opposition to the legislation, referred to as Measure B. Their actions reveal it is possible to bring the adult community together politically, especially among performers who could benefit from a stronger voice. As Dana DeArmond suggests, "I think we will stand together and become activists. I will exercise my right of free speech. I will do it [have sex on-screen] without wearing a condom." If her activist prediction is true, adult talent will discover a power it did not previously acknowledge or was not interested in exercising. As a result, a more formal performer organization within the adult film community may become possible.

* * *

Feminist directors have a pro-condom reputation and there is no de-prioritization threat. Nica Noelle insists condoms are a staple on her sets, leaving them "within view." Because veteran performers understand their risks and have their own safer sex practices, Nica rarely brings up the topic with them. On the other hand, if she is working with a new performer, especially one she has recruited, Nica reviews informed choices. Concerning the rehire dilemma, Nica claims she has not "seen it first-hand" but rumors abound that it happens. Tristan Taormino also has condoms available for her shoots and encourages their use. Most performers ignore them, she comments, relying on the industry's blood testing protocol.[23]

For Erika Lust the condom issue is straightforward. She always discusses condoms with actors and if her storyline portrays two people meeting for the first time, she supports the safer sex message. European male pornographers are similar to their stateside counterparts regarding de-prioritization. "Unfortunately that happens often," Erika notes. And, the ratio-nalizations are the same. "Male fantasies do not allow the regular use of condoms," she says.[24]

Nica Noelle, who still occasionally performs, believes heightened awareness of STIs among models tends to ensure safe shooting conditions. Her concern is with people outside the porn orbit who hook up with adult models. Civilians seem uncon-cerned about protecting their lovers, Nica says, and keep their health history to themselves. "I'd be much more worried about sleeping with a civilian than I would an adult performer," she declares.

A Little Extra on the Table

At the 1986 *Consumer Electronics Show* in Las Vegas, a Brit named

Alana took a restroom break from her floor stint as a receptionist for *Superior Video*. In the ladies room, a handful of "starlets" were recreating with a little chemistry. Not unusual, in those days porn and drugs were inseparable. It was their conversation that Alana noticed. The girls were divvying up their hotel room time to accommodate convention patrons they met during the day. In the halcyon days of 35mm film actresses did not openly hustle outside business opportunities nor did they purposely use their status to troll for clients. The popularity of the VCR brought changes to the industry.[25]

Conventions and trade shows afford a girl the opportunity to meet potential clients. For a broader appeal, online sites make escorting services available worldwide. Fees are by the hour, night or weekend and can run into thousands of dollars. One company, *Dreamgirls*, advertises an elite service and touts a "portfolio" containing "Playmates, Penthouse Pets, fashion models, actresses, [and] adult film stars." The agency lists eighty-five adult performers and is pricey. Customers pay $1500 for one hour and $4,000 for four hours, length brings a bit of a discount apparently. The "model of your choice" will travel, the company says, but rates begin at $8,000 a day. The site does not mention condoms and may not need to, assuming the clientele understands protective barriers are an expectation.[26]

Adult film women not represented by escort services have alternatives. Selected agents and promoters can assume a pimping role and a model may deliberately choose one based on that service. Researcher Corita Grudzen quotes one performer whose opinion of agents is not generous. "'An agent is nothing more than a glorified pimp,'" the model claims, adding some agents consider girls to be "'nothing more than sides of beef.'" Another girl mentions agents provide their models with places to stay and "provide everything for them." In return the performers are expected "to sleep with them or their friends." If a girl refuses, she is passed on to someone else.[27]

There is a fine line between the adult film business and prostitution. The 1989 Freeman ruling affirms that a porn model's paycheck is for acting, not for gratifying her costars, though some people may see no difference. Bobbi Starr is a performer, not a prostitute, she says, because a civilian is not exchanging money for sex with her. She is paid a negotiated rate for a shoot, an exchange with a "third party" which is within the bounds of the Freeman decision.

Tara Lynn Foxx jokes she is frequently asked about prostitutes and porn stars. "We are both having sex for money," she declares, but the main distinctions for her as a porn performer are legality and safety. Thanks to Freeman, filming a sex scene is legal in California and the set is a secure environment, something that prostitutes do not have. Imani Rose, who uses her business degree to brand her name, finds escorting confusing and "scary", but knows performers who exchange sex for money off the set. In her mind, prostitution and acting for a paycheck are far apart. A porn set is "staged," she says, "everything is timed [and] prepared." Imani lists requirements that vacate the prostitution label: "paperwork, identification, lights [and] camera."

Jiz Lee understands that some people might consider pornography to be a type of prostitution, but the conclusion is short-sighted. An adult film performer is a "sex worker" in the larger regard, a profession that covers both legal and illegal activities. Like the others, Jiz emphasizes that adult film is produced within a controlled setting of crew, director and cast and sold for profit. To clarify adult film's legality, Jiz stresses the "transparency of information: 2257 forms, legal names, proof of identification, social security information." A prostitute is not responsible for government required paperwork.[28]

Traditional prostitution covers streetwalkers, brothel workers and pimps of all varieties, an implied manifestation of a hidden underworld of crime, drugs and violence. Though high-end in many cases, escorting is sex work and undeniably linked to prostitution. From a legal perspective modern adult film does not fit within those parameters. That notion draws a line in the sand allowing performers to rationalize they are not sex workers in that regard. However, for some women the easy and profitable transition from on-screen sex to off the set cash is an unambiguous connection that encourages ancillary work as escorts. For them there is little difference between the overt and the concealed.

Escorting is so closely linked to porn that it may be the endgame of a model's accumulated filmography. Some girls walk onto the porn set so they can boost the rates they demand for their private time. Their goal, as Tara Lynn Foxx relates, is to become a high-end escort rather than building an adult film repertoire. Sasha Lexing claims porn models can make double or triple their regular expected income by escorting. "It's ridiculous," she says, girls "are just dying to get famous" so they can supplement their income beyond the set. Instead of being a perk of filmed sex work, escorting's "porn star experience" may be the marketable paydays of a girl's financial aspirations.[29]

Each time an adult film performer provides sex for hire beyond the shooter's lights, it's a personal decision reflecting an individualized moral universe. But she must consider the backwash of her choices. Within the adult community extracurricular behavior, especially when it endangers the health and working availability of the closed circle of tested individuals, can be devastating.

Sex off camera with industry people may complicate the separation of work sex from personal sex, creating unwanted entanglements and obliterating boundaries between the two. Potential rewards encourage behind the scenes arrangements , testing a girl's resolve to resist the intimidation of the casting couch. According to Dylan Ryan, a director may promise a performer more shoots and potential stardom in exchange for certain favors. Cash or checks may not be offered, Dylan says, but a "future monetary gain" is implied. When pressed to estimate how frequently this happens, Dylan guesses enough to make it a concern for performer well-being.[30]

Sex under this umbrella is a subtle form of coercion, Dylan says. She's heard of girls being told they should "hang out" with studio people, implying that earning potential hinges on a willingness to cross lines all performers tacitly acknowledge. The threat is thinly veiled, "If you don't, you won't work here again," Dylan says, illustrating another avenue de-prioritization can take. Bobbi Starr warns new girls who cave to such demands, careers will be short, novelty will quickly fade and new bookings will become scarce.

After peeling away the top layer of performers, what about the next level? Here resides Sasha Lexing, a San Francisco bondage model who shoots sporadically around her day job. Sasha admits to dealing with "casting couch ethics," but has no broad assessment of how widespread it is. Because Sasha is not an upper echelon player, getting hired requires effort and de-prioritization never goes away. "The amount of my work has dropped during certain times because I didn't want to go to this place or this party," she says.

Sasha is a free agent and estimates half the girls she knows are as well. She expends "a lot of energy" in securing her gigs. "You get what you put in," Sasha says, emphasizing the positive. The part-time college student maintains a straightforward proactive attitude, "if you go after the director, you get a little bit more work." Fortunately Sasha's willingness to be tied up, flogged and penetrated elevates her employability in the San Francisco area where she films for BDSM websites.

Porn girls can increase their non-shooting paydays through self-advertising on the internet. A booking agent can also offer similar services, and some do, but an aggressive model can run her own extra work, exercising her free will to build an escorting business that profits her. As Annie Sprinkle demonstrated in the 1980s, a porn performer can be a feminist and a prostitute and control her future. Of course, attitude is important. Tara Lynn Foxx believes porn facilitates escorting because being sexually "open minded" and free spirited is beneficial to a girl who chooses to go that route.[31]

How many performers actually escort for a little extra on the table? Estimates are all over the map. Tara Lynn Foxx comments some girls get annoyed and offended when the subject is mentioned, limiting her reckoning to guesswork. The practice is widespread, Imani Rose says, though "most girls are quiet about it." When pressed for a number, Sasha Lexing guesses "about seventy-five percent." Popular internet porn producer Billy Watson is cavalier, but honest. "Over time," he says, "they all do," underscoring escorting's broad acceptance in the industry.[32]

Adult Industry News editor Steve Nelson reports about half of the models he can count "at random" do so and protective barriers are part of the deal. "They use condoms as a strict rule when escorting," Steve declares, emphasizing in that regard at least, escorting is safer than shooting a scene. Noting her personal life is fluid bonded and protecting her significant other is important, Sasha Lexing agrees that condoms are imperative beyond the set for everyone's safety. Casey Calvert is shaded and less certain. "There might be a condom, but the john isn't tested," she says.

Ira Levine reinforces that "escort work is barrier protected" and underlines a common misconception, models are "a bunch of wild nymphomaniacs out to screw everybody." In fact, Ira says performers tend to be "monogamous" in their personal lives because "that's about all they have energy to maintain."

Nevertheless, porn is a money monster, writes Journalist Dennis Romero, a materialistic high-end lifestyle glorified by "social media." Cyberspace bluster entices new talent with unrealistic expectations. In a recession weary business, job offers are a fraction of what they used to be and reduced pay for routine sex acts is an expectation. Couple these factors with the constant supply of new faces the industry craves, and escorting offers a way to maintain a lifestyle or perhaps just survive.[33]

The Night Before

Pursuing money beyond the camera opens a Pandora's Box of troubles. Civilians can be perceived as clean and risk free, particularly troublesome when a non-condom private solicitation occurs. There are other gambles. Imani Rose and Sasha Lexing reference sex parties, otherwise known as swing, adult or lifestyle parties, attended by non-industry people. Wannabe starlets can break into the business at these get-togethers. Significant health risks are present if condoms are ignored, though "the swinger community is very, very careful about safer sex," Casey Calvert declares.

Performers are obliged to honor the safety net everyone covets and the thoughtlessness of some is perplexing. Imani Rose doesn't understand how girls can come onto the set if they escorted bareback the night before. They are careless and inconsiderate. Casey Calvert, who does not escort, refuses to hide her annoyance. Models go out, she says, "boasting that they are porn stars, fucking whoever they meet at the bar that night, and then coming back to work. It puts every single one of us at risk." Consequences can be tragic. Referencing an unidentified actress who reportedly contracted HIV in 2009, Bobbi Starr says the model was "either extremely unlucky or simply not exercising a reasonable amount of caution in her off-camera endeavors." The girl "displayed a blatant disregard for the safety of her fellow sex workers."[34]

Is there breathing space surrounding escorting? Chanel Preston thinks so. A native Alaskan by way of Hawaii, Chanel is an adult film superstar who electrifies a room with her presence. Though she does not openly identify as a pornography feminist, this former community theater actress is every bit the empowered woman one finds within these pages.

Chanel makes a salient and sensible point about escorting. "You would think porn people would be more tolerant [of escorting] because they're in an industry that [the outside world] stigmatizes. But unfortunately, that's not the case. We still stigmatize *within* the industry," she says. Performers belittle their own with whispers of "'that girl escorts.'"

"I don't look down on girls who escort," the 5'8" brunette says, because "performers can make a business out of it." In fact, Chanel believes condemnation is counterproductive. "Whenever you push industries underground, safety is eliminated and people do stupid things." Chanel suggests a change in attitude would help everyone. "If we embrace it [escorting] and empower those women they'd be more apt to protect themselves. Instead of shunning the girls," she continues, "we should teach them to be safe and mindful of what they are doing and let them know there are repercussions if they don't."

Joining the collective voices about escorting's consequences, Chanel reminds everyone, "When you're in porn there is a responsibility to maintain that homeostasis amongst the performers." Bringing STIs onto the set is "harming people," she insists. "People have families."

For the record, Chanel Preston does not escort. "I don't enjoy it," she says, "but I have no problem with girls who do." Her preference is the camera. "I like performing," Chanel beams, "I get off on doing really crazy and intense things" like "getting gangbanged, I love doing that."[35]

* * *

On a sunny January morning in 2010, Bobbi Starr and I are

walking the crowded Vegas Strip to the Sands Convention Center. We've wrapped up breakfast and she is due for her four-hour stint on the floor for *Evil Angel*, her primary employer. Greeting her fans eager for a few words and a photo is something Bobbi enjoys. Like her contemporaries, recognition and accolades are the financial fuel that keeps her universe expanding. Our breakfast conversation covered many topics, Bobbi's musical talent, her take-charge feminism, her attitude on fame and the fantasy of pornography. Bobbi Starr is unassuming and sweet with the warmest of smiles. Our fellow customers in the hotel's coffee shop would never guess this fresh-faced girl in a warm up suit and carrying a backpack is a well respected adult film personality.

As we near the Sands, my comfort level with Bobbi is established and perhaps she feels likewise. We met briefly the previous day and agreed to extend our talk to this morning. Picking up the pace, we banter on various topics including her family and how they are comfortable with her profession. Then without a question from me, Bobbi offers nonchalantly, "You know, ninety percent of the girls in this business escort." I mentally pause and before I can comment, Bobbi is approached by two industry affiliated men who solicit her attention. After a brief conversation we move on and I decide to not pursue her escorting remark with the follow-up she probably expects. It does not seem appropriate and I, quite frankly, prefer not to know.

Over the next year Bobbi talks more extensively about the women in her family whose support she values and the possibility of having her own children. Bobbi Starr lives on solid ground, more than most women in the business. Though I never reference our conversation on that pleasant Las Vegas day, over breakfast in another city I get the answer I know I could have written without inquiry.

"A lot of girls now in the industry could care less about what they are doing or where they are doing it," Bobbi says. "They care more about the paycheck, more about just doing porn so that they can charge higher rates when they escort."

Bobbi describes the magic of a box cover appearance and how it translates into escorting status. "That's the motivation for being in this industry," she says, repeating her opinion if it were an indictment.

After a moment she comments almost casually, "Girls feel like they have no other options."

"Why?" I ask.

The industry perpetuates stereotypes, Bobbi explains, resignation creeping into her voice. Performers feel trapped in oversimplified images they believe they are powerless to alter and consequently "not interested in fighting." Frankly, Bobbi is not overly vocal about her opposition to the stereotype either. She considers herself to be a "silent activist," doing her part by offering a positive example to others. This stunning brunette is a moral voice in a business easily condemned for lacking integrity and ethics.

Perhaps feeling the need to clarify her thoughts on that conversation we never finished in Las Vegas, Bobbi adds, "I don't escort. I don't think that is right." No one, she insists, regardless of their status in society should "be able to buy that type of service."

Even in a marginalized world where bodies and souls are displayed for profit and extra paydays are offered away from the camera, Bobbi Starr insists that there should be boundaries.

"There is a need for some black and white," she concludes, "the industry has too much gray."

Chapter 10

A Safe Place for All of Us

"I love it here. It's like a piece of home to me."
Bobbi Starr on filming at *Kink.com* from a pre-shoot interview
for *Hogtied.com*, April 27, 2010

An Exchange of Energy

Deep in the caverns of a hundred-year old fortress, real life lovers
are performing for Princess Donna's *Wired Pussy* website. Electro
play, electrical stimulation on exposed female body parts, is the
theme of *Wired Pussy* episodes. One of the performers is Jiz Lee.
This is Jiz's first shoot with Donna and Jiz is understandably
nervous. "I didn't really see myself fitting in; I wasn't sure if I'd
be enough of a 'pain slut,'" Jiz remembers. *Wired Pussy* is a big
step for another reason. Some of *Kink*'s requirements discouraged
Jiz from completing a model application "until Princess Donna
invited me and said I didn't have to shave," Jiz says, "I could be
myself!"

Before the shoot begins, Jiz is reminded that an unforseen or
uncomfortable turn of events will stop the action. Such an
unanticipated moment does occur. "I enjoy moderate spanking,"
Jiz says. "The spankings in this shoot were going well, until they
got to a certain level ... [M]y mind shot straight back to my
childhood ... I felt so angry that I screamed long and loud."
Donna halts the scene momentarily to give Jiz time to recover. An
appreciative Jiz later describes how Donna secures a model's
"trust" and then uses her skills to find "challenges" for the
performer to produce a rewarding experience.

The shoot ends on an up note and Jiz's excitement carries over
to the green room, the performers' lounge, where a public

address announcement reminds the talent they need to pick up their checks. Jiz exclaims, "I had so much fun that I almost forgot about the money! Sweeeet."[1]

Referencing the *Kink* shoot over breakfast in Toronto in 2011, I ask Jiz if Jiz is a BDSM lifestyler.

"I identify as a kinky person," Jiz replies. "My relationship at *Kink* is pretty fluid. I'm still experimenting with a lot of things." A lover introduced Jiz to San Francisco's leather scene and the BDSM community. Jiz admits to liking bondage, but isn't interested in the 24/7 aspect of the lifestyle. Nevertheless, the *Kink* experience was mind blowing and returning to the facility for future shoots is high on Jiz's list.[2]

* * *

The success of *Kink* shoots depends on the directors. Princess Donna is a maven of finesse, testing performer limits with a gentle word or caress. James Mogul is methodical, using heavy doses of psychological play to challenge his performers. Interrogator, warden and professor are among his personas. *The Training of O* under James's direction is a sexual self-discovery that tackles a performer' hidden apprehensions and subdued desires. Lochai, on the other hand, is like a kid playing hooky at the ballpark, he knows why he came and what he wants to see in the limited time he's there. The native Baltimorean is a rope artist, a highly regarded rigger among BDSMers. "We'll have fun" is his demeanor in a *Hogtied* shoot. His talent is orchestrated with endearing smiles as he binds and suspends a model, chatting amiably all the while.[3]

Donna, James and Lochai are specialists in a team of directors who handle their websites with an infectious workman-like enthusiasm. *Kink's* sex is rough, extreme and fetish oriented, catering to models and customers who have a taste for an alternative sexual circus. Though critics can easily misinterpret its BDSM scenes as violently degrading and humiliating to women, the fanciful creation of entrepreneur Peter Acworth is much admired for respecting and caring for its staff and the performers it hires.

Kink's shoots can be intoxicating and BDSM oriented pornography feminists frequently mention its woman friendly atmosphere. Dana DeArmond praises the environment as "positive and friendly." "They know my body of work and they treat me nicely," she says. Dylan Ryan agrees, "They're so aware of whether or not I'm ok, if I'm enjoying myself, what my boundaries are." Returning to *Kink* is a treat for Dana and Dylan, directors and crews support their rough sex propensities and craft scenes accordingly. Intense BDSM play is not for the timid or fainthearted and *Kink* works hard to ensure performers are safe in acting out their fantasies.[4]

Peter Acworth believes *Kink.com* is philosophically different from the Southern California scene. He describes Porn Valley gonzo as "fast food," a simple recipe mass produced. Madison Young concurs insisting much of LA porn is "disposable" because of its predictable formula; directors can "plug in" any girl based on her appearance and acrobatic skills. As a result, performer expendability promotes stereotyping. Tara Lynn Foxx offers a supporting opinion, commenting that some gonzo cinematographers just pay models to "come in, fuck, and leave." "There's nothing about you," she says with disappointment. In contrast Madison exclaims sex-positive feminist porn is "real sex," a filmed documentary that emphasizes "connection" and an "exchange of energy" between performers. It's the soul of the San Francisco adult film palette, be it the heart of queer porn or the work of Peter Acworth, whose multi-layered approach dominates a niche market.[5]

A Porn Taj Mahal

Residing in the Old National Guard Armory on Mission Street, *Kink.com* is an established internet trademark. Peter Acworth's enterprise celebrates the last sexual bastion to be breached, the final debauchery released from the Victorian secret museum. The British born businessman composes his product with a panache that stylizes the San Francisco adult scene, a porn that feminist scholar Dr. Carol Queen proclaims is "sexually intense [and] more likely to be queer, trans-inclusive, and kinky."[6]

Unlike eastern cities dominated by an Old World bluenose tradition, San Francisco's tolerance recalls its frontier days. Drinking, gambling and bordellos were ensconced in a cultural landscape that catered to miners, sailors, salesmen and charlatans of every ilk. San Francisco's "local color" revolved around the commercialization of sex. From the early 1900s Irish washerwoman advertisements (prostitution) to infamous madams, the city took pride in its open-minded attitudes, a revolutionary culture distinct from other American cities.[7]

The 1960s flower children brought drugs, free love and the inevitability of filmed sex. An early notable was Mary Rexroth, the hippie daughter of renowned poet Kenneth Rexroth. A student of ballet, Mary's other stage was the loop, her means of paying the rent. She remembers filmmakers were locals, often college students honing their craft. In the waning days of the sexual revolution denizens of the city's Haight-Ashbury scene picked up extra cash performing for the camera. The overriding fear in the pre-Viagra era was losing an erection. Silence ruled the shoot: a far cry from today's *Kink* productions. Mary recalls pre-filming discussions defined limits and she had few. Oral, anal, sex toys, it didn't matter. She was enthusiastically affirmative, reflecting a feminist-like control of her body and her desires. Unfortunately sadomasochistic scenes were considered taboo at the time, Mary recalls, apparently disappointed that the psychiatric community still considered BDSM a perversion.[8]

Another San Francisco porn institution took hold during Mary Rexroth's time. A sundry of adult theaters produced their own explicit shows. Noted directors flourished; among them were Lowell Pickett, Bob Chinn and Alex de Renzy. Smut merchants in those days discovered San Francisco's liberal attitudes to be good for business. Relying on the "community standards" guidelines set down by *Miller*, pornographers were relatively immune from prosecution, though not free of police harassment.[9]

Enter Jim and Artie Mitchell. Artie had a penchant for the creative; Jim a flare for turning it into a profit. The libertine environment provided female models who would bare it all for less money than professional hookers, prompting Jim to recruit hippie girls for topless photos and the eventual loops he peddled to local grindhouses. The brothers had a knack for concocting a provocative atmosphere at their O'Farrell Theater and celebrating the resulting notoriety. Live sex shows, such as those starring Nina Hartley, brought frequent police raids. Business boomed, nonetheless. But it was feature film that seduced Jim and Artie, the pornographers' quest for the Golden Fleece to challenge the newly released *Deep Throat*. Their version opened the *Green Door*; Marilyn Chambers demonstrated her oral skills and the Mitchells greeted fame.[10]

Journalist John Huebner writes porn stars are made by pushing limits and Marilyn Chambers, like Mary Rexroth, was game. Building a reputation meant crossing boundaries. In Marilyn's case that translated into shows featuring strong BDSM scenes. She packed the house with everything imaginable from whipping to oral sex to hot wax to vaginal and anal fisting.[11]

Using the O'Farrell as their porn Taj Mahal, the Mitchells' forte was to control each step of production from shooting to exhibition. Today Peter Acworth, who traded his pursuit of an Ivy League PhD and a career in finance for hardcore sex, solidifies that vertical integration model into San Francisco's modern

Taj Mahal. His vehicle is cyberspace, his stage international and his debt is to the past.

One of *Kink's* most popular websites, *Public Disgrace*, employs a variant of the *Green Door* motif. Reminiscent of an O'Farrell show, the sexual escapade plays out before a live audience although *Kink* makes no pretense that the performer is an unaware "victim." Every *Public Disgrace* number has a pre-shoot interview to establish the model's consent and delineate her sexual boundaries. When filming begins, pre-selected spectators and carefully screened individuals, some of whom are professionals, interact with her according to her check list preferences. Performer satisfaction is the cardinal rule and the show is always under the watchful eye of Princess Donna who sometimes participates. Similar to Marilyn Chambers' stellar exhibitions, *Public Disgrace* poses the question of who is entertained more, the audience or the actors.

An intense BDSM shoot can cause stomachs to flutter, no matter how desired the experience may be. A 2009 *Public Disgrace* episode featuring Dylan Ryan reinforces the gentle monitoring of *Kink* employees. Nervous in the pre-shoot interview, Dylan hesitatingly walks into the arena to meet her fantasies. Once there she gets into the setting quickly thanks to pre-arranged persons who offer physical comfort, especially in the early minutes when Dylan is immobile, kneeling in wooden stocks. Throughout the filming Dylan is encouraged by a warm and supportive crowd. By the shoot's conclusion, she is beaming. Dylan is cognizant of how others might misinterpret her *Kink* performances. "If there's really something painful going on or there's degradation happening," she says, "it's completely consensual [and] intentional. Everybody is very present in the moment."[12]

Feminists in Pain?

On the second day of her *The Training of O* shoot, Dylan Ryan's confrontation with James Mogul is ratcheted up. She will yield to his master/disciplinarian persona knowing the resistance she hopes to quell in herself will rear its ugly head. This is a personal journey for her, transforming a porn shoot into a therapeutic experience. Before she begins, Dylan talks of rage and the BDSM stage as a psychological force.

"When I am in super amounts of pain [during a BDSM session]," she says, "I get a hateful and nasty feeling ... and then I just shut off." Her goal is to give up control and release a broader need "to determine everything all the time."

The Day Two test begins with a nude Dylan standing on a slightly raised wood platform. Resembling a barbarian queen captured in battle, her feet are shackled wide apart; her cuffed and chained hands are at her side. Her neck is encased in a wide black leather collar. The chains permit some mobility; Dylan is able to stand or sit according to James' will. She's the image of a prisoner prepared for public display and torture. Dylan will struggle with her fury, but she cannot escape.

James' plan includes flogging and the inevitable Hitachi to conclude the session. The scene ends with a *Kink* cinematic hallmark: the frozen moment, the psychological resolution. A kneeling and chained Dylan is facing a wall, hands attached above her bowed head. The whipped and emotionally beaten prisoner, she is drained of all resistance. It is a visual classic, reproduced for decades in graphic novels and bondage prints.

This final denouement is the result of a titanic struggle. Dylan fights the session, wildly thrashing around and firing angry visual darts at James, verbally assaulting him with profanities. At one point James snaps Dylan's hands behind her back, forces her into a sitting position, legs splayed, and presses her downward with his foot on her upper back. A disentangling results with

James as the antagonist. Dylan's physical and emotional explosiveness builds and she is suddenly engulfed in a revelation. Her eyes look directly at James with the slightest of smiles that reads, "I've arrived." She relaxes and an ethereal calm descends on the scene. Dylan later explains "the room was full of energy and emotion." James was "pushing" her beyond her limits, leaving only "pure emotion and intensity and energy and violence." At that point, an irresistible force moved into Dylan's psyche and she started to laugh. "It was absolutely overwhelming... I'm not sure I've ever had a feeling quite like that before."

The drama releases Dylan; the payoff is an invigorating renewal. In the final debriefing, James references the scene, admitting he took chances, refusing to take timeouts at crucial moments. He comments to Dylan, "You were searching for something that you couldn't articulate." Dylan replies she wasn't sure what she expected to discover, but she did want to learn more about herself. The shoot, Dylan concludes, was the most difficult she has ever filmed.[13]

Admiration for James Mogul runs deep. "James is very gentlemanly, polite," says a smiling Dana DeArmond. "He's great at tying, he's a cool guy." She recalls contacting James about a shibari shoot and meeting him for the first time in his LA hotel room. Though he chastised her for coming to a strangers' room, she took a chance and was rewarded; they became friends. Casey Calvert explains James Mogul's demeanor. He is very professional and "extraordinarily respectful," chatting with his performers "on the first day about some issue they want to work on," she says. That becomes the theme of the four days. When the scene begins, James uses "predicament bondage," quizzing his model about her strengths and weaknesses to guide his construction of the remaining episodes. In her shoot, he was unwilling to risk much at first because they had recently met, Casey comments, but James quickly recognized her kinks and "started pushing all the right buttons" after that.[14]

In a white room that could pass for a futuristic world, Casey Calvert is in rope suspension with electrodes taped to her body. Soon she will be kneeling on a bed with hands bound behind her, electrodes attached to her nipples. Bobbi Starr will penetrate Casey vaginally and anally with a strap-on that carries an electric stimulation Bobbi will fire up as the shoot progresses. Accentuating over an hour of film, Casey's long slow moans and ecstatic screams announce repeated orgasms. This is not for the timid, but it is a side of adult film feminism in the new century.

In the pre-shoot interview for this *Electrosluts* episode, eagerness describes Casey while Bobbi is watchful and subdued. Questioned about why bondage appeals to her, Casey replies, "the helplessness." Is she familiar with electricity play, Bobbi asks? Casey smiles affirmatively mentioning cattle prods and violet wands in her private life.

"Have you ever cried on camera?" Bobbi is touching all the bases.

Casey pauses for a moment. "Sort of, kind of," nodding slightly as if admitting to a weakness she finds embarrassing.

Bobbi explains the safeword protocol and stresses electricity play can be "psychologically confusing," consequently she will monitor everything closely. Bobbi does not want Casey to be a pain heroine. "No matter how tough you are, tell us if something is going on," she says.

"Sounds good," Casey replies with a huge grin.

Casey yearns for erotic pain and her anticipation enthralls the viewer. Using constant and intermittent shocks, some administered unpredictably, Bobbi manipulates Casey with a sexual teasing that keeps her off balance. The wanton submissive soon travels into her own chamber of thrills, eyes closed, seemingly dissociated from her surroundings. Like a parent soothing a child, Bobbi keeps verbal contact with her feminist sister. Casey's screams and curling toes punctuate her orgasms as Bobbi drives her to ecstasy.

In the post-shoot debriefing, Casey describes the electricity as "a good thing," using "amazing" and "incredible" to underscore her satisfaction. The shocks moved through her body, Casey says, reinforcing BDSM as a total physical and emotional experience. Like a coach rewarding an athlete, Bobbi tells Casey she is proud of her. They celebrate with infectious laughter.

Casey Calvert is quick to praise Bobbi Starr's topping ability. "[She's] so smart and kinky [with] the ability to read a bottom and know exactly what she can and cannot take. I trust her." Casey explains that she and Bobbi are "perfectly compatible" because they have the same mentor, famed bondage master and rigger, Lew Rubens, who ran *Kink*'s *Waterbondage* site in its early years. Asked about the difference between the two feminists, Lew indicates they are "apples and oranges." Each girl is a treat in her own way. Casey required no "baby steps" to get into the BDSM scene, Lew remembers, the diminutive model went into subspace quickly. During his first bondage and whipping session with her, she was "completely drunk on endorphins" and totally "euphoric." "Candy for a little girl" is how he likens Casey Calvert's response to pain. She's a masochist, Lew says, "pure and true on."[15]

Submissives vary in what they like, some are into pleasing, others, like Casey, prefer pain. But all must be agreeable to what happens in a scene because BDSM is a mutually negotiated activity in which participants discuss the degree of power each possesses and how it will be used. Psychotherapist Charles Moser relates that there is an "illusion of control" that demands cooperation by all players. Scenes are monitored; safety and consent are paramount. No one suffers for the entertainment of another because the play space has its rules.[16]

Close analyses of *Kink* narratives underscores that performers are psychologically equipped to create the scenes the directors cultivate. A strong sense of self-worth, a distinguishing character-istic of pornography feminists, and a powerful imagination are valued. If a performer is not a professional bondage model or her personal life is not BDSM oriented, grasping the nuances of submissive behavior is necessary to convincingly perform on film. The pinch of nipple and labia clamps, the appropriate size of ball gags and the impact of canes, single tails or the softer floggers can be off putting if the model is unaware of what to expect. The formulas for BDSM adult film are more complex than those of vanilla pornography and require models to be flexible (literally, some recommend yoga) so that periods of immobility are less taxing. Tolerance for a degree of physical discomfort and patience with riggers is a given. Needless to say, awareness of dominant and submissive power exchange is requisite or the shoot loses any authenticity it purports to achieve.

Preparation and negotiation are linchpins in BDSM play because the fetish's excitement dwells partly in the fantasy of the *setting* as well as its accoutrements. Peter Acworth's facility satisfies this vital psychological element. The Armory contains a vast basement equipped to serve multiple BDSM narratives, a controlled environment that accommodates the fantasy roleplay found in BDSM clubs and local events.

Because the risk of public exposure drives caution in BDSM communities, part of *Kink's* mission is to alleviate misunder-standing and minimize public apprehension. Peter Acworth validates the fetish community, providing *Kink* with a ready-made audience and amateurs willing to be filmed in exchange for the use of his facility.

They're Really Here for Me

In her pre-shoot interview, BDSM model Sasha Lexing explains that she does "a ton of bondage" at local Bay area clubs. *Hogtied* director Lochai wants to know if today's shoot is her first BDSM film experience. "Yes," Sasha answers with a broad smile, "You are breaking my cherry." Others who film at *Kink* may admit to pre-shoot jitters, but not Sasha. The 5'9" former exotic dancer is accustomed to being tied up and showing off her sharply toned body. Sasha's extroverted personality wins over Lochai as she gladly submits to his rigging. Sassiness enlivens her performance; she laughs tauntingly through floggings and hot wax. Later Sasha is bound in a standing spread-eagled position. With an irrepressible audacity, she brazenly arches her back for Lochai, pumping impudence and eroticism into the scene.

In the post-shoot debriefing an amused and perplexed Lochai wants to know why Sasha giggles in situations that sometimes cause other girls distress. "Because it eggs people on" is the coquettish answer. Her play partner will hit her harder, she says, driving her to the next level. Sasha loves being flogged on her back. It "feels good" and if the dominant is "really intense" with his work, the experience morphs into a form of meditation. "I'm submissive. I like the pain ... I get pleasure from the way that it turns other people on," she explains, plus it releases stress and accumulated emotions. "I can take an immense amount of marking [and] when I walk away from a session I feel a hundred times lighter. It really is just pleasurable for me."

What would Sasha tell others who might have a fascination about the BDSM lifestyle? She is direct, unwavering and reflective of Peter Acworth's mission.

"Don't be afraid of your fetish, enjoy it and embrace it."[17]

A *Kink* shoot is a stark contrast to traditional female friendly erotic films, but is no different in its respect for women. Recalling her first *Public Disgrace* shoot, Tara Lynn Foxx comments she had "a wonderful time." The scene was "empowering," though an audience member stepped over the line and Princess Donna halted the action, asking Tara if she wanted to continue. "Amazing," Tara says, "most people would have just kept shooting." Impressed with Donna's respect for her boundaries, Tara ranks the experience as "awesome."

Kink rarely loses sight of model care. BDSM interposed with hardcore sex is tough on the body. Breaks are necessary. Shae Simon describes the crew's reaction to her exhaustion during a shoot. They insisted she wear her flip-flops to avoid the concrete floor and made sure she kept her energy level up. "They always have granola bars and juices for us," Shea says, "They are so on top of it." Jiz Lee and Casey Calvert voice similar praise. Jiz appreciates comfort items such as "food, apple juice, gum, tooth-brushes." Robes and disposable slippers are a nicety because the basement is chilly. Casey praises *Kink* for taking care of models far better than any other company. They "have everything from makeup and wardrobe to a fully stocked bathroom," she says, not to mention their "amazing sandwiches."[18]

Safewords are the stock in trade of BDSM and *Kink* encourages performers to use them. Models can break the action, regain their composure and resume if they desire. Payton Bell explains that the intense stimulation of filming raises her emotional level. Tension begs to be released and tears flow, a common occurrence unrelated to distress or pain. Sexuality is brain based and performers report experiencing an overwhelming arousal and excitement that by any measure confounds the viewer's perspective. During a *Device Bondage* shoot Sasha Lexing remembers she began to cry when the director was pushing her limits. Her outburst was an invigo-rating "emotional release" and she didn't want to stop. The crew expressed concern but Sasha insists, "I was laughing at the same time I was crying," and assured everyone she was just fine.[19]

Performers sometimes end a shoot because it exceeds what they anticipated. This can happen with girls who show up at the Armory because their agent insisted they take the booking. At other times, the model may not want to be there at all. Bobbi Starr confesses she has difficulty working with performers who'd rather be someplace else, pointing out that she does nothing "that would warrant them using a safeword." Casey Calvert supports Bobbi's observation. She is openly critical of performers who accept a *Kink* booking when they have no feel for the fetish. "LA porn girls," as she calls them, arrive at the Armory "solely for the paycheck." Their experience tumbles downward because they "don't even know what BDSM is," the Florida native scoffs. Quickly "overwhelmed," they become fearful and lose control of the situation because "their bodies can't take the physical stress."

On the other hand, performers can experience real discomfort during a shoot, as Casey implies, particularly if suspension is involved. "Muscle strain is common," Bobbi says. Stress on the joints can create shoulder and hip pain. As the endorphin rush wears off, the pain becomes more acute, necessitating a halt. Especially risky are seasoned performers who refuse to take a timeout. "There are girls who are vets that should call their safewords but don't out of pride or competition," Bobbi states, putting pressure on director and crew to monitor the shoot closely.

Safewords are rare for James Mogul because he has developed "filters" to read what is happening with a performer. Asking "lots of questions" facilitates communication, he says. Occasionally a safeword may come from a newbie who is not giving any "signals" that her personal "red zone" is approaching. Even then, he comments, it's "nothing alarming." With Casey Calvert there are no worries. A James Mogul shoot produces soreness after the first day, she says, and a lot of hurt by the end of Day Four. Though most models are glad to wrap things up by then, Casey is different. It was "really sad to have to go home," the true masochist says with disappointment because her energy level remained high.[20]

The BDSM play scene can be a heady experience. By giving up all responsibility and trusting another person, an accomplished submissive's neurochemistry can produce an altered state of consciousness known as "subspace." Dominants are always pressured to keep an eye on the scene. A sub's physical and emotional stress can slowly melt away, producing exhilaration that blocks safewords. *Kink*'s directors frequently check on a model's coherence, a touch, a whisper in the ear, to insure everything is going well. Limits are respected. Dana DeArmond, who now switches, underscores that topping is "mentally stressful." The need to plan ahead is extremely demanding because submissives must always be "aware of their surroundings," she says.

For seasoned bondage models, filming can border on the transcendental. Tara Lynn Foxx characterizes a *Kink* shoot as a "mindfuck." She loves to push her boundaries and believes the company offers a self-discovery found nowhere else in adult film. However, "mindfuck" is determined by a girl's psychological parameters. Self-identified pain devotees like Casey Calvert sometimes reserve the rarified state for their personal lives, preferring to stay in control during a professional shoot. Casey wants to know what is coming because if she enters subspace and her cognizance escapes her, she might get hurt. *Kink*'s "responsible directors," Casey says, are careful enough to not "mess up a girl's head," something she appreciates.

The pre- and post-shoot interviews are designed to reinforce the consensual play of a *Kink* shoot. Central to a shoot's success is the model's checklist that is reviewed before filming begins. Emphasizing "It NEVER gets violated," Casey Calvert says the document is several pages and covers anything that "could potentially happen." Reinforcing the checklist's importance, Payton Bell points out constructing a scene that meets her expectations and respects her limits makes *Kink* unparalleled. "They're really here for me," she says.

After her scene is filmed, the model takes a short timeout before reappearing on camera for debriefing. Chatting with the director, the performer enumerates what gave her pleasure and comments on whatever she found objectionable. Striving for transparency, there is no script for the post-shoot interview. Peter Acworth insists everyone talk freely. The message is upfront: everything was agreed upon in this snapshot of a BDSM fantasy. Skeptics notwithstanding, it appears genuine.

Part of *Kink's* transparency is the company's Model Rights, a document posted online. To be woman friendly is more than a paycheck; it involves a secure on set environment that protects the performer's health and safety. Persuading a girl to go beyond her stated guidelines is off limits because emotional and physical arousal can influence a model to "agree to something she previously didn't want to do," Peter Acworth says.[21]

Protective barriers is a valued model right. *Kink* maintained a condom mandatory policy until 2006. Performers now have options and are not pressured to go bareback. If they choose the safer sex route, there is "no debate, it's a condom shoot," Peter Acworth says. Also, performers who insist on condoms never face a rehire risk. An unscientific review of *Kink* shoots reveals about a third of participants decide on latex. *Kink* offers a display of condoms, Tara Lynn Foxx notes, and the company provides non-latex for models with allergies. Casey Calvert, who supports *Kink's* condom policy, appreciates the Armory's overall health conscious attitude. Production assistants monitor cleanliness and biohazard buckets are always present. "Everything, including rope that might have touched bodily fluids," she says, is collected and sanitized. Casey gives *Kink* the highest compliment, "I have never once felt unsafe on a *Kink* set."

Finally, *Kink* pays for blood tests, one of the few companies that does. Performers shoot for a host of studios, Peter Acworth remarks, and many companies feel they have no responsibility to reimburse test expenses, "but we always have." *Kink* also follows OSHA guidelines to maintain a safe work environment. The argument that health regulations put an undue economic burden on adult studios is not a concern at *Kink* where viewers remain loyal. Condoms apparently have little effect on their willingness to spend their dollars, an indication it is the fetish that sells.

Flags and Lights

In 2006 Peter Acworth seized a momentous opportunity to expand his company from its existing facility at the time, the "Porn Palace." He purchased the Old National Guard Armory in San Francisco's "South of Market" district. Erected in 1912 during the city's post-earthquake resurrection, the edifice was abandoned sixty years later and sat derelict, pockmarked with broken windows and graffiti defaced walls. The once proud sentinel was the gem Peter sought. Its 200,000 square foot interior offered a dungeon-like underground that beckoned to be converted into fantasy sets and an expansive top floor where an English manor house of bondage and pleasure could be recreated.

The Moorish Revival fortress dwarfs the neighborhood just as a medieval castle dominated its surrounding countryside. With a brown brick façade and corner turrets resembling defense towers, the Castle, as it is sometimes called, is bathed in the decadence appropriate for the BDSM imagination. Possessing a look of "palatial depravity," *New York Times Magazine* journalist Jon Mooallem writes that the Armory offers the "exact aesthetic" that *Kink* tried to duplicate in its previous facility.[22]

The old facility's foreboding interior, a Disney Corporation acquisition, is authentically recreated at the Armory. Queried about the Disney connection, Peter Acworth recounts that *Kink* constructed a dungeon out of "molds which came from the Disney scene shop." With a twinkle in his eye, he adds *Kink* has a "history of collaboration" with the Disney people. Bondage meets Cinderella and Snow White.

The transition into the Armory was not hassle free. The Mission District is one of San Francisco's seedier areas. Street hookers, homelessness, substance abuse and property destruction plague the neighborhood. Once the private sale was complete, *Kink* quietly began shooting until the media caught wind of the story. Suddenly the citizen alarm sounded; opposition mobilized. Because no exterior changes except for beautification were planned, the city was powerless to mollify public concern other than listen politely in an open forum. To mitigate apprehension about its presence, *Kink* announced its plan to replace windows, clean up the exterior, increase building security and install outdoor lighting, essential in a neighborhood inundated with vandalism.[23]

The citizen gathering experienced a moment of history revisited. Among the speakers was Melissa Farley, anti-porn feminist zealot from the old sex wars days. Pulling out a photo of Abu Ghraib prison torture, she compared it to a *Kink* shoot. Typical of vintage WAP and WAVPM slide shows, Farley sought to indict BDSM porn as violence against women. Displaying a *Wired Pussy* still, Farley suggested performer participation was non-consensual and abuse was rampant. Preferring assumptions and preconceived notions, she spoke with no one connected to the company, Peter Acworth remembers. He explained to the city commission that performers appreciate filming for *Kink*. The work environment is positive and models are well compensated with the benefit of government mandated worker protection laws.[24]

Kink's owner believes the company is a boon to the Mission neighborhood. The block was "very dark, a frightening area to walk around at night," he says. *Kink* now protects its investment with twenty-four hour lights and security. To accommodate the homeless, security personnel open the roll-up door each night. Local residents "feel there's been a definite improvement," Peter Acworth says, pointing out that flags on the turrets are awash in brightness. "This corner of 'The Mission,'" he boasts, is "safer."

Nevertheless, images and myths persist. Like China's

Forbidden City, the Armory dominates its neighbors and filming remains mysterious though the pornographer's door is open. The public may peek, or if bold enough, walk into a world that is not what it seems. Securing the status of an ethical, performer friendly sanctuary in a morally questionable industry is still a work in progress. But a pornography business and a neighborhood can coexist in an accepting environment.

Today the Armory is vibrant with a second renaissance fueled by an entrepreneur's vision. It is also a fortification and an outreach, shielding its inhabitants from the barbarians at the gates, those who accuse and vilify, while reinforcing the friendships that build *Kink*'s worldwide community.

A Cyberspace Community

Peter Acworth's interactive product lives in cyberspace. *Kink* members are offered live events and can join a chat room that obliges consumer desires when possible. An omnipresent computerized voice announces viewer requests and accommodations are made provided suggestions are within each performer's pre-established boundaries.

A live *Device Bondage* shoot is classic *Kink*. Viewers converse directly with the models as they are being fitted to the contraptions that will restrain them. Dressed in black jumpsuits, workmen secure metal grips and harnesses to the performer's dimensions. In various states of undress, the girls banter about their favorite shoots and their private lives. Slowly locking models into sexually seductive positions, the crew frequently checks to assure comfort is maintained. When the show is underway the "victims" are appropriately disciplined according to member interests. The set is in constant flux, creating a surreal viewing experience. Bondage positions change necessitating down time; performers are reconfigured while the creepy, haunting computer voice overrides the entire show.

Kink has a reality TV/webcam flavor that combines the casual and the bizarre. Site users watch fetishes come alive in an ambiance that is extraordinary, yet seemingly routine. Sometimes the viewer is distracted by the busyness around the models, especially on *Public Disgrace* and *Device Bondage* episodes. Conversation resembles party chitchat and extroverted performers can take control of a show. When the pace slows, the viewer gets the urge to jump in and lend a hand to move things along. Members comment on what they like and dislike, just as the models do in post-shoot interviews. On set or online, everyone is involved, creating a community that stretches around the globe.

A *Kink* shoot is an erotic interplay and a psychological composition, a drama steeped in heavy doses of multitasking. Proficient in acrobatic bondage positions, sexual performance and emotional coping skills, over 1400 models have filmed at the Armory. Popular girls frequently revisit the facility with feminist performers accumulating almost a thousand shoots among them, Lorelei Lee at 300 and Bobbi Starr with 250 leading the group. Their repeated appearances cultivate the atmosphere Peter Acworth strives to achieve because *Kink* is about professional relationships and performer well-being.

Mentioning that an Armory shoot is "almost like a real movie set," Chanel Preston praises *Kink* as "the most professional company" she has encountered in her career and she understands why. "They want people to come to work for them," she says, and they know "not everyone shoots BDSM," so their reputation is integral to their success. To produce the "high volume" of shoots they need, Chanel notes, everyone has to be comfortable. That means an efficient operation that emphasizes performer respect, first and foremost.[25]

And, it shows. Jiz Lee remarks *Kink* is "very professional" and "transparent" in dealing with models. Dana DeArmond appreciates the Armory's environment. They "aren't shady" and "don't try to trick you into anything." Performers can make more money in Southern California, but *Kink* is family. Shae Simon, a diminutive local girl who is literally and figuratively distant from Porn Valley A-listers, reveres the Armory as "a comfort zone, a safe place for all of us." Payton Bell, another local who films as a submissive, appreciates the community atmosphere. "I'm working with people who know who I am and want to know who I am," the former college cheerleader declares. Payton does live shows, real time events that supply "regular work" in a business where steady employment is a premium. Critical for her is the feeling of being "spoiled." During our interview, a *Kink* employee brings Payton a bottle of water and a check for her latest shoot.

A Feminist Disposition

Kink reflects the Silicon Valley corporate culture that is its neighbor. Many of the company's employees are graduates of the University of California system and its respected film school. They have 401k plans and health insurance. Taking pride in the *Kink* product, the talented workforce mirrors the diversity of San Francisco's various communities. Peter Acworth summarizes, "We're normal people in a normal business" who believe "porn can be produced respectfully and positively." Marketing expert John Sander is well compensated but could command a higher salary elsewhere, noting that "porn is not as profitable as people think." But at *Kink* he is helping a "friend build a business," an invigorating process that is preferable to laboring for distant shareholders.[26]

While many studios cling to patriarchal attitudes, there is little doubt that *Kink*'s disposition is feminist. From studying the company's shoots and talking personally with performers, I have a sense of how far feminism in pornography/erotica has come since the days of Club 90. While the sex may be edgier with health risks always an insertion away, today's model is proclaiming a personal aegis over her career, a characteristic inherited from past feminists that is coming into its own. Though doubts remain, Princess Donna answers the criticisms of anti-porn second wavers, telling them "I make porn *because* I am a feminist."[27]

Casey Calvert lays everything on the line. "Feminism is all about the right to choice," she says, pounding home her message in the unabashed, crisp staccato style of her sister feminist Dylan Ryan. "I choose to be tied up, I choose to be humiliated, I choose to be submissive, I choose to be beaten. It is *my* choice. How is that not feminist?"

* * *

With an astute business sense and a willingness to engage in a dialogue about his product, Peter Acworth removes the shroud from once forbidden fetishes, demystifying sexual preferences that operate outside our culturally validated heteronormative world. Anyone persuaded that adult film models are degraded, humiliated and abused for the viewer's deviant fantasies will find their assumptions dismissed at *Kink*. Once distant and unknowable decades ago, performers now put their personal expressions, attitudes, fetishes and foibles out there for all to examine. Candor encourages familiarity, familiarity fosters tolerance, and tolerance is the road to acceptance, a humanizing process that escapes pornography's critics who shout down the industry out of hand without knowing those involved in it.

Conclusion

Once Was

The following account is borrowed with some alterations from an article I wrote for *Adult Industry News*, June 2012.

Rumbling northward on Amtrak, I'm headed for the Big Apple. Settling into the train's swaying and clacking, I remember my first visit some years ago. A couple of pals and I ventured to the old Times Square for a taste of urban porno land, taking care to avoid winos, druggies, hookers and other assorted street people.

This time I'm following up an Annie Sprinkle invitation. Club 90 is gathering for a special event, Veronica Vera's wedding. The ladies are going to be in town for a week, their first full reunion in seventeen years. On this cool and rainy June evening, Manhattan's *Museum of Sex* on 27th and 5th Avenue is hosting the group via a panel discussion. Billed as a reunion of the "Golden Girls of Porn," it's a celebration of camaraderie and longevity.

"We stayed in porn on our own terms," Annie tells an audience of friends, admirers and the curious. Gloria Leonard nods in agreement and with her political voice proclaims that Club 90 "defied" the "bimbo" stereotype of porn women. Later during the Q&A session, an audience query on the definition of pornography gives Gloria another shot. Pornography is "a platform for the political," she asserts, reinforcing adult film as an agitator of society's moral and legal waters.

Candida Royalle stands up for a woman's right to watch porn, but approaches it through her "ambivalence" over her career as a performer. When she retired Candida knew that porn needed a remake, the infusion of a woman's voice. Out of this determination came the first feminist adult film company.

The room floats between the past and present with memories

fondly recounted. Annie Sprinkle describes her career as an "amazing journey" and updates her goal for the future. "I want to get to fifty years in sex!" she muses to amiable vocal support from the audience.

With the evening winding down and attendees milling about, among the Club 90 well wishers are old acquaintances who themselves were once the toast of the adult film industry. Observing them reunite with the five golden goddesses, my imagination retreats through the portal of time to erase the nasty joke played on all of us: age, something the young firmly believe will never happen to them. I fancy the women and their old friends in just such a room with youthful sparkle as they set up for a porn shoot. Hustling around are director, PAs, grips and cameramen. Perhaps a makeup artist is adding some final touches to faces destined for wear in a business that can grind away the years. In that moment the past and present drift together, age defeated and accomplishments measured.

This Manhattan evening wraps itself around Club 90 with confabulations where facts are hazy and musings endorsed, assuming there is unanimity of memory. Among skyscrapers and traffic punctuated with omnipresent yellow cabs, the affair negotiates the small town feel of neighbors recollecting "the good ole days" as urban sprawl consumes the land around them. The past will never be the present; but it is forever in the present, swirling below the level of consciousness. Adult film reflects such a history. The fledging enterprise that was the heyday of Club 90 is now an international business. The tentacles of companies, actors, technology and cultural mainstreaming have absorbed and eroded adult film's institutional memory. Only flickers and glimpses remain, preserved in a few who "remember when." Club 90 is representative of such a few and on this occasion a storefront museum dwarfed in an urban canyon becomes a brief glimmer of their "once was" and a celebration of their "still is."

As I head back to the train station, rain pelts ever hectic New Yorkers scurrying under umbrellas to get from here to there. The scene is a stage, a living history illuminated by lights embedded in mist and shrouded in the past, appropriate for an evening when pornography feminism is forward looking and backward reaching in search of its place in the larger narrative of American feminism.

Final Thoughts

The new century is establishing its sexual identity though the intimate garden of female liberation is not in full bloom. Old condemnations hang on. Candida Royalle believes the story of women has stagnated. Stamped into our national psyche, the double standard of "Madonna versus whore" is unwilling to validate female sexual pleasure. Social training is steeped in traditional gender roles, circumscribing female sexual behavior and persuading women to cling to hearth and home. As Candida correctly implies, women who define their own sexual agenda are quickly labeled sluts, whores and tramps.[1]

Nevertheless, a woman's reality is her sexual power and the fear it generates. A libertine miss poses a threat to the social institution of family, history tells us, challenging a morally based interpretation of domesticity that cannot be tolerated. The suppressive anchor keeping female eroticism at bay is fear, a woman's fear of humiliation for expressing her longings and society's fear that she will realize she is the only one who can truly determine her future.[2]

A sociology professor in my undergraduate years impressed upon his students that a society's power structure dictates how that culture treats those whose influence is secondary. A simple concept for me, I represented the powerful: white, middle class, male ... and heteronormative. My university legitimized the male/female binary and assumed students would do little to upend the social and political forces in place. Gay/queer students and anyone of any sort who harbored a fetish were silent. Decades later I stand before my own students whose attitudes have moved only slightly from my undergraduate years. Are women more aggressive and empowered today? Yes. Do twenty-first century females take the right to pornography and a career in adult film for granted? Without doubt, but do they *feel* more equal? I am uncertain because conservative attitudes culturally programmed in every child historically survive holocausts of storm and stress.

Pornography feminism is a voice for change because the sexual will forever be political and patriarchy will always enrage a woman's voice. The parabolic tale of Lilith, who preferred to be on top, and her rejection in favor of Eve, dutifully assigned to the bottom, is political to the core. Adam's refusal to negotiate sex with Lilith is an injustice and an insult to every woman, but it's a confrontation she is destined to lose. Because of her rebellion Lilith is driven into the fires of the mythological evil; she becomes the pornographic, stalking the night to torment men and seduce innocent children. Lilith is, if anything, the first moral panic.

Denigrated and punished because she demands equality, Lilith is conveniently replaced by a yielding and controllable version of womanhood who fares no better. The docile, yet beguiling, Eve is blamed for the expulsion from the allegorical Garden. Further punishment is inflicted and woman becomes childlike, man becomes the father and female sexuality is closeted, periodically emerging as sinful and salacious should it act on its own. The myth is emboldened and the suffering endures because civilization creates its own padded room shut out from the light of day. A culture that gives up its right to view, consume and seek pleasure in the erotic loses a part of its humanity in the name of taming immorality.

Pornography feminists are throwing off this paradigm,

replacing it with a sexual and political freedom that refuses to legitimate a Victorian legacy and its "Secret Museum." Whether under the feminist label or some yet undefined vision, every woman has the right to step into the erotic and become as powerful as she wants to be.

* * *

The adult film people I met survive and often prosper in an industry that sits on the edge of whatever we call a normalized society. This is particularly true of Bobbi Starr, who is the muse for this book. I owe Bobbi a debt of gratitude for her time in Las Vegas when an inquisitive academic made his way to the *Evil Angel* booth uncertain of what he would find.

Endotes

Introduction: Neglected Stepchildren

1. Wendy McElroy, *XXX: A Woman's Right to Pornography* (New York: St. Martin's Press, 1995), ix.

2. Veronica Hart, interview in Las Vegas, January 19, 2012.

3. Whitney Strub, *Perversion for Profit: The Politics of Pornography and the Rise of the New Right* (New York: Columbia University Press, 2011), 251; McElroy, *XXX*, vii.

4. Ellen Willis, "Toward a Feminist Sexual Revolution," in *No More Nice Girls: Countercultural Essays*, ed. Ellen Willis (Hanover and London: Wesleyan University Press, 1992), 28; Carmine Sarracino and Kevin M. Scott, *The Porning of America: The Rise of Porn Culture, What It Means, and Where We Go from Here* (Boston: Beacon Press, 2008), xviii.

5. Annie Sprinkle and Gloria Leonard, A reunion of the "Golden Girls of Pornography" at the Museum of Sex, New York City, June 6, 2012. For an overview of the event see Rich Moreland's "When New York was Grand," *Adult Industry News*, July 17, 2012. http://ainews.com/Archives/Story 21539.phtml.

6. Jiz Lee, "Sleeping with Cissies, Coming out as Queer," *Jiz Lee Blog*, September 23, 2010. Accessed October 6, 2010, http://jizlee.com/wordpress/.

7. Dylan Ryan, interview in Toronto, April 8, 2010.

Remember Where You Started

1. The shoot was titled *Public Gangbang 4* and posted on the company's website, September 5, 2008. It was re-released on March 14, 2012 as *Bobbi Starr Helpless and Destroyed by Cocks and Crowd*.

2. Bobbi Starr, interview in Toronto, April 15, 2011 and email to the author, February 9, 2013 and February 23, 2014.

Chapter 1: *Real* Sex Merchants

1. Al Di Lauro and Gerald Rabkin, *Dirty Movies: An Illustrated History of the Stag Film, 1915-1970* (New York: Chelsea House, 1976), 26; *Smokers I: A Free Ride* (Las Vegas, NV: Erotic Heritage Museum Film Club, Exodus Trust Archives, n.d.); John Heidenry, *What Wild Ecstasy: The Rise and Fall of the Sexual Revolution* (New York: Simon & Schuster, 1997), 50; Kenneth Turan and Stephen F. Zito, *Sinema: American Pornographic Films and the People Who Make Them* (New York: Praeger Publishers, 1974), 4.

2. David Hebditch and Nick Anning, *Porn Gold: Inside the Pornography Business* (London: Faber and Faber Limited, 1988), 23-26; Dave Thompson, *Black and White and Blue: Adult Cinema from the Victorian Age to the VCR* (Toronto: ECW Press, 2007), 78-79.

3. Di Lauro and Rabkin, 26; Thompson, 119-20; Thomas Waugh, "Homosociality in the Classical American Stag Film: Off-Screen, On-Screen," in *Porn Studies*, ed. Linda Williams (Durham and London: Duke University Press, 2004), 136.

4. Eric Schlosser, *Reefer Madness: Sex, Drugs, and Cheap Labor in the American Black Market* (New York: Houghton Mifflin Company, 2004), 126; Thompson, 43, 75.

5. Di Lauro and Rabkin, 60-61.

6. Constance Penley, "Crackers and Whackers: The White Trashing of Porn," in *Porn Studies*, ed. Linda Williams (Durham and London: Duke University Press, 2004), 314-15.

7. Waugh, 136; Di Lauro and Rabkin, 26.

8. Whitney Strub, *Perversion for Profit: The Politics of Pornography and the Rise of the New Right* (New York: Columbia University Press, 2011), 86-88; Eric Schaefer, *"Bold! Daring! Shocking! True! A History of the Exploitation Films, 1919-1959"* (Durham and London: Duke University Press, 1999), 153.

9. Eddie Muller and Daniel Faris, *Grindhouse: The Forbidden World of "Adults Only" Cinema* (New York: St. Martin's

Griffin, 1996), 9; Schaefer, 2-6; Linda Williams, *Screening Sex* (Durham and London: Duke University Press, 2008), 88.

10. Schaefer, 119, 132; Muller and Faris, 17. During my 2010 visit to the Center for Sex and Culture in San Francisco, curator Dr. Robert Lawrence showed me some exploitation film posters, explaining that local authorities would determine what was acceptable for advertising. Anything too risqué was concealed with a black ink makeover.

11. Muller and Faris, 30; Schaefer, 234-35, 261-64.

12. Muller and Faris, 25.

13. Muller and Faris, 42; Turan and Zito, 41; Schaefer, 69.

14. Turan and Zito, 5; Muller and Faris, 43.

15. Di Lauro and Rabkin, 55; Thompson, 105.

16. Muller and Faris, 7; Schaefer, 305.

17. Chuck Kleinhans, "The Change from Film to Video Pornography: Implications for Analysis," in *Pornography: Film and Culture*, ed. Peter Lehman (Brunswick, N.J. and London: Rutgers University Press, 2006), 156; Legs McNeil and Jennifer Osborne, *The Other Hollywood: The Uncensored Oral History of the Porn Film Industry* (New York: HarperCollins Publishers, 2005), 10-11; Muller and Faris, *Grindhouse,* 36-39.

18. Carmine Sarracino and Kevin M. Scott, *The Porning of America: The Rise of Porn Culture, What It Means, and Where We Go from Here* (Boston: Beacon Press, 2008), 58-59.

19. Schaefer, 312, 322, 324.

20. Schaefer, 300, 333; Turan and Zito, 7-8.

21. Turan and Zito, 15.

22. Schaefer, 8-9; Turan and Zito, 10-11, 31.

23. Turan and Zito, 33.

24. Schaefer, 326.

25. Di Lauro and Rabkin, 72-73; Hebditch and Anning, 18; Luke Ford, *A History of X: 100 Years of Sex in Film* (Amherst, NY: Prometheus Books, 1999), 16; John Hubner, *Bottom Feeders:*

From Free Love to Hard Core, The Rise and Fall of Counterculture Heroes Jim and Artie Mitchell (New York: Doubleday, 1992), 56; *Smokers II: A Smart Aleck Part 1* (Las Vegas, NV: Erotic Heritage Museum Film Club, Exodus Trust Archives, n.d.), DVD; Penley, 316; Jim Holliday, *Only the Best: Jim Holliday's Adult Video Almanac and Trivia Treasury* (Van Nuys, CA: Cal Vista Direct Ltd, 1986), 194.

26. Gregg Barrios, "Risque Business: The complicated life of Texas' most famous stripper," *The Texas Observer*, January 17, 2011, Accessed August 14, 2011, http://www.texasobserver. org/culture/risqu%C3%A9-business; *Smokers II: A Smart Aleck Part 1*.

27. Muller and Faris, 60.

28. Edward de Grazia, *Girls Lean Back Everywhere: The Law of Obscenity and the Assault on Genius* (New York: Vintage Books, 1992), 321-25; *Jacobellis v. Ohio*, 378 US 184 (1964).

29. *Stanley v. Georgia*, 394 U.S. 557 (1969).

30. de Grazia, 549.

31. Susie Bright, *Susie Bright's Erotic Screen: The Golden Hardcore & the Shimmering Dyke-Core* (The Erotic Screen: Bright Stuff, 2011) Kindle edition, part 1.

32. Turan and Zito, *Sinema*, 21, 24; Muller and Faris, 128.

33. Bright, part 1; Erika Lust, *Good Porn: A Woman's Guide*, trans. X.P. Callahan (Berkeley, California: Seal Press, 2010), 92.

34. Muller and Faris, 101-103; Sarracino and Scott, 78.

35. Muller and Faris, 95.

36. Turan and Zito, 45-46.

37. Turan and Zito, 136; Holliday, 14; *Mona: The Virgin Nymph* (1970), (1997: Something Weird Video, Special Video) Accessed 19 August, 2012, http://xhamster.com/movies/ 738363/mona_the_virgin_nymph_1970.html.

38. *Mona* (1970).

39. Muller and Faris, 135.

40. Hubner, 90.

41. Gonzo pornography relies heavily on sex and de-emphasizes plot (models appear as themselves). In our interview on January 18, 2012, John Stagliano explained that decades ago he drifted away from features (big budget film with plot and script) to shoot independent scenes. As a result, his popular "Buttman" series became gonzo's defining example. The girl looks squarely at the camera while performing sexually, sometimes on the shooter himself. Today gonzo is broadly defined as anything that "isn't a feature," Stagliano said. Paul Fishbein, founder of *Adult Video News*, credits the term gonzo to *AVN* editor Gene Ross. In a February 4, 2012 email, Fishbein recalls that in the 1980s a film genre we would call "reality porn" today gained momentum. In tribute to Hunter Thompson's gonzo journalism, Ross suggested the name for the new filming style. "It stuck," Fishbein remembers, quickly becoming "the industry standard." Eric Schaefer, "Gauging a Revolution: 16 mm Film and the Rise of the Pornographic Feature," in *Porn Studies*, ed. by Linda Williams (Durham and London: Duke University Press, 2004), 376-377.

42. Turan and Zito, 78, 128; Eric Schaefer, "Gauging," 381.

43. Turan and Zito, 80-81, 132; Holliday, 14; Heidenry, 85; Hebditch, 192.

Chapter 2: A "Gaze" of Their Own

1. Linda Williams, *Screening Sex* (Durham and London: Duke University Press, 2008), 347 ftn; "Playboy magazine back issue August 1973," *Downtown: The Unbound Magazine*, January 11, 2012, Accessed January 11, 2012, http://www.dtmagazine.com/cmopg1924/pb873.html.

2. Kenneth Turan and Stephen F. Zito, *Sinema: American Pornographic Films and the People who Make Them* (New York: Praeger Publishers, 1974), 179; Veronica Hart, interview in Las Vegas, January 19, 2012. In our interview in Los Angeles

on October 5, 2012, agent Chris Cane claims a girl can make a substantial amount of money if she is willing to work hard for three to four years.

3. John Hubner, *Bottom Feeders: From Free Love to Hard Core, The Rise and Fall of Counterculture Heroes Jim and Artie Mitchell* (New York: Doubleday, 1992), 163-64, 166, 168.

4. Georgina Spelvin, *The Devil Made Me Do It* (Los Angeles: Little Red Hen Books, 2006), 32, 54; Georgina Spelvin's remarks are from emails to author, December 2, 2009 and January 23, 2010 and an interview in Los Angeles, October 4, 2012.

5. Hubner, 238-41.

6. Veronica Hart's remarks are from an interview in Las Vegas, January 19, 2012 and emails to the author, December 11, 2009 and September 24, 2013.

7. Susie Bright, *Susie Bright's Erotic Screen: The Golden Hardcore & the Shimmering Dyke-Core* (The Erotic Screen: Bright Stuff, 2011), Kindle Edition, introduction; Nina Hartley, interview in Las Vegas, January 18, 2012.

8. See Walter Kendrick's *The Secret Museum* (New York: Viking Penguin Inc., 1987) for a look at Victorian attitudes toward pornography and the development of the secret museum.

9. Robert J. Stoller, *Porn: Myths of the Twentieth Century* (New Haven: Yale University Press, 1991), 216; Robert J. Stoller and I. S. Levine, *Coming Attractions: The Making of an X-Rated Video* (New Haven and London: Yale University Press, 1993), 210, 215, 220-21.

10. Jill Nagle, "First Ladies of Feminist Porn: A Conversation with Candida Royalle and Debi Sundahl," in *Whores and Other Feminists*, ed. Jill Nagle (New York and London: Routledge, 1997), 157, 159; Legs McNeil and Jennifer Osborne, *The Other Hollywood; The Uncensored Oral History of the Porn Film Industry* (New York: HarperCollins Publishers, 2005), 373.

11. Unless otherwise cited, Annie Sprinkle's remarks are from emails to the author, October 15 and December 31, 2009, June 28, 2012 and January 21, 2013; McNeil and Osborne, 371.

12. Annie Sprinkle, *Post-Porn Modernist: My Twenty-Five Years as a Multimedia Whore* (San Francisco: Cleis Press, 1998), 13, 17; Annie Sprinkle, Keynote Presentation, "Visions of Feminism" Conference (American University, Washington, D.C. April 4, 2009).

13. John Heidenry, *What Wild Ecstasy: The Rise and Fall of the Sexual Revolution* (New York: Simon & Schuster, 1997), 155.

14. Annie Sprinkle, "Annie's Films," Accessed June 16, 2011, http://anniesprinkle.org/about/films.html; Annie Sprinkle, "Visions."

15. Sprinkle, 153; Unless otherwise cited, Gloria Leonard's remarks are from a telephone interview, October 23, 2009 and emails to the author, December 24, 2011, April 16, May 31 and June 4, 2012.

16. Elizabeth M. Stephens, "Annie Sprinkle: Cumulative Biography," n.d.

17. Jim Holliday, *Only the Best: Jim Holliday's Adult Video Almanac and Trivia Treasury* (Van Nuys, CA: Cal Vista Direct Ltd, 1986), 111.

18. Annette Fuentes and Margaret Schrage, "Veronica Hart, Gloria Leonard, Kelly Nichols, Candida Royalle, Annie Sprinkle, and Veronica Vera interviewed: Deep Inside Porn Stars," *Jump Cut: A Review of Contemporary Media*, 32 (April 1987), 41.

19. McNeil and Osborne, 372; Sprinkle, 69.

20. "Franklin Furnace in Time," in *Franklin Furnace: On a Mission to Make The World Safe for Avant-Garde Art*, Accessed September 10, 2009, http://www.franklinfurnace.org/top.html.; Arlene Raven, "Star-Studded: Looking Beneath the Surface: Deep Inside Porn Stars," *High Performance* 28

(1984), 25-27; Sprinkle, 150.

21. Sprinkle, 150.

22. Unless otherwise cited, Candida Royalle's remarks are from an email to the author, December 11, 2009 and a telephone interview, April 28, 2010; Raven, "Star-Studded," 25.

23. Shannon Bell, *Reading, Writing, and Rewriting the Prostitute Body* (Bloomington and Indianapolis: Indiana University Press, 1994), 144-47.

24. Ibid.

25. "Franklin Furnace in Time"; Edward de Grazia, *Girls Lean Back Everywhere: The Law of Obscenity and the Assault on Genius* (New York: Vintage Books, 1992), 660-62, 665.

26. Whitney Strub, *Perversion for Profit: The Politics of Pornography and the Rise of the New Right* (New York: Columbia University Press, 2011), 136; "Franklin Furnace in Time"; de Grazia, 662-65.

27. Ellen Willis, "Hard to Swallow: *Deep Throat*," in *Beginning to See the Light: Sex, Hope, and Rock-and-Roll*, ed. Ellen Willis (Hanover and London: Wesleyan University Press, 1992), 71, 73-74.

28. Wendy McElroy, *XXX: A Woman's Right to Pornography* (New York: St. Martin's Press, 1995), 171-72; Ann G. Sabo, "A Vision of New Porn: How Women are Revisiting Porn to Match a Time of Greater Gender Equality," in *Generation P? Youth, Gender, and Pornography*, eds. Sven-Axel Mansson, Lotta Lofgren-Martenson and Susanne V. Knudsen (Copenhagen: Danish University of Education Press, 2007), 224.

29. McElroy, 172.

30. Sabo, 226-27; Linda Williams, *Hard Core, Power, Pleasure, and the "Frenzy of the Visible"*; (Berkeley, Los Angeles, London: University of California Press, 1999), 250-52.

31. Williams, *Hard Core*, 253, 261.

32. McElroy, 172-73; Bright, part 1.

33. Holliday, 79; An "inside" movie focuses on one performer

and her interpretation of the sex she has on film.

34. Holliday, 115; Sprinkle, 33.

35. Sprinkle, 34; Annie Sprinkle, *"Annie's Commentary," Deep Inside Annie Sprinkle, Disc 2* (Evart Enterprises, 2006), distributed by Video-X-Pix, DVD.

36. Sprinkle, *"Annie's Commentary."*

37. Ibid.

38. Ibid.

39. Louis Landeira, "Porno for Women," *GQ Spanish*, February 5, 2009, 5.

Chapter 3: My Body, My Rules

1. Georgina Spelvin, emails to the author, March 23 and 27, 2010.

2. Eric Schlosser, *Reefer Madness: Sex, Drugs, and Cheap Labor in the American Black Market* (New York: Houghton Mifflin Company, 2004), 181-82; Harris Gaffin, *Hollywood Blue: The Tinseltown Pornographers* (London: B.T. Batsford Ltd, 1997), 31, 43.

3. Unless otherwise cited, Nina Hartley's remarks are from an email to the author, September 28, 2009 and an interview in Las Vegas on January 18, 2012.

4. Ryan Shaffer, "Atheism, Ethics, and Pornography: An Interview with Nina Hartley," *The Humanist: A Magazine of Critical Inquiry and Social Concern*, September/October 2010, Accessed July 6, 2011, http://thehumanist.org/humanist /10_sept_oct/Shaffer.html.

5. Robert J. Stoller and I. S. Levine, *Coming Attractions: The Making of an X-Rated Video* (New Haven and London: Yale University Press, 1993), 212.

6. Unless otherwise cited, Veronica Hart remarks are from an interview in Las Vegas, January 19, 2012 and Gloria Leonard's remarks are from an email to the author, April 16, 2012 and a telephone interview, October 23, 2009.

7. Drucilla Cornell, *The Imaginary Domain: Abortion, Pornography & Sexual Harassment* (New York & London: Routledge, 1995), 97, 116.

8. The independent contractor issue is examined in the following: De Cesare, M.R. (2006), "Rxxx resolving problems of the performer health and safety in the adult film industry," *Southern California Law Review* 79: 667-710; and Wilmet, Holly J. (1998-1999), "Naked Feminism: The Unionization of the Adult Entertainment Industry," *Journal of Gender, Social Policy & the Law* 7: 465-498.

9. Wendy McElroy, *XXX, A Woman's Right to Pornography* (New York: St. Martin's Press, 1995), 4-5, 40; John Stagliano's remarks are from an interview in Las Vegas, January 19, 2012.

10. The remarks of Jesse Jane, Jessa Rhodes, Tasha Reign, and Chanel Preston are from interviews in Las Vegas, January 15-17, 2014.

11. Carol Queen, email to the author, June 16, 2010.

Chapter 4: Her Own Amateur Porn Movie

1. E. A. Armstrong and S. M. Crage, "Movements and Memory: The Making of the Stonewall Myth," *American Sociological Review* 71, 5 (2006): 728, 737, EBSCOhost; D. Carter, "Stonewall Stories," *Advocate* 1027/1028 (2009): 94, EBSCOhost.

2. John Heidenry, *What Wild Ecstasy: The Rise and Fall of the Sexual Revolution* (New York: Simon & Schuster, 1997), 102-103; Sewell Chan, "Police Records Document Start of Stonewall Uprising," *CityroomBlog*, June 22, 2009, Accessed June 24, 2011, http://cityroom.blogs.nytimes.com/2009/06/22 police-records-document; Armstrong and Crage, "Movements," 737; Carter, 94.

3. S. Dooley, *Advocate*, 941 (2005): 36, EBSCOhost; Armstrong and Crage, 737-38; Carter, 94.

4. Diane Silver, "Stonewall's Unfinished Revolution," *Lesbian News*, 34,12 (2009): 14, EBSCOhost.

5. Heidenry, 18-19, 22, 34; Nan D. Hunter, "The Pornography Debate in Context" in *Caught Looking: feminism, pornography, and censorship*, eds. Katie Ellis, et al. (Seattle: The Real Comet Press, 1988), 26.

6. Alice Echols, *Daring to Be Bad: Radical Feminism in America, 1967-1975* (Minneapolis: University of Minnesota Press, 1989), 382; Lynn Chancer, "Pornography Debates Reconsidered," *New Politics*, 2,1 (1988): 73.

7. Wendy Kaminer, "Feminists Against the First Amendment," *The Atlantic*, November 1992, 1, Accessed August 24, 2009, http://theatlantic.com/doc/199211/feminism-censorship/2.

8. Echols, 239; Wendy McElroy, *XXX, A Woman's Right to Porn* (New York: St. Marin's Press, 1995), 84; Rosemarie Tong, *Feminist Thought: A More Comprehensive Introduction*, 2nd ed. (Boulder, Colorado: Westview Press, 1998), 42-43.

9. Tong, 70; Susie Bright, *Sexwise* (Santa Cruz, California: Bright Stuff, 2008), 145.

10. Gayle Rubin, "The Leather Menace: Comments on Politics and S/M" in *Coming to Power: Writings and Graphics on Lesbian S/M*, eds. Members of Samois, Lesbian/Feminist S/M Organization, 3rd ed. (Boston: Alyson Publications, 1987), 212-214; Ellen Willis, "Toward a Feminist Sexual Revolution," in *No More Nice Girls: Countercultural Essays*, ed. Ellen Willis (Hanover and London: Wesleyan University Press, 1992), 26-27.

11. Hunter, 27; Laura Lederer, "Introduction," in *Take Back the Night: Women on Pornography*, ed. Laura Lederer (New York: William Morrow and Company, Inc., 1980), 15; Alison Lee, "The new face of porn: a new generation of feminists are reclaiming porn as consumers and producers." *This Magazine* November-December 2008, 2-3, Accessed April 4, 2009, http://thismagazine.ca/issues/2008/11/newporn.php.

For an further look at the anti-porn feminist argument, the reader is directed to Andrea Dworkin's *Pornography: Men Possessing Women* (1981) and Catharine MacKinnon's *Only Words* (1993).

12. Hunter, 28; Whitney Strub, *Perversion for Profit: The Politics of Pornography and the Rise of the New Right* (New York: Columbia University Press, 2011), 240.

13. Lee, 3; Verta Taylor and Leila J. Rupp, "Women's Culture and Lesbian Feminist Activism: a Reconsideration of Cultural Feminism," *Signs*, 19,1 (1993), 33, ftn 3; Carol S. Vance, "More Danger, More Pleasure: A Decade after the Barnard Sexuality Conference," in *Pleasure and Danger: Exploring Female Sexuality*, ed. Carol S. Vance (London: Pandora Press, 1992), xxi; Carol S. Vance, "Epilogue," in *Pleasure and Danger: Exploring Female Sexuality* ed. Carol S. Vance (London: Pandora Press, 1992) 431; Tong, 28.

14. Vance, "More Danger," xxii.

15. Marcia Pally, *Sex & Sensibility: Reflections on Forbidden Mirrors and the Will to Censor* (Hopewell, New Jersey: The Ecco Press, 1994), 16.

16. Nadine Strossen, *Defending Pornography: Free Speech, Sex, and the Fight for Women's Rights* (New York: New York University Press, 2000), 77-79.

17. Vance, "More Danger," xxvi-xxvii; Strub, 255. Anthony Comstock was U.S. Postal Inspector who fought obscenity from 1873 to 1915.

18. Edward de Grazia, *Girls Lean Back Everywhere: The Law of Obscenity and the Assault on Genius* (New York: Vintage Books, 1992), 552; *The Report of the Commission on Obscenity and Pornography.* 2nd print. (New York, NY: Bantam Books, 1970), 31, 59, 61; Strub, 133.

19. *The Report of the Commission*, 456, 458, 461, 464, 489; Strub, 83, 129, 131; Philip Shenon, "Justice Dept. Pornography study Finds Material Tied to Violence," *The New York Times*, May

14, 1986, A17; Eric Schlosser, *Reefer Madness: Sex, Drugs, and Cheap Labor in the American Black Market* (New York, NY: Houghton Mifflin Company, 2004), 133-35; de Grazia, 559.

20. Richard Nixon, *381-Statement About the Report of the Commission on Obscenity and Pornography*, October 24, 1970, Accessed February 21, 2011, http://www.presidency.ucsb.edu/ws/index.php?pid=2759.

21. Veronica Vera, "Ms. Vera Goes to Washington," *Adam Magazine*, April 1985, 29, 4, 29.

22. Veronica Vera, email to the author, April 20, 2009.

23 Vera, "Ms. Vera," 28.

24. *U.S. Congress, Senate Committee on the Judiciary United States Senate, Juvenile Justice Subcommittee, Effect of Pornography on Women and Children.* Hearings. *Oversight on Pornography, Magazines of a Variety of Courses, Inquiring into the Subject of Their Impact on Child Abuse, Child Molestation, and Problems of Conduct Against Women,* 99 Cong., 2 sess., October 30 1984. 317-18.

25. Ibid. 319.

26. Ibid. 320.

27. Heidenry, 341; Strub, 142-43.

28. *Final Report of the Attorney General's Commission on Pornography* (Nashville: Rutledge Hill Press, 1986), 465-70; David Jennings, *Skinflicks: The Inside Story of the X-Rated Video Industry* (Bloomington, IN: 1st Books Library, 2000), 342; Richard Stengel, "Sex Busters," *Time Magazine*, July 21, 1986, 4, Accessed February 1, 2011, http://www.time.com/time/magazine/article/0,9171,961781,00.html.

29. Brian Wilcox, "Pornography, Social Science, and Politics: When Research and Ideology Collide," *American Psychologist*, 42 (1987): 941; Heidenry, 332; Andy Pasztor, "Pornography Commission's Report Calls for Nationwide Crackdown on Obscenity," *Wall Street Journal*, July 10, 1986, 1. ProQuest.

30. Wilcox, 941-942; *Final Report*, 205.

31. *Final Report*, 471.

32. Strossen, 187-88; Carol S. Vance, "Negotiating sex and gender in the Attorney General's Commission on Pornography," in *Sex Exposed: "Sexuality and the Pornography Debate,"* eds. Lynn Segal and Mary McIntosh (New Brunswick, NJ: Rutgers University Press, 1993), 47.

33. Strossen, 187; de Grazia, 584, 586; Vance "Negotiating Sex," 32.

34. Vance, "Negotiating Sex," 32-33; de Grazia, 586.

35. *Final Report*, 198-199.

36. Strub, 231-32; Linda Williams, *Hard Core: Power, Pleasure, and the "Frenzy of the Visible"* (Berkeley, Los Angeles, London: University of California Press, 1999), 191, 193; McElroy, 7-8; Bright, 149.

37. Williams, 16-17, 19-20.

38. Vance, "Negotiating Sex," 43.

39. Rubin, 216-17; Ellen Willis, "Toward a Feminist Sexual Revolution," in *No More Nice Girls: Countercultural Essays*, ed. Ellen Willis (Hanover and London: Wesleyan University Press, 1992), 28.

40. Kathleen Currie and Art Levine, "Whip me beat me and while you're at it cancel my N.O.W. membership—feminists war against each other over pornography," *Washington Monthly*, June 1987, 1, Accessed January 29, 2009, http://findarticles.com/p/articles/mi_m1316/is_v19/ai5010445.

41. Rubin, 217.

42. Williams, 320, ftn 14; Vance, "More Danger," xxvi; Dorchen Leidholdt, "When Women Defend Pornography," in *The Sexual Liberals and The Attack on Feminism*, eds. Dorchen Leidholdt and Janice Raymond (New York: Teachers College Press, 1990), 125-126; Wendy Stock, "Toward a Feminist Praxis of Sexuality," in *The Sexual Liberals and The Attack on Feminism*, eds. Dorchen Leidholdt and Janice Raymond (New

York: Teachers College Press, 1990), 149, 152.

43. Joan Kennedy Taylor, "Feminism for Free Expression," in *Whores and Other Feminist*, ed. Jill Nagle (New York, NY: Routledge, 1997), 256-58; "FFE Mission," *Feminists for Free Expression*, Accessed January 6, 2013, www.ffeusa.org; Marcia Pally, email to the author, August, 28, 2009.

44. Naomi Wolfe, *The Beauty Myth: How Images of Beauty are used Against Women* (New York: Harper Collins Publishers, Inc. 2002), 2.

45. Tamar Lewin, "Furor on Exhibit at Law School Splits Feminists," *The New York Times*, November 13, 1992, B16; Strossen, 212-14; Veronica Vera, "'Whoriculture' A Video by Veronica stirs up a controversy at the University of Michigan Law School," *Adam Magazine*, April 1992, 37, 4, 11.

46. Strossen, 213-14; Vera, "'Whoriculture,'" 10-12.

47. Lewin, "Furor"; Strossen, 212; Vera, "'Whoriculture,'" 11.

48. Lewin, B16.

49. Ibid.

50. Porn 'Im' Age "Ry" at University of Michigan, Accessed September 30, 2009. http:www.ed.sc.ehu.es/FileRoom/doc uments/Cases/118pornImAge.html.

Chapter 5: An Attitude, Not a Movement

1. Unless otherwise cited, the remarks of Tina Horn, Jiz Lee, Dylan Ryan and Courtney Trouble are from a roundtable interview held in Toronto, April 8, 2010.

2. Erika Lust, *Good Porn: A Woman's Guide*, trans. X. P. Callahan (Berkeley, California: Seal Press, 2010), 150.

3. J. D., "Interview with Ilana Rothman," *HotMoviesForHer.com*, September 10, 2010, Accessed August 25, 2011, http://www. hotmovieswforher.com/?s=ilana+rothman&x=25&x=25&y=1 7; Andi Zeisler, *Feminism and Pop Culture* (Berkeley, California: Seal Press, 2008), 133.

4. Jessica Valenti, *Full Frontal Feminism: A Young Woman's Guide*

to *Why Feminism Matters* (Berkeley CA: Seal Press, 2007), 167, 180; Kristin Rowe-Finkbeiner, *The F-Word: Feminism in Jeopardy* (Emeryville, CA: Seal Press, 2004), 66, 89-90; Melissa Klein, "Duality and Redefinition: Young Feminism and the Alternative Music Community" in *Third Wave Agenda: Being Feminist, Doing Feminism*, eds. Leslie Heywood and Jennifer Drake (Minneapolis/London: University of Minnesota Press, 1997), 207-08, 221.

5. Leslie Heywood and Jennifer Drake, "Third Wave Activism and Youth Music Culture," in *Third Wave Agenda: Being Feminist, Doing Feminism*, eds. Leslie Heywood and Jennifer Drake (Minneapolis/London: University of Minnesota Press, 1997), 204; Zeisler, 106-07.

6. Zeisler, 136-37; Molly Merryman, "Not All Feminists Look/(Think) Alike in the Dark," *Gauntlet*, 18 (1999), 32; Klein, 220. In 2014, Duke University freshman Miriam Weeks emerged as an adult entertainment sensation performing under the name Belle Knox. The women's studies major and sex-positive feminist used her porn income to meet her college costs.

7. Unless otherwise cited, Alison Lee's remarks come from an email to the author, May 5, 2009; Heywood and Drake, 204.

8. Zeisler, 87.

9. Merryman, 32.

10. Rowe-Finkbeiner, 99; Carol Guess, "Deconstructing Me: Being [Out] in the Academy," in *Third Wave Agenda: Being Feminist, Doing Feminism*, eds. Leslie Heywood and Jennifer Drake (Minneapolis/London: University of Minnesota, 1997), 156; Carol Queen, *Real Live Nude Girl: Chronicles of Sex-Positive Culture* (San Francisco: Cleis Press, 1997), 113-14, 118; Carmine Sarracino and Kevin M. Scott, *The Porning of America: The Rise of Porn Culture, What It Means, and Where We Go from Here* (Boston: Beacon Press, 2008), 97.

11. Scarlot Harlot (aka Carol Leigh) is a sex worker activist,

writer, and director residing in San Francisco.

12. Joanna Angel, "... On Being a Feminist With a Porn Site," in *Naked Ambition: Women who Are Changing Pornography*, ed. Carly Milne (New York: Carroll & Graf, 2005), 234.

13. Tristan Taormino, "About Tristan," *Puckerup.com: Tristan Taormino's Sex-Positive Salon*, Accessed January 9, 2010, http://puckerup.com/about/about-tristan/.

14. Unless otherwise cited, Tristan Taormino's remarks come from a seminar at Goucher College, Baltimore, Maryland, April 2, 2009.

15. Tristan Taormino, "... On Crossing the Line to Create Feminist Porn," in *Naked Ambition; Women Who Are Changing Pornography*, ed. Carly Milne (New York, NY: Carroll & Graf, 2005), 91.

16. Taormino, "...On Crossing," 93-94.

17. "Inside Tristan Taormino," *Inside the Porn Stars Studio*, August 24, 2006, Accessed November 22, 2008, www.xrentdvd.com/Porn_Star_Interviews/Tristan_Taormino.html.

18. Unless otherwise cited, Nica Noelle's remarks are from emails to the author, May 10-11, 2010.

19. Dan Miller, "Nica Noelle Forms Partnership with AEBN, Launches Candy Girl, Hard Candy Films," *XBIZ: The Industry Source*, October 14, 2011, Accessed August 10, 2012, http://www.xbiz.com/news_piece.php?id=139683&mi=all&q

20. Unless otherwise cited, Erika Lust's remarks are from emails to the author, May 19, June 3, June 11, July 8, 2009 and from "Erika Lust: European Entrepreneur, Pornographer, and Feminist," a biography by Rich Moreland published June 29, 2010, Accessed December 28, 2011, http://media.lust films.com/media/press_room_files/lust%20profile%20for%2 0distribution.pdf.

21. Ann G. Sabo, "A Vision of New Porn: How Women are Revising Porn to Match a Time of Greater Gender Equality,"

in *Generation P? Youth, Gender, and Pornography*, eds. Sven-Axel Mansson, Lotta Lofgren-Martenson, and Susanne V. Knudsen (Copenhagen: Danish University of Education Press, 2007), 233; Linda Williams, "Blogspot Erika Lust," November 5, 2007, Accessed December 9, 2009, http://erikalust.blogspot.com/2007/11/best-award.html.

22. *Five Hot Stories for Her*, directed by Erika Lust (Thagson Digital Media in association with Lust Films of Barcelona, 2007), DVD.

23. Jacky St. James' remarks are from an email to the author on September 9, 2013.

24. Penny Pax, email to the author, August 12, 2013.

25. Carlyle Jansen, interview in Toronto, April 15, 2011; Tasha Reign, interview in Las Vegas, January 15, 2014.

Chapter 6: Space for Everyone

1. Unless otherwise cited, the remarks of Dylan Ryan, Jiz Lee and Tina Horn are from a roundtable discussion held in Toronto, April 8, 2010. Included is Jiz Lee, interview in Toronto on April 15, 2011, and emails to the author, May 24, 2009 and August 26, 2011.

2. John Stagliano, interview in Las Vegas, January 19, 2012.

3. Bobbi Starr's remarks are from interviews on January 8, 2011 in Las Vegas and April 15, 2011 in Toronto. At a Las Vegas seminar on January 9, 2010, feminist leaning Sasha Grey explained that she gave careful thought to a porn career, studying the industry for a year before taking the plunge.

4. Dana DeArmond's remarks are from an interview in Las Vegas, January 17, 2013.

5. Tara Lynn Foxx's remarks are from interviews on October 1, 2010 in San Francisco, January 8 and 9, 2011 in Las Vegas and a telephone interview, May 23, 2012.

6. After turning twenty-one, Tara spent time away from porn, admitting the unscrupulous aspects of the industry had

taken its toll. By 2012 she returned the business.

7. Casey Calvert's remarks are from emails to the author, August 22, September 4, 6, 7, 2013.

8. Jiz Lee, "I got to see the piece of the industry, from the inside," *Jiz Lee Blog*, January 13, 2010, Accessed October 6, 2010, http://jizlee.com/wordpress/; Jiz Lee, "I got to bring visibility to myself and queers," *Jiz Lee Blog*, January 13, 2010, Accessed October 6, 2010, http://jizlee.com /wordpress/.

9. Lux Alptraum, "Jiz Lee: Lesbian adult actress talks ejaculation, porn politics and shooting with Belladonna," *Bizarre Magazine*, September 2009, Accessed April 4, 2013, http//www.bizarremag.com/alt-girls/pin-ups/8149/jiz _lee.html.; Jiz Lee, "Postcard from the Feminist Porn Awards: The Boundary Breaker!" *Jiz Lee Blog*, April 11, 2010, Accessed March 21, 2014, http://jizlee.com/the-boundary-breaker/

10. Alptraum, "Jiz Lee."

11. Rosalie Scolari, "Gender feminist porn star: Jiz Lee," *The Scavenger*, August 27, 2010, Accessed, http://www.thescavenger.net/queer/genderqueer-feminist-porn-star-jiz-lee-74398.html.

12. Scolari, "Genderqueer feminist;" Jiz Lee, "Sleeping with Cissies, Coming out as Queer," *Jiz Lee Blog*, September 23, 2010, Accessed October 6, 2010, http://jizlee.com/word press/.

13. Scolari, "Genderqueer feminist."

14. Nica Noelle, "Queer Nation: Porn's Queer Mafia," *National Sexuality Resource Center*, April 4, 2011, Accessed May 1, 2011, http://nsrc.sfsu.edu/article/queer_nation_porns_quee r_mafia. Unless otherwise noted, Annie Sprinkle's remarks are from an interview in San Francisco, October 1, 2010 and an email to the author, September 21, 2013.

15. *Linda/Les & Annie: A Female-to-Male Transsexual Love Story*,

directed by Albert/Annie/Johnny (1989: Pacific Media Production, 2008), DVD.

16. Ibid.

17. Chris Straayer, "The Seduction of Boundaries: Feminist Fluidity in Annie Sprinkle's Art/Education/Sex," in *Dirty Looks: Women, Pornography, Power*, eds. Pamela Church Gibson and Roma Gibson (London: British Film Institute, 1994), 163-64.

18. Jiz Lee, "Fuck Competition," *Jiz Lee Blog*, May 23, 2009, Accessed October 6, 2010, http://jizlee.com/wordpress/page/11/

19. "Dyke Porn and Trans Porn, in Bed Together," *Pink and White Productions*, July 14, 2008, Accessed September 3, 2011, http://pinkwhite.biz/PWWP/dyke-porn-and-trans-porn-in-bed-togther/.

20. April Flores and Carlos Batts, interview in Los Angeles, October 4, 2012.

Chapter 7: *Real* People *are* the Medium

1. "About Us," *Good for Her*, Accessed November 10, 2011, http://goodforher.com/about_us. Carlyle Jansen's remarks are from an interview in Toronto, April 15, 2011.

2. "About Us," *Good For Her*.

3. "About Good Vibrations," *Good Vibrations: Making the World a Sexier Place*, Accessed November 15, 2011, http://www.goodbvibes.com/content.jhtml?id=about-good-vibrations.

4. Lynn Comella, "Selling sexual liberation: Women-owned sex toy stores and the business of social change," *Electronic Doctoral Dissertations for UMass Amherst*; PaperAA13152682 (2004), Accessed July 12, 2010, http://scholarworks.umass.edu/dissertations/AA13152682. "About Good Vibrations," *Good Vibrations*.

5. Alison Lee, "The new face of porn: A new generation of feminists are reclaiming porn, both as consumers and

producers," *This Magazine*, Nov-Dec, 2008, 1, Accessed April 4, 2009, http://thismagazine.ca/issues/2008/11/newporn. php.

6. Lee, 4.

7. Ibid.

8. The other major industry group, the *X-Rated Critics Organization*, initiated its awards show a year later on February 14, 1985. "History," *XRCO: X-rated Critics Organization*, Accessed December 6, 2013, http://www.xrco. com/

9. Rich Moreland, "Toronto: A Crossroads of Two Porn Cultures," *Adult Industry News*, May 9, 2011, Accessed November 5, 2012, http:ainews.com/Archives/story19421 .phtml.

10. Graham Ponante, "Feminist Porn Awards Return to Toronto," *Valley Porn Observed*, March 18, 2010, Accessed July 12, 2010, http:gramponante.com/feminist-porn awards-return to Toronto/.

11. Ponante, "Feminist Porn Awards Return to Toronto."

12. Dusty Horn, "The 2010 Feminist Porn Awards," *Carnal Nation*, April 28, 2010, Accessed July 12, 2010, http://carnal-nation. com/content/53859/501/2010-feminist-porn-awards. The 2013 Awards program was relocated to Toronto's Capital Event Theater on Yonge Street in the city.

Chapter 8: My Porn-Art Daughter

1. "The Training of Madison Young, Day One," directed by James Mogul (San Francisco, CA: *Kink.com*, September 6, 2007), Accessed November 21, 2010, http://www.thetrain-ingofo.com/site/clips_flash.jsp?nats=MTA0MDk1MTozOjE1, 125,0,0,0&shootId=4680.

2. Brian Alexander, *America Unzipped: In Search of Sex and Satisfaction* (New York: Harmony Books, HarperCollins Publishers, 2008), 196-97; "Inside Madison Young," *Inside the*

Porn Stars Studio, September 24, 2008, Accessed November 11, 2008, www.xrentdvd.com/Porn_Star_Interviews/Madison_young.html.

3. *Madison Young's Tail of a Bondage Model*, directed by Madison Young (San Francisco, CA: Madison Bound Production in Association with Blowfish Video, 2006), DVD.

4. Francesca Gentille, "TRANSCENDENTAL BDSM; THE TANTRA OF DOMINANCE & SUBMISSION with Madison Young," *Personal Life Media*, Episode 73, March 1, 2009, 3, Accessed April 22, 2009, http://personallifemedia.com .podcasts/225-sex-tantra-and-kama-sutra/e.

5. Marrow, "Madison Young; fetish and bondage model," *Bind Me*, May 25, 2008, Accessed June 28, 2009, www.bindme .nl/efeaturemadison.php.

6. Gentille, 4.

7. *Tail of a Bondage Model.*

8. Gentille, 3, 8; Alexander, 198.

9. Gentille, 6-7; Bobbi Starr, interview in Toronto, April 15, 2011.

10. Marrow, "Madison Young."

11. Candida Royalle, "Porn in the USA," in *Feminism and Pornography*, ed. Drucilla Cornell (Oxford: Oxford University Press, 2000), 545.

12. "Inside Madison Young"; Unless otherwise noted, Madison Young's remarks are from emails to the author, January 12, 15 and 28 and May 4, 2009, October 5, 10 and November 29, 2010.

13. *Tail of a Bondage Model.*

14. Alexander, 193.

15. Marrow, "Madison Young."

16. Ibid.

17. *Tail of a Bondage Model.*

18. "About Us," *Femina Potens Art Gallery*, Accessed December 12, 2012, http://feminapotens.org/about/

19. Ibid.

20. Courtney Trouble, "Femme Fatale: This lesbian feminist pornographer has us all tied up," *Curve Magazine*, 19,1 (January/February, 2009): 46; Gram Ponante, "Madison Young Talks with Gram Ponante," n.d., *Gram Ponante's Porn Stash*, Accessed June 8, 2009, http://www.gamelnk.com/naked_truth_.jhtml$id=Madison-young-interview; "Inside Madison Young."

21. Trouble, 47; Cooper, "Interview: Madison Young," *Social Kink*, May 21, 2008, Accessed June 8, 2009, http://www.social kink.com/articles.php?do=view&id=336.

22. Trouble, 47.

23. Marrow, "Madison Young."

24. Lynn Chancer, "Pornography Debates Reconsidered," *New Politics*, 2,1 (1988), 82-83.

25. Ibid.

26. Cooper, "Interview: Madison Young."

27. Wendy McElroy, *XXX, A Woman's Right to Porn* (New York: St. Martin's Press, 1995), 128-29.

28. Marrow, "Madison Young."

Chapter 9: Too Much Gray

1. P.J. Huffstutter, "See No Evil," *Los Angeles Times*, January 12, 2003, Accessed March 22, 2010, http://www.aegis.com/news/Lt/2003/LT030110.html; Mark Kernes, "Brook Ashley Workers Comp Hearing Continues," *Adult Video News*, July 20, 2007, Accessed May 17, 2010, http://business.avn.com/articles/Brooke-Ashley-Workers-Comp-Hearing-Continues-3094.html.AVN; Media Network Home Page, "Cash Markman: 'The Brooke Ashley Shoot Was One of Those Jobs I Regret Taking,'" *Adult Video News*, March 12, 1999, Accessed April 23, 2010, http://business.avn.com/articles/13763.html.

2. Huffstutter, "See No Evil."

3. Eric Slater, "Movies' New Dress Code: Condoms; HIV-Positive diagnoses Prompted Action," *Washington Post*, May 2, 1998, C.03. Credit: *Los Angeles Times*. ProQuest; Unless otherwise cited, Gloria Leonard's remarks are from a telephone interview, October 23, 2009 and an email to the author, April 30, 2010.

4. Ira Levine's remarks are from a telephone interview, January 29, 2012.

5. Slater, C.03.

6. Ibid.

7. Legs McNeil and Jennifer Osborne, *The Other Hollywood: The Uncensored Oral History of the Porn Film Industry* (New York: HarperCollins Publishers, 2005), 533. Bill Margold learned of Savannah's attempt on her life from director Ron Sullivan (Henri Pachard). She was taken to the hospital where she survived until late morning. (Bill Margold, email to the author, March 30, 2013).

8. In *Hollywood Blue; The Tinseltown Pornographers* (London: B.T. Batsford, Ltd, 1997), Harris Gaffin writes that Sharon Mitchell was feminist oriented until she entered the adult industry and mainstream feminists disapproved of her career (91).

9. Nick Madigan, "Voice of Health in a Pornographic World," *The New York Times*, May 10, 2004, A14. ProQuest.

10. Corita Grudzen, et al., "Pathways to Health Risk Exposure in Adult film Performers," *Journal of Urban Health Bulletin of the New York Academy of Medicine*, 86,1 (2008), 69; Melanie M. Taylor, et al., "Epidemiologic Investigation of a Cluster of Workplace HIV Infections in the Adult Film Industry: Los Angeles, California, 2004," *Clinical Infectious Diseases* 44 (January 15, 2007): 302; Sharon Mitchell, "How to Put Condoms in the Picture," *The New York Times*, May 2, 2004, WK 11. ProQuest.

11. Grudzen, 69, 72. This chapter is not intended to be a detailed

examination of the STI issue in adult film. For a further review of research, see the studies listed in endnote 10 and K.M. Coyne, et al, "Sexual health of adults working in pornographic films," *International Journal of STD & AIDS* (2009) 20, issue 7: 508-9; Binh Y. Goldstein, PhD, et al., "High Chlamydia and Gonorrhea Incidence and Reinfection Among Performers in the Adult Film Industry," *Journal of the American Sexually Transmitted Diseases Association* (July 2011) 38, issue 7: 644-48; Corita Grudzen and Peter R. Kerndt. "The Adult Film Industry: Time to Regulate?" *PloS Medicine*, (2007) 4, issue 6: 993-96.

12. Grudzen, "Pathways to Health Risk," 73: Cristina Rodriguez-Hart's remarks are from a telephone interview with the author, May 26, 2010 and an email to the author, May 31, 2011.

13. Unless otherwise cited, Bobbi Starr's remarks are from interviews in Las Vegas, January 9, 2010 and Toronto, April 15, 2011 and emails to the author January 27, 2010 and April 29, 2010.

14. Huffstutter, "See No Evil;" M.R. De Cesare, "Rxxx resolving problems of the performer health and safety in the adult industry," *Southern California Law Review* 79 (2006): 705.

15. Nina Hartley's remarks are from an interview in Las Vegas, January 18, 2012; Dana DeArmond's remarks are from an interview in Las Vegas, January 17, 2013.

16. Imani Rose's remarks are from an interview in Los Angeles, October 5, 2012; Casey Calvert's remarks are from emails to the author September 9 and 10, 2013.

17. Tara Lynn Foxx's remarks are from an interview in Las Vegas, January 8 and 9, 2011.

18. Susannah Breslin, "They Shoot Porn Stars, Don't They?" *HOME CREDITS*, 2009, Accessed April 23, 2010, http://theyshootpornstars.com.html.

19. De Cesare, 703; Grudzen, "Pathways to Health Risk," 73;

Christina Jordan, "The XXX-Files: CAL/OSHA's Regulatory Response to HIV in the Adult film Industry," *Cardozo Journal of Law and Gender*, 12, 1 (2005), 432-33; Dylan Ryan's remarks are from an interview in Toronto April, 8, 2010.

20. Steve Nelson's remarks are from an email to the author, January 12, 2011.

21. Courtney Trouble, interview in Toronto, April 8, 2010.

22. Candida Royalle telephone interview, April 28, 2010.

23. Tristan Taormino, seminar at Goucher College, April 7, 2009; Nica Noelle's remarks are from an email to the author, May 10, 2011.

24. Erika Lust, email to the author, June 29, 2010.

25. David Jennings, *Skinflicks: The Inside Story of the X-Rated Video Industry* (Bloomington, Indiana: 1st Books Library, 2000), 267.

26. Chris Hedges, *Empire of Illusion: The End of Literacy and the Triumph of Spectacle* (New York: Nation Books, 2009), 67-68; The Original Dreamgirls Agency International, Accessed September 2011 http://www.the girlofyourdreams.com /new_site/services.html. In our Los Angeles interview on October 28, 2013, performer Andy San Dimas explained that some industry girls are attracted to the "girlfriend experience," a type of escorting that is "three minutes of sex and fifty-seven minutes of conversation."

27. Grudzen, "Pathways to Health Risk," 75.

28. Jiz Lee, interview in Toronto, April 15, 2011.

29. Sasha Lexing's remarks are from a telephone interview, February 10, 2011.

30. In our interview in Los Angeles on October 5, 2012, Chris Cane, whose talent agency is a member of LATATA, (Licensed Adult Talent Agency Trade Association) points out he rarely has casting couch issues with his clients. Should that situation arise, he would expect a call from the model. Chris mentions that with unlicensed and unmonitored agencies irregular activities might occur just as they could

with girls who operate as free agents.

31. Drucilla Cornell, *The Imaginary Domain: Abortion, Pornography & Sexual Harassment* (New York & London: Routledge, 1995), 119.

32. Billy Watson, interview in Los Angeles, October 28, 2013.

33. Dennis Romero, "Porn Defends the Money Shot: Critics gain ground, demanding condom use to control AIDS," *LA Weekly*, September 29, 2011, Accessed April 18, 2012, http://www.laweekly.com/2011-09-29/news/porn-defends-the-money-shot/

34. Bobbi Starr, "Rubber Lovin'," *Popporn.com*, June 6, 2009, Accessed April 28, 2010, http://popporn.com/node/108.html.

35. Chanel Preston, interview in Las Vegas, January 17, 2014.

Chapter 10: A Safe Place for All of Us

1. Jiz Lee, "New experiences and a New Collection on WiredPussy.com," *Jiz Lee Blog*, May 4, 2009, Accessed October, 6, 2010, http://jizlee.com/wordpress/page/11/; "Collection Part 2: Jiz Lee," directed by Princess Donna (*Kink.com*, May 28, 2009), Accessed October 30, 2010, http://www.wiredpussy.com/site/search.jsp?search=jiz+lee&searchButton=sear.

2. Jiz Lee's remarks are from an interview in Toronto, April 15, 2011.

3. Lochai no longer works for *Kink.com*, but was active when I was given access to the company's websites in the fall of 2010. This chapter is a snapshot in time as some personnel included here have changed over the years.

4. Dylan Ryan's remarks are from an interview in Toronto, April 8, 2010 and Dana DeArmond's remarks are from an interview in Las Vegas, January 17, 2013. Not every model has a positive experience at *Kink*. For some it's just another booking. As one performer told me, the company does not pay her enough to beat her.

5. Peter Acworth's remarks are from a telephone interview on July 14, 2010 and an interview in San Francisco, October 1, 2010; Madison Young's remarks are from an interview in Las Vegas, January 8, 2010; Tara Lynn Foxx's remarks are an interview in San Francisco, October 1, 2010.

6. Carol Queen, email to the author, June 16, 2010.

7. John Hubner, *Bottom Feeders: From Free Love to Hard Core, The Rise and Fall of Counterculture Heroes, Jim and Artie Mitchell* (New York: Doubleday, 1992), 81.

8. Kenneth Turan and Stephen F. Zito, *Sinema: American Pornographic Films and the People Who Make Them* (New York: Praeger Publishers, 1974), 100-03.

9. Eddie Muller and Daniel Faris, *Grindhouse: The Forbidden World of "Adults Only" Cinema* (New York: St. Martin's Griffin, 1996), 142; Hubner, 82.

10. Hubner, 103; Muller and Faris, 144.

11. Hubner, 305, 309.

12. "Dylan Ryan and John Strong," directed by Princess Donna (*Kink.com*, September 18, 2009), Accessed January 13, 2010, http://www.publicdisgrace.com/site/clips_flash.jsp?shootId=7176

13. "The Training of Dylan Ryan, Day Two," directed by James Mogul (*Kink.com*, January, 9, 2009), Accessed November 10, 2010, http://www.thetrainingofo.com/site/clips_flash.jsp?shootId=5724; "The Training of Dylan Ryan, Day Four," directed by James Mogul (*Kink.com*, March 20, 2009), Accessed November 10, 2010, http://www.thetrainingofo.com/site/clips _flash.jsp?shootId=5726.

14. Casey Calvert's remarks are from emails to the author, August 21 and 22 and September 4 and 9, 2013.

15. "Electrotest for Casey Calvert," directed by Bobbi Starr (*Kink.com*, May 27, June 17, July 24, 2013), Accessed October 13, 2013, http://www.kinkondemand.com/kod/clips_flash.jsp?shoot=29375, 29376, 29377; Lew Rubens email to the

author, November 1, 2013.

16. Charles Moser and J.J. Madeson, *Bound to be Free: The SM Experience* (New York: Continuum, 2005), 32, 103.

17. "Sasha Lexing takes a beating in stride and then some," directed by Lochai (*Kink.com*, Dec 2, 2008), Accessed December 6, 2010, http://www.hogtied.com/site/clips_flash.jsp:shootId=5740.

18. Shea Simon's remarks are from an interview in San Francisco, October 1, 2010.

19. Peyton Bell's remarks are from an interview in San Francisco, October 1, 2010.

20. Bobbi Starr's remarks are from an interview in Toronto, April 15, 2011 and an email to the author, February 23, 2014; James Mogul, email to the author, September 9, 2013.

21. Details about company values and model rights can be found at http://www.kink.com/k/values.jsp and http://www.kink.com/k/model_rights.jsp.

22. Jon Mooallem, "A Disciplined Business," *The New York Times Magazine*, April 29, 1997. Accessed July 9, 2010, http://www.nytimes.com/2007/04/29/magazine/29kink.t.html?_r=2/

23. Steve Robinson, "50 protest porn business inside old Mission Street armory," *SF Gate: home of the San Francisco Chronicle*, February 8, 2007, Accessed August 2, 2010, http://www.sfgate.com/cgi-bin/article.cgi?f=/c/a/2007/01/26/BAG5RNPKIVI.DTL.

24. Marisa Lagos, "No welcome mat for adult film studio: Activists prefer building be used for housing," *SF Gate: home of the San Francisco Chronicle*, January 26, 2007, Accessed August 1 2010, http://www.sfgate.com/cgibin/article.cgi?f=/c/a/2007/01/26/BAG5RNPKIVI.DTL.

25. Chanel Preston, interview in Las Vegas, January 17, 2014.

26. "Career Opportunities," *Kink.com*, Accessed December 20, 2011, http://wwwskink.com/k/jobs.jsp?c=1; "Kink.com Celebrates its 10-Year Anniversary." (*BehindKink.com*,

February 2, 2009) Accessed July 30, 2010, http://news.behin dkink.com/blog/default/skip/40/; John Sander, interview in San Francisco, October 1, 2010.

27. Brian Alexander, *America Unzipped: In Search of Sex and Satisfaction* (New York: Harmony Books, HarperCollins Publishers, 2008), 210.

Conclusion: Once Was

1. Candida Royalle, "Biography," *Candida Royalle.com*, Accessed December 21, 2010, http://www.candidaroyalle.com/index 2.html.

2. Jill Nagle, "First Ladies of Feminist Porn: A Conversation with Candida Royalle and Debi Sundahl" in *Whores and Other Feminists*, ed. Jill Nagle (New York and London: Routledge, 1997), 161.

Contemporary culture has eliminated both the concept of the public and the figure of the intellectual. Former public spaces – both physical and cultural – are now either derelict or colonized by advertising. A cretinous anti-intellectualism presides, cheerled by expensively educated hacks in the pay of multinational corporations who reassure their bored readers that there is no need to rouse themselves from their interpassive stupor. The informal censorship internalized and propagated by the cultural workers of late capitalism generates a banal conformity that the propaganda chiefs of Stalinism could only ever have dreamt of imposing. Zer0 Books knows that another kind of discourse – intellectual without being academic, popular without being populist – is not only possible: it is already flourishing, in the regions beyond the striplit malls of so-called mass media and the neurotically bureaucratic halls of the academy. Zer0 is committed to the idea of publishing as a making public of the intellectual. It is convinced that in the unthinking, blandly consensual culture in which we live, critical and engaged theoretical reflection is more important than ever before.